Cosmopolitanisms in Enlightenment Europe and Beyond

P.I.E. Peter Lang

Bruxelles · Bern · Berlin · Frankfurt am Main · New York · Oxford · Wien

Mónica García-Salmones and Pamela Slotte (eds.)

Cosmopolitanisms in Enlightenment Europe and Beyond

Multiple Europes
No.49

Cover picture: © Marie Jo Lafontaine.

Éditions scientifiques internationales
Brussels, 2013
1 avenue Maurice, B-1050 Brussels, Belgium
www.peterlang.com; info@peterlang.com

Printed in Germany

ISSN 1376-0904
ISBN 978-2-87574-065-6
D/2013/5678/54

CIP also available from the British Library, GB and Library of Congress Cataloging-in-Publication Data

Bibliographic information published by "Die Deutsche Nationalbibliothek"

"Die Deutsche Nationalbibliothek" lists this publication in the "Deutsche Nationalbibliografie"; detailed bibliographic data is available on the Internet at <http://dnb.d-nb.de>.

Acknowledgements

The editors want to thank BIARI at Brown University (USA) and the Erik Castrén Institute of International Law and Human Rights (Finland) for their contribution to funding this publication and María José Belmonte Sánchez and Tero Lundstedt for their help in editing the manuscript.

From Peter Lang we would like to thank Hagen Schulz-Forberg and Emilie Menz for their support and for their interest in our project. We are especially indebted to Martti Koskenniemi and Bo Stråth for their help in different ways and moments in the path of this publication.

Finally, we want to thank all the contributors for embarking in this project and for their rich and enlightening pieces.

Table of Contents

Introduction

Mónica GARCÍA-SALMONES & Pamela SLOTTE

The invitation to think of oneself as a "citizen of the world" will strike most modern individuals as eminently reasonable, indeed something so self-evident that it is hard to find anything beyond platitude to justify it. In an age of globalisation, we are all "cosmopolitans". And yet when we think about this more closely, most of us will find the invitation hard to take in full seriousness. We may even come to think of it as a facile suggestion to overlook those other local identities that all of us have and whose pull often feels more tangible and more urgent than that of an abstract call to feel oneself one with the world. Though a classical theme of intellectual history, cosmopolitanism is rarely treated in all its complexity. Seldom is highlighted not only cosmopolitanism obvious attractiveness but also its intricate and demanding character. What indeed might it *really* be to feel no allegiance beyond that to the world at large? Or might it be that the abstract universalism of the invitation to cosmopolitanism may itself be contextualized as part of some clearly definable local and temporal moment? What indeed is its relationship to the various European philosophical vocabularies in which it is often expressed?

This volume offers critical, historical and theoretical perspectives on cosmopolitanism, with reference also to its implications and forms of appearance outside Europe. It also enquires about the links between cosmopolitanism and teleological understandings of Europe: there is an idea of "progress" not far below the surface of the notion, but what does it mean? Where is it pointing to? Through this analysis we have discovered several cosmopolitanisms playing out and originating in different periods of European history – most conspicuously the Antiquity and the European Enlightenment. We recognize, of course, that some of the cosmopolitan languages did not originate in or locate themselves exclusively in Europe; but we believe that they nonetheless spread through linkages with that continent, most commonly through the colonial encounter. There have been many types of cosmopolitanism, and the cultural and political meaning of the notion has changed in the course of time. Cosmopolitanism has sometimes been related to liberal individualism, sometimes to capitalism, perhaps also to socialism, even to religion. It has been espoused by artists and workers, writers and bankers.

We have highlighted the semantic polysemy of the expression by analysing *different cosmopolitanisms* in and beyond Europe.

One familiar starting-point is the cosmopolitanism put forward by Immanuel Kant (1724-1804). This builds on the idea of human interdependency and puts forward a normative vision for human co-existence that purports to be ultimately universal in reach. Kant's ideas about a global order, including cosmopolitan law, serve as a reference point in much of the historical and contemporary reflection on our theme. They are also touched upon in essays in this volume. The German philosopher's visions are grounded in his philosophical and ethical thinking. At its core is the principle that we should "act only according to the maxim whereby you can at the same time will that it should become a universal law".[1] The proper reference group when contemplating how to act and how to organise society, Kant claims, is that of all humans. This does not mean that we should actually ask all humans or need to do so, nor would we be able to. However, when contemplating on how to live in the world, we should choose on the basis of how it is that everyone would want to live. Here cosmopolitanism is translated into an enormously demanding command to think in terms of universal rules.

Another way to put this is to suggest that the whole of humanity should be our moral concern – at least in the sense just mentioned – and this foundational idea serves as a justification for action taken towards the fulfilment of a moral duty with universal scope. It is in light of this that Diogenes' famous exclamation that he was a "citizen of the world", reiterated by many ever since, becomes useful as a portrayal of the cosmopolitan mindset. These normative foundations are visualised and translated into forms of action via, for example, ideas about codification of cosmopolitan law or about economic expansion and trade. To put it briefly, and as Martti Koskenniemi remarks in his contribution to this volume, cosmopolitanism works as "a language of *identity*" but also "invokes a *project* about the world".

But cosmopolitanism was not invented by Kant. It is an old European language. It is often linked with Stoic philosophy – this is the perspective in which it today appears in the influential writings inspired by Martha Nussbaum, for example[2] – but we typically refer to many other streams of thinking as "cosmopolitanism", too. They include sixteenth century humanism, Enlightenment rationalism, nineteenth century pacifism and perhaps also the various forms of cultural internationalism

---

1 Kant, Immanuel, *Grounding for the Metaphysics of Morals*, transl. by James, W. Ellington, Cambridge, MA, Hackett Publishing Company, 1981, p. 30 [4: 421].

2 See e.g. Cohen, Joshua (ed.), *For Love of Country. Debating the Limits of Patriotism. Martha C. Nussbaum with Respondents*, Boston, Beacon, 1996.

of the twentieth century. It is precisely this cross between its "European" pedigree and its universalistic reach that creates its *ambivalence*. What might its relationship be to imperialism, for example? Much of this ambivalence lies in the heart of the essays in the book. The texts of this volume recognize valuable aspects of cosmopolitan thinking. However, the contributors simultaneously insist that cosmopolitan projects are ambiguous and often indeterminate in their outcomes. They may be used to buttress imperial policies and blind us to the violence sometimes intrinsic in uprooting humans from their local contexts and alignments. Cosmopolitan projects must be assessed not only on the basis of the visions that they carry but also on the fruit that they reap.

We have deliberately refrained from embarking on a normative project of our own by proposing our own view of cosmopolitanism, together with our own universalistic project. Instead, we have set ourselves the task in this volume to situate cosmopolitanism in history and in this fashion to enquire into the ambiguities of the cosmopolitan imagination. This includes also trying to tackle what could be called the sociologies of cosmopolitanism. For no less than its philosophical incarnations, cosmopolitanism is also sociologically polysemic. We can, for example, distinguish between an informal, spontaneous, "cultural" cosmopolitanism on the one hand, and an official and institutional, "political" cosmopolitanism on the other. The former is illustrated in many citizens' movements and for example, the intrinsic internationalism of science and the arts – the latter is illustrated in the internationalism of diplomacy and official international institutions, such as the United Nations for example.[3] This proliferation of practices understanding themselves – or being understood by others – as intrinsically "cosmopolitan" tells much about the historical and political contexts in which they appear. The image of the cosmopolitan artist, for example, travelling with her exhibition around the world is very different from that of the cosmopolitan investment banker, moving between business class lounges. Both appear equally distant from the activist of an environmental group meeting yesterday in Copenhagen and Porto Alegre, today in Durban. It would be impossible to understand cosmopolitanism today without reflecting it against such different contexts and activities.

This example highlights the fact that cosmopolitanism is also the mode of living of a certain group of people: the *cosmopolitans*. Situating the cosmopolitans is an important part of trying to grasp the phenomenon itself. A typology of three easily suggests itself. Once cosmopoli-

---

[3] For a specific treatment of this question, Pierik, Roland, and Werner, Wouter G. (eds.), *Cosmopolitanism in Context. Perspectives from International Law and Political Theory*, Cambridge, Cambridge University Press, 2010.

tans were part of an aristocratic movement; educated European men travelled around, and like Diogenes, felt themselves to be "citizens of the world". They spoke many languages and had contacts all over the world. Thereafter, in the twentieth century, another type of cosmopolitism emerged – that of the traveling merchant first, banker then, and the representative of the business enterprise. The expansion of trade and commerce brought forward a cosmopolitanism that was very different from the old, aristocratic-intellectual one. More recently, a third type of cosmopolitanism has emerged which is that of refugees and especially of migrant workers. They are today the true cosmopolitans. This is a "proletarian" type of cosmopolitanism, an absence of firm patriotic allegiance. It is a Third World phenomenon rather than one of European high culture, but one for which Europe has become at the very least a stopover for the experiences of life.

Cosmopolitanisms in Enlightenment Europe and Beyond provides a fresh reading of key political concepts – cosmopolitanism, progress, teleology – put in circulation by the European Enlightenment in the eighteenth century and then transplanted into different environments and contexts, through the force of repetition and innovation, across the nineteenth and twentieth centuries. As such it is loaded with an incredible wealth of intellectual history. Probably not by chance, the findings of this volume go in various different directions and cannot be compressed in a single conclusion. Like any interesting and important language, the vocabulary of cosmopolitanism is irreducibly ambiguous; both ambitious and short sighted at the same time, appealing as a cultural or sociological association and yet indeterminate in its political (or indeed economic) effects. Nevertheless, with their contributions the authors have begun the work of dissecting a fascinating and a complex notion – a notion that is both a concept and a practice, a vocabulary and a project – so as to pave the way for imagining what it might mean to invite us to be "citizens of the world" in the twenty first century.

* * * * *

In the opening essay, Koskenniemi traces critically the uses and misuses of the cosmopolitan project in Western political thought. Cosmopolitanism has been both a source of inspiration and of destruction, even self-destruction due to the overwhelming demands that it imposes on the cosmopolitan. How could one possibly be able to love the whole world? Why would one do so? And with what cost? One of the more problematic aspects of cosmopolitanism has been its identification with the "universal". This brings forward the *political* nature of cosmopolitanism. According to Koskenniemi, it has been singularly committed against state sovereignty in its different forms, and thereby in favour of institutions and policies that have presented themselves as "international". That is a problematic position, Koskenniemi argues, for what in a globalized world does it mean to be in favour of the "international" today? Koskenniemi recognises nonetheless a great value in cosmopolitanism: the way it invites opening oneself to the world in terms broader than oneself.

Law has been one carrier of the cosmopolitan project, and Kant's idea of a cosmopolitan law offers a hugely influential historical conceptualisation of it. However, interestingly, from the perspective of the hypothesis of a common European law, in the early modern period, Europe appears not to have been itself cosmopolitan, as Jan Schröder argues. Private law stands out as the most important element of *jus commune* and seems to be the most cosmopolitan law that we find in Europe during the Middle Ages. Still, it was concentrated in Romanic states and in the German Empire, and it left vast areas of the continent untouched. With regard to natural law, the argument that Schröder puts forward is that as soon as the early seventeenth century it began to be intertwined with a strong sense of philosophical positivism. While for a long period of modernity it was unquestioned that God was the creator of natural law, the positive legislator was given so much precedence from the beginning that, Schröder argues, the cosmopolitan aspect of natural law was in fact doomed to disappear.

Gabriella Silvestrini presents us with one of the most powerful efforts of European Enlightenment, the development of a cosmopolitan normative order for the states of the world. This is Jean-Jacques Rousseau's theory of war. Silvestrini manages to articulate the core of a new vision of war in which "only the winner can choose to be just". At the same time she complicates our understanding of Rousseau, who has been often understood as the one who for the first time eliminated the doctrine of just war and thus contributed to the neutralisation of natural law. But Rousseau developed his argument in line with the position of the theorists of just war rather than of the supporters of "perpetual peace". Together with non-aggressive forms of patriotism Rousseau proposes a moral-political cosmopolitanism that ought to limit the natural right to war. As Silvestrini suggests, rather than being an inspiration for today's cosmopolitan project, Rousseau's work seems to warn us about the limits of the combination of realism and ethical-universalism, and the species of realist-cosmopolitanism that it proposes.

Demin Duan disentangles different expressions of the encounter of liberalism with the world and its *becoming* "cosmopolitan". As he argues, more often than not, albeit for several reasons, liberal cosmopolitan narratives contain an imperialist germ. The liberal world of Alexis de Toqueville on which Duan concentrates, appears to be thoroughly and shamelessly imperialist. To take part in the imperialist race came close to a necessity as part of the love for his country. That is one of the reasons why Duan does not accept the relativistic reading of liberalism of some authors, who state that liberals could have done *well*, if only historical circumstances would have been more favourable. With his own reading Duan is unburdening the examination of European history by previous teleological readings from an artificial fate. It might be the case, he seems to suggest, that it is "we" who are constructing the cosmopolitan historiography of Europe. In order to be able to look at the soul of someone like Tocqueville one might need to accept his imperialism but also the fact that he thought that freedom is no abstraction but exists only in the very structure of power.

Unexpected but not unwise is Francisco Ortega's description of the *parochialism* of European cosmopolitanism. It was that very parochialism, which, when adopted by the Ibero-American republics, limited their emancipatory potential of what independence from Spain might have offered. However, there as well appeared creative and original thinkers like Simón Rodríguez, whose legacy Ortega analyses. Rodríguez embodies a type of revolutionary intellectual that defies the image of a nineteenth century naïve cosmopolitan.[4] He had no problem stating that the enemies of freedom of thinking in America were Europe's Enlightenment and the prosperity of the United States. Tutor, fellow traveller and life-long friend of Simón Bolívar, Rodríguez was an extraordinarily cultivated person, innovator and entrepreneur of the education in South America. He was also a profound observer of a highly complicated society with many races; the solution to the problems in state making he saw – how could it be otherwise? – in cosmopolitanism, in mixing the blood of the citizens to unify the nation. Rodríquez is surely an impressive – and perhaps under-appreciated – figure in the history of cosmopolitanisms.

From South America we travel to the Ottoman and Russian empires during the nineteenth centuries in order to examine the complex and fascinating cluster of reactions produced by the exposure of those empires to Western cosmopolitanism, both cultural and economic. The Russian and Ottoman empires were on their part also confronted with issues typically dealt with by cosmopolitan sensibility such as national plurality, identity and openness, as Adrian Brisku discusses in his essay. What Briskus's text also demonstrates is that the notion of "cosmopolitanism" might sometimes be too simple an analytical tool in the study of

4 That might be interpreted as hinted by Koskenniemi when dealing with some of the founders of modern international law in the nineteenth century, Koskenniemi, Martti, *The Gentle Civilizer of Nations. The Rise and Fall of International Law, 1870-1960*, Cambridge, Cambridge University Press, 2002.

very rich cultural and political environments. On the other hand, however, cosmopolitanism does play a significant role – together with other languages such as those of the "nation" and of "development" or "security" – in the formation of political identities of large territorial entitles that like to think of themselves as empires.

Markus Prutsch invites us to revisit the *grandeur* of Napoleon's constitutional politics, through which, paradoxically, the soil of Europe itself became a laboratory for cosmopolitan ideas. In this case, cosmopolitanism appears as a servant and supporter of nationalism and political modernity. But the cosmopolitan dream for Europe visible in Napoleon's writings from his exile in Elba and later Saint Helena became at best terribly nostalgic. What should one think of the claim that the French conqueror had a cosmopolitan vocation? Did his attitude simply camouflage his inexhaustible ambition for power under a typically "French" language? Probably not – for how else to explain Napoleon's personal commitment and involvement in the promotion of modern constitutions in the territories under French influence? Undoubtedly this is a topic worth revisiting in an exploration of cosmopolitanism's trajectory through nineteenth century Europe.

What made the French and the Haitians revolutions different? Liliana Obregón poses this question in her piece on the non-recognition of Haiti by the cosmopolitan elite, providing another insight into the nineteenth century cosmopolitan imagination: its troubled relationship with the question of race. The problem started with the incapacity of some races to *understand* the "beautiful", the "sublime" or "religion", as Kant put it. The Enlightenment thinkers decided that a fixation of the principles of knowledge was necessary, and when they looked around they found out that they finally possessed them. The centre of history, they felt, "is here and now with us and with those that are like us". The Haitian revolution carried out by the slaves that had been transported from Africa was a reason to break this pattern into thousand pieces. Not only mental stagnation but also the high politics of the day resisted taking up the challenge that paradoxically the cosmopolitan ideal posed to them when it came true in the Haitian revolutionaries.

From the African point of view, Adedokun Ogunfulu argues, the darkest side of cosmopolitanism lies in its economic side, the perpetuation of the Western dominance as the example of Nigeria shows. Ogunfulu follows the well-known narrative of Gallagher and Robinson on British imperialism in Africa.[5] This concentrates on putting emphasis on "informal empire" and the operation of private actors under British

5 Gallagher, John and Robinson, Ronald, with Denny, Alice, *African and the Victorians. The Official Mind of Imperialism*, London, Macmillan, 1961.

protection. What is repeated is the process of jettisoning the modes of economic, cultural, political and legal life of the communities in which the "cosmopolitans" arrived to do their business. While empire has faded, economic cosmopolitanism remains.

In a manner not unrelated to Ogunfulu's critical essay Bo Stråth concludes the collection with a reflection on the possible reason for the failure of cosmopolitanism as a theoretical concept: its incapacity to deal with the social question. The challenge in the nineteenth century was about how to unify the nation with the cosmopolitan, and this took place in the liberal idiom by assuming that everyone participated in the world through their nations, their particular alignments. The question today is how to make cosmopolitanism compatible with the demands of the social: this is an aspect of the globalisation problem, of course, the tension between the essentially universal – hence cosmopolitan – demands of economics and technology and the local allegiances and preferences of particular communities. It is certainly appropriate to end the collection with a strong appeal for thinking hard about how to make cosmopolitanism compatible with the lives and dreams of real humans, always situated intrinsically "somewhere" instead of "everywhere".

Cosmopolitanism's power was always greatest when most of the world espoused patriotic, intensely nationalist ideologies. But with globalisation, those sentiments have become less important so that in a relevant sense, everyone *must* become cosmopolitan now. Otherwise, you will miss the boat. The old distinctions do not work in a new environment in the way they used to. Nevertheless, if one thing has survived in cosmopolitanism, it is its ambiguity, its emotional appeal for many and its indeterminacy as a political project. Connected with old European languages about being a "citizen of the world", it has taken historically many forms, provided personal identities and projects of political reform that have differed from one period to another. The language of cosmopolitanism is of course present today as well but in a moment of globalisation, its specific meaning is difficult to fathom. Poised between nostalgia and activism, cosmopolitanism still speaks to many audiences. Perhaps there is a novel sense of the expression, however, that no longer links with worn-out narratives, old geographical (or geopolitical) allegiances and stereotyped class positions but to cultural and political preferences of a novel moment. If this is the case, then it must be welcomed in a world where there are not too many alternatives to the colonisation of the global imagination by the languages of mindless consumerism and political apathy.

Part I

Theorising Cosmopolitanisms

Cosmopolitanism[1]

Martti KOSKENNIEMI

Cosmopolitanism is a big word. It has especial attraction to academics who like to travel to places and to characterise themselves through words with a pedigree from European antiquity. To think that one in some ways resembles a Stoic sage able to say, "I am a citizen of the world" – an intrinsic aspect of the image of the (European) intellectual. The world is me; I am the world. But this, to borrow another Greek word, is *hubris* and none the less so for the moral or moralistic radiation of such vocabularies: I am speaking in the name of all. And whoever appointed you to that position?

In this paper I would like to examine two environments where that vocabulary is at home. Cosmopolitanism is, first of all, a language of *identity*. One identifies oneself, or one's neighbour or perhaps one's ideal hero as "cosmopolitan". On the other hand, cosmopolitanism also invokes a *project*, a vocabulary with which to speak about the world as a whole. It integrates the human universe as a moral or political criterion for thought and action. The cosmopolitan is not neutral but "good". I want to suggest that in both respects, cosmopolitanism is profoundly ambivalent, however. It opens an admirable, perhaps in some respects even unavoidable, perspective on ourselves and the world. But it may easily end up suicidal or tyrannical: a moral trap or a prologue to oppression. The cosmopolitan is a hard vocabulary to manage, and it can never be managed alone without being accompanied by its apparent opposite, the local that carries it, through which the cosmopolitan declares itself and becomes known. Even Stoic sages, after all, were creatures of a very specific time and place. But when the balance between the global and the local is right, the cosmopolitan vocabulary may provide the channel to a powerful and appealing aesthetic and political experience.

---

1 This is text only slightly modified from the opening address. I have preserved its colloquial tone.

1. Identity

Cosmopolitanism as identity, first. What is it? Here is a recent catalogue from the upscale Helsinki Department store, Stockmann:

In this advertising image, cosmopolitanism is made to connote all kinds of positive things; leisure, individualism, wealth, travels to exotic environments. Cosmopolitanism, the image suggests, is an aesthetic attraction to frequent change of scenery, openness to the alien to the extent it can be tamed in domesticated representations. The placing of the self is central – it exists in the collection of things it is surrounded with. This is an identity that sees itself moving about but in a controlled way; not the mass tourist, perhaps, but the man or the woman of the wayward path, measured excitement, anthropology of the amateur.

Of course, this type of cosmopolitanism – the cosmopolitan of the "Rough Guide" reader, the world music fan – is a cliché, and an Orientalist and a commercialised cliché at that. Look at the zebra stripes on those pillows. Few of us academics think that such attributes, visible in countless travel brochures, would depict an identity that is actually valuable or desirable. It is after all part of *our* identity to point to the sensibilities in evidence among European middle classes (of which we are a part) we would loathe being associated with…That latter identity, too, is a cliché. It is a reaction formation by a left humanist or social science oriented intelligentsia that feels its own aesthetic and cultural sensibilities violated by advertising images of this sort. The cliché of *épater les bourgeois* by taking objects such as the image on the Stockmann catalogue as platforms for the exercise of interpretive skill. No less academic is its right-wing equivalent in market studies: "What should Stockmann now put in the middle of its spring catalogue?" It would be a mistake to think that the expertise and experience that goes to *make* a catalogue would be any less sophisticated about what it does than any *analysis* of it. Each is a marker for the fact that we are in the presence of (a wholly cosmopolitan) community of professionals.

The cosmopolitan want to communicate "I am a citizen of the world". This is a familiar Stoic slogan, of course, but what does it *mean* in today's context? A recent philosophical examination suggests that cosmopolitanism as a moral disposition seeks to communicate that "life of everyone matters, and matters equally".[2] This is Immanuel Kant's universalism translated into the language of universal equality, an undivided right for attention and concern. Treat everyone as you would want yourself to be treated – and give no normative or epistemological priority to those you like or who are nearest to you. As far as philosophical algorithms go, this is nice. But as a moral predisposition it is a trap, ending its protagonist in frustration and bitterness, perhaps cynicism, perhaps aggression. Some years ago, the Finnish novelist Anu Kaipainen wrote a play with the name *Magdalena and the Children of the World*. It is a common enough story.

Magdalena had learned about the starving children of Africa; about their swollen stomachs, enormous eyes, about the sand and heat they had as their environment. To her the call of cosmopolitanism was trans-

---

2 Couture, Jocelyne and Nielsen, Kai, "Cosmopolitanism and the Compatriot Priority Principle," in Gillian Brockand Harry Brighouse (eds.), *The Political Philosophy of Cosmopolitanism*, Cambridge, Cambridge University Press, 2005, pp. 180-197, p. 184.

lated into a normative agenda: what possible justification would she have to live for anything else than to help those children? What could possibly be more important or urgent for her to devote her life? And yet, all her efforts showed themselves insufficient, even pathetic. She was always called upon to do more, and still more. The pragmatic question, "How much of her time should she devote to relieve the plight of starving children?" was transformed into the compelling moral question, "How could she possibly think of doing anything else?" If she burned from the inside – was that not just proof that she should do more, always more for those who have nothing, while she has been blessed with so much? In the end, the absoluteness of the cosmopolitan call destroyed her.[3]

She fell in a moral trap, one that is familiar to the critics of Kantian absolutism, the morality of universal duty. The golden rule "treat everyone as you would wish yourself to be treated" and the prohibition against making arbitrary distinctions between humans is a recipe for disassembly of identity, or alternatively for bitterness and cynicism. Nobody can live under such a weight. We need to distinguish, to choose whom to prefer and whom to forget, at least for the moment. In a moral or political world where one is called upon to treat everyone as worthy of equal concern, any priority, any principle of moral distinction will ultimately be found unjustifiable. Tragedy – or perhaps xenophobia – follows from the attempt to follow a political principle that accepts the necessity of distinction but has no language for making it?

Cosmopolitanism is popular on the academic Left and the academic Right because it expresses in identity terms the Protestant sensibilities invoked by Kantian duty which are much appreciated by Western academics: to be larger than oneself. On the Right, this desire appears in the Stockmann image: consumerism as the reality of cosmopolitanism. Ikea is surely universal in a way that few things of this world are. And what is the Left's preferred gesture? Perhaps it is made towards Filipino maids in the households of Dubai-based Indian professionals, or a Bangladeshi construction worker in Hong Kong, or Romanian gypsies begging in the corner of Stockmann. More anxiety here of course – and an ironic commitment to locality as part of the critique of the "irresponsible detachment" of the universal standpoint of the Kantians.[4]

Cosmopolitanism has come to carry contrasting meanings in a way that few other words can, replacing such more technical terms as univer-

---

3 Kaipainen, Anu, *Magdaleena ja maailmanlapset*, Porvoo, WSOY, 1969.

4 For "post-colonial cosmopolitanism", see Cheah, Pheng & Robbins, Bruce (eds.), *Cosmopolitics. Thinking and Feeling beyond the Nation*, Minneapolis MN, Minnesota University Press, 1998.

salism, internationalism, globalism. Its success lies in that none of the latter is sufficiently loose and sentimental – should I say light? – to carry the associations and identities that cosmopolitanism can. "Universalism" is too loaded with philosophy, purchasing its scope at the cost of its weight. Besides, a "universal person" offers the merest sketch of a person; a set of general features, a computer image; an ideal type without an anchoring-point in the real world. As Michael Walzer has put it, someone who prefers living in a hotel rather than at home.[5] Internationalism, again, evokes the image of the unending flow of black limousines in front of the UN headquarters on the third Tuesday of every September. Grandiloquent speeches made in the General Assembly, and forgotten as soon as the crowd retreats to enjoy drinks in the Indonesian lounge. *Esprit d'internationalité* – this is how late nineteenth century liberal activists labelled their shared sensibility, their optimism and belief in progress as they were struggling to get the work of arbitration going five minutes before the Great War reduced that late-Victorian sensibility to ashes.[6] "Internationalism" lives on in a certain European mindset, as nostalgic as the inevitable *hôtel moderne* that you can find in every French village – familiar and very affordable, and more than a little dull.

And globalism? Well, this is the Stockmann image of a new generation: Facebook, Twitter, and Erasmus exchange programs around the world. For slightly older boys and girls the "global" opens up into financial markets and job opportunities in Hong Kong or Beijing, Mumbai, Mexico City, perhaps Washington – probably not Brussels: the metropolis as the cosmopolis. These gestures could not be further away from eighteenth century Königsberg – the contours of the future are hardly those of a cosmopolitan federation, but rather of *Blade Runner*.

It seems to me that as a foundation for identity – "to be cosmopolitan" – the word offers either too much or too little. It is too heavy as a morally serious anchoring of selfhood: *Magdalena* is sad, and dead. But it does work well as a cultural vignette – useful as long as it stays elusive enough to avoid being pinned down as being in fact the same as universalism, internationalism, globalism. We appreciate its nostalgic feel. But the stripes on the pillows in that Stockmann image convey no feeling for any *real* Africa. Nor does it embody any real commitment to whatever it may be that "Africa" may signify as a focus for political activity and activism. It is an ironic nostalgia that knows itself to be

---

5 Walzer, Michael, *Interpretation and Social Criticism*, Cambridge MA, Harvard University Press, 1987, pp. 14-15.

6 I have discussed this in my book, *The Gentle Civilizer of Nations. The Rise and Fall of International Law 1870-1960*, Cambridge, Cambridge University Press, 2002.

unsustainable and is therefore immune to standard (Leftist) critiques. It was never even supposed to be associated with development work in Tanzania. The condition is that of "enlightened false consciousness"; the point is the feeling, not whatever invokes it. How uncool it is to believe otherwise!

But I do not think the ontological status of the corresponding Left alternative is in any way different from this; reading Naomi Klein or Immanuel Wallerstein on the way to the next cultural studies seminar is a very particular, easily localisable habitus. There is hardly a more popular conference theme than cosmopolitanism, updated in a post-colonial tone within the Anglo-American academia; that is to say, the universal academia, the cosmopolitan arrogation for speaking for all. Here, too, I am afraid "enlightened false consciousness" has long ago trumped any belief in "authentic" representation.[7]

2. Projects

A key part of cosmopolitanism is the way it seeks to enlarge human activity (or perhaps human nature) to embrace the whole world. For that purpose, cosmopolitanism becomes a project and a set of institutions – institutions of the "international" or the "global" usually, engagement in world politics. Often these institutions justify themselves by what could be called the cosmopolitanism of the ancients.[8] This view (by no means a vocabulary confined to the ancient world but very present today) begins with the suggestion that the world is always already united by something and that the political project should be to seize and express and that something in terms of institutions of law and education.[9] What the "real" or underlying unity consists of has been stated in different ways at different times: perhaps it is the underlying *telos* of creation or the way nature can be understood as an integrated whole; maybe the intrinsic laws of human society or communication, the embedded logic of the market, the desire for power or the rational principles of human value. The cosmopolitanism of the ancients understands the world as always already containing the secret of its unity. It then becomes the

7 For a useful reflection of this theme in Europe ("depth") vs. the United States ("energy"), see Bewes, Timothy, *Cynicism and Postmodernity*, London, Verso, 1997, pp. 104-172.

8 See further Cheneval, Francis, *La Cité des peuples. Mémoires de cosmopolitismes*, Paris, Cerf, 2005, pp. 248-250 and *passim*.

9 An influential embrace of the ancient "Stoic" position as the basis for advocacy of cosmopolitan education is Nussbaum, Martha C., "Patriotism and Cosmopolitanism," in Martha C. Nussbaum (ed.), *For Love of Country. Debating the Limits of Patriotism*, Boston, Beacon, 1996, pp. 3-17. The rest of this useful little book consists of various reactions to Nussbaum's stoicism.

task of political institutions to give expression to that unity, to be always poised towards transcending their particularity. The cosmopolitanism of the moderns by contrast believes that the world is united by history as open horizon. This is Kant's teleology rightly understood – universal history's "cosmopolitan purpose" not as a natural force but a presupposition that reasonable humans must make in order to make sense of what we know of the world.[10] Kant concluded that the lessons of the French Revolution thus could no longer be forgotten. The way to progress for humankind had been opened, and this meant life under a constitution that would make reality of everyone's freedom – conceived as the intrinsic meaning of the world.[11] The cosmopolitan would be a *creation* and not just an expression of something already "there".

The cosmopolitanism of both the ancients and the moderns have positioned themselves historically in a different way: the former advocating liberation as spiritual clarity about the unchanging truths of humanity (perhaps return to a Golden Age); and the latter constructing its institutions *de novo* so as to escape from the weight of the past. To the extent that Western political theory has been "cosmopolitan" it has oscillated between the two, in Leo Strauss' famous (though of course biased) formulation, between natural law and history, each choice accompanied by a particular institutional representative – perhaps the university, perhaps the political party or a particular relationship of domination: through merit, need, interest or entitlement – or then "by unpredictable experiences or decisions".[12]

The biggest problem with cosmopolitan projects has to do with their arrogant theory of representation – namely, that they are entitled to speak for the whole world. Why should anyone believe this? The problem is familiar: the cosmopolitan has no representative of its own; it can only be represented by some particular, local entity. But why should we believe this of any particular entity? What could possibly lift that something out of its (local) particularity into something larger than itself? Why not instead be suspicious of the way the claim will inevitably enhance the authority of that entity? The cosmopolitanism of the ancients – the language of the European upper classes – will automatically

---

10 Kant, Immanuel, "Idea for a Universal History with a Cosmopolitan Purpose," in Hans S. Reiss (ed.), *Kant. Political Writings*, 2nd ed., Cambridge, Cambridge University Press, 1991, pp. 41-53.

11 Kant, "On the Relationship of Theory to Practice in Political Right," in *Political Writings*, pp. 87-92 and "The Contest of the Faculties", *ibid.*, pp. 182-185.

12 Strauss, Leo, *Natural Right and History*, Chicago, Chicago University Press, 1950, p. 19.

appear as imperialism for anyone not already convinced.[13] And the cosmopolitanism of the moderns – capitalism above all – will appear to threaten everything salvaged from history's wreckage.[14]

Take the home of cultural cosmopolitanism; the Rome of Seneca, Cicero and the Stoics. Here the view of all human beings united in a community of equal respect and dignity was articulated by a theory of natural reason and represented by Roman law, especially the *jus gentium*. The threefold division by Gaius – *jus naturae*, *jus gentium*, *jus civile* – postulated in its middle term the practices of the *praetor peregrinus*, that Romans handily saw in terms of "common sense, or 'natural reason', which all men shared as part of their human nature".[15] For Cicero, there was no doubt who represented these. For, he wrote, all humans share reason and they therefore also share law. And all who share law "must be considered members of the same state".[16] And so Roman law, and with it the Roman Empire, become the representatives of reasonable humanity.

The story of Roman law and institutions as representative of universal reason was happily combined with Pauline Christianity, which understood humankind as united in view of its having been created by God. "There are no longer Jews or Greeks, no longer slaves or freemen; there is neither man nor woman" (Gal. 3: 14. See also Rom 10: 13-14). Before God, all such distinctions became meaningless. Even pagan peoples carry natural law in their hearts (Rom 2: 14). This was not just theory, but the starting-point of Christian missionary practice. In a cosmopolitan world, there would be no limit to Christian evangelism. Rome and Christianity appeared inextricable: Christian Rome as the *Civitas Maxima*, represented jointly by the Emperor, and the Pope.[17] The gap between the idea and its representative broke wide open in the investiture

---

13 From many critiques, see e.g. Wallerstein, Immanuel, *European Universalism. The Rhetoric of Power*, New York, New Press, 2006. I have dealt with this theme also in my "International Law in Europe. Between Tradition and Renewal," 16 *European Journal of International Law* (2005), pp. 113-124.

14 See e.g. Cheah, Pheng, "The Cosmopolitical – Today," in Cheah and Robbins (eds.), *Cosmopolitics*, pp. 30-38.

15 Stein, Peter, *Roman Law in European History*, Cambridge, Cambridge University Press, 1999, p. 13.

16 Cicero, "On The Laws," in Cicero, *On the Commonwealth and On the Laws*, James E.G. Zetzel (ed.), Cambridge, Cambridge University Press, 1999, pp. 105-175, p. 113.

17 This is a big theme, of course, but starting on it, one might benefit from reading Pagden, Anthony, *Lords of All the World. Ideologies of Empire in Spain, Britain and France c. 1500-1800*, New Haven, Yale University Press, 1995, pp. 24-27 and pp. 29-31; and Muldoon, James, *Empire and Order. The Concept of Empire 800-1800*, London, Macmillan, 1999, especially pp. 46-86.

struggle: mankind may have been a single unity, but was access to it open from the side of the institutions of the Church or those of the empire?

The answer to this question played itself out differently depending on where in Europe one happened to live. In Northern Italy in the late thirteenth and early fourteenth centuries one's view on it must have reflected how one viewed the incessant warfare between the city-states. As Dante Alighieri saw it, in his *De Monarchia* written around 1310, the only escape from the chaos lay in the re-affirmation of the universal authority of the Emperor.

> [...] mankind is most a unity when it is drawn together to form a single entity, and that can only came about when it is ruled as one whole by one ruler.[18]

This view is underlain by a familiar metaphysical premise: "Unity seems to be root for what it is to be good, and plurality the root of what it is to be evil."[19] In Dante's ideal, as in the view of countless Western cosmopolitans following him, the empire was the political realisation of cosmopolis. The task of any future politics was to recreate the conditions of empire while learning the reasons for Rome's fall – "empire and liberty" as the English republican tradition was to formulate the predicament.[20]

Writing some years before Dante, Thomas Aquinas would have agreed but would also have stressed the presence of the universal in a natural law that can be grasped by all human beings by reason; the project was to turn reason's commands into law.[21] During the Thomist revival in sixteenth century Spain this view was used to articulate the ground of Spaniards' encounters with populations in the New World. Were the Indians humans, just like the Spanish? They were humans and governed by the laws of reason just as the Spanish were, according to the foremost theologian of the realm, Francisco Vitoria. Unfortunately for the Indians, however, those laws included a universal right to travel and trade, and if the Indians were to prevent its exercise – well then, a just war could be waged against them. The cosmopolitan embrace came

---

18 Dante, *Monarchy*, transl. and ed. by Prue Shaw, Cambridge, Cambridge University Press, 1996, Bk I, viii (13). For the context of *Monarchy*, see Skinner, Quentin, *The Foundations of Modern Political Thought. Vol. I: The Renaissance*, Cambridge, Cambridge University Press, 1978, pp. 12-18; D'Entrèves, Alessandro Passerin, *Dante as a Political Thinker*, Oxford, Clarendon, 1952, pp. 26-51 (stressing Dante's knowledge of Roman law as inspiration for his imperialist views).

19 Dante, *Monarchy*, Bk 1, xv, p. 26.

20 For the latter, see e.g. Armitage, David, *The Ideological origins of the British Empire*, Cambridge, Cambridge University Press, 2000, especially pp. 125-198.

21 Aquinas, Summa Theologiae Ia IIae Q 91 A 2, in R.W. Dyson (ed.), *Political Writings*, Cambridge, Cambridge University Press, 2007, pp. 85-86.

with a cost. It bound Indians into a normative system under which they would find themselves under European discipline.[22]

For Vitoria as for most Counter-Reformation intellectuals, reason's universal laws allocated to each individual the right of *dominium* that they could use to rule themselves in separate commonwealths and even, if necessary, to resist (especially Protestant) tyrants.[23] Neither the Pope nor the Emperor would enjoy universal lordship. Independent commonwealths would represent God's universal design. From Vitoria to the French revolutionaries – and beyond – the national community has not existed in contrast to the universal or the cosmopolitan but as an *expression* of it. Kings and peoples would be the decentralised rulers of the universe, ruling with "reason", of course. And who might have authority to say what reason demands? Referring again to the Spanish expansion in the Indies, Vitoria noted simply that "since this is a case of conscience, it is the business of the priests, that is to say the Church, to pass sentence upon it".[24] The Church's cosmopolitan voice enabled religious scholars such as Cardinals Bellarmine or Richelieu to become advisors to their princes, and also enabled Jesuits such as Molina or Suárez to consolidate the spiritual authority of the Church under a vocabulary of universal natural law.[25]

As cosmopolitanism seeks to intervene in the world, it must take a stand between rival political institutions and local contestants for power. Among the cosmopolitan tracts of the early seventeenth century, the *Grand Design* by Henri IV's Foreign Minster, Duc de Sully (1638-1662) was designed to limit Habsburg pretensions by moving the centre of the Empire from Vienna to Paris. It also suggested the complete reorganisation of the European political order by expelling Turkey and Russia and by coordinating European colonial conquest.[26] The "design" involved a full territorial reworking of European space, together with the establishment of a "general council" to decide issues of general im-

---

22 See generally Anghie, Antony, *Imperialism, Sovereignty and the Making of International Law*, Cambridge, Cambridge University Press, 2005, pp. 13-31.

23 Vitoria, Francisco de, "On Civil Power," *Political Writings*, Anthony Pagden and Jeremy Lawrence (eds.), Cambridge, Cambridge University Press, 1991, §§ 1-11, pp. 4-19.

24 *Ibid.*, p. 238.

25 Reibstein, Ernst, *Die Anfänge des neueren Natur- und Völkerrechts. Studien über den 'Controversiae illustres' des Fernandus Vasquius* (1559), Bern, Haupt, 1949, pp. 56-57.

26 For a discussion of the content and context of the proposals, see Hinsley, Francis Harry, *Power and the Pursuit of Peace. Theory and Practice in the History of Relations Between States*, Cambridge, Cambridge University Press, 1963, pp. 20-29; Bois, Jean-Pierre, *L'Europe à l'époque moderne. XVIe-XVIIIe siècle*, Paris, Colin, 2004, pp. 186-199.

portance and six particular councils to decide on local affairs. For it, like for Emeric Crucé's *Nouveau Cynée* (1623), Europe's reorganisation became the decisive instrument for world peace and unity. It was precisely because of its worldwide significance that peace between Christians seemed such a necessity.[27]

For most of the seventeenth and eighteenth centuries, cosmopolitan designs pointed to universal monarchy – an idea associated with Louis XIV, and perhaps more generally with French foreign policy. On the German or generally Protestant side, nothing seemed worse.[28] But the Protestants had their own cosmopolitan laws, too, which were invoked by Hugo Grotius against the Portuguese monopoly on trade in the East Indies. In fact, as Grotius made clear in the (unpublished) *De jure praedae* (1604-1606), the Dutch war against the Iberians' monopoly was waged to avenge the violation of everyone's rights and thus on behalf of humanity itself.[29] His mature work *De jure belli ac pacis* (1625) was written as a vigorous apology of warfare in defence of universal property rights. If there is no express theory of the international community in Grotius, the implicit construction is crystal-clear: natural law guarantees to everyone basic subjective rights, particularly the right of property, and the faculty to defend it by force if necessary: "This is most certain, that every Man has the natural Right to revenge himself, and therefore were Hands given to us."[30] Grotius' cosmopolitanism was that of private ownership and exchange. To protect these, everyone, including commonwealths and commercial companies, had the right to go to war.

For a long time, cosmopolitanism was intellectually represented by the natural law tradition whose different careers were pursued at German universities and Parisian salons in the eighteenth century in different directions. In Germany, Grotius' vocabulary was taken up by the Saxon jurist Samuel Pufendorf in whom reason grounded a universal natural law of sociability that coincided with the clever management of the "reason" of each State – its security and welfare. Pufendorf's civil philosophy posited techniques of ruling independent commonwealths at the heart of his natural law, and led a whole stream of experts on *jus naturae et gentium* at Gottingen to speculate on principles of statecraft

27 See also Bély, Lucien, *L'art de la paix en Europe. Naissance de la diplomatie moderne XVIe-XVIIe siècle*, Paris, PUF, 2007, pp. 103-130.

28 See e.g. Leibniz' ironic, "Mars Christianissimus," in Patrick Riley (ed.), *Political Writings*, Cambridge, Cambridge University Press, 1981, pp. 121-145.

29 Grotius, Hugo, *Commentary on the Law of Prize and Booty* [*De jure praedae*], ed. and with an Introduction by Martine Juliavan Ittersum, Indianapolis, Liberty Fund, 2006, Ch. XIV pp. 448-452.

30 Grotius, Hugo, *The Rights of War and Peace*, Richard Tuck (ed.), Indianapolis, Liberty Fund, 2005, Bk. I, Ch. V, Section I, p. 384.

and comparative politics in thick Latin volumes.[31] By contrast, at Halle, Christian Wolff's *Civitas Maxima* projected a hypothetical community of nations as reason's highest cosmopolitan representative. Unlike Wolff, his student Emer de Vattel operated in diplomatic circles and felt compelled to reject such an elevated ideal in favour of a soberer and much more influential *Droit des gens* in which the primary duties of the nation were directed towards their own self-perfection, and in which twentieth century jurists and diplomats would recognise the contours of the modern, state-based international system as the always somehow insufficient realisation of our cosmopolitan ideas.[32]

As the tradition of *jus naturae et gentium* rose and fell at German universities, French intellectuals were busy translating their cosmopolitan sentiments into popular pamphlets, didactic novels and encyclopaedia articles that sought to speak to the masses by making fun of the antiquated mores of the ruling class.[33] When Abbé Sieyès then relabelled the third estate as the universal estate, he gave a description of the emerging bourgeoisie as the truly cosmopolitan class, no longer tied by oppressive local traditions. Like intellectuals everywhere, however, French revolutionary thinkers were divided about the role of commerce and especially of the attractions of "luxury" in the new world of "civil society".[34] They knew that although the *Déclaration des droits de l'homme et du citoyen* may have emanated from a powerful sentiment of universal humanity, the revolution had been launched by the Parisians' need for bread. Even if they had no doubt that the French nation was the true bearer of enlightenment and civilisation, they were divided about what those words really meant. It took the better part of the nineteenth century for them to figure out whether to be truly cosmopolitan would mean to advocate enterprising commercial individuality *à l'anglaise*, or whether it denoted solidarity in tune with the collective "social" emerging at industrial centres outside Paris.

Where Kant broke with his eighteenth century predecessors was with his introduction of an open-ended historical perspective – the idea of

---

31 See e.g. Hunter, Ian, *Rival Enlightenments. Civil and Metaphysical Philosophy in Early Modern Germany*, Cambridge, Cambridge University Press, 2001.

32 See de Vattel, Emer, *The Law of Nations*, Bela Kapossy and Richard Whatmore (eds.), Indianapolis, Liberty Fund, 2008, Preliminaries § 13-15 and Ch. II § 13-25 (pp. 73-74, 85-91). For all this, see my "International Community from Dante to Vattel," in Vincent Chetailand Peter Haggenmacher, *Vattel's International Law in a 21st Century Perspective*, Leiden, Brill, 2011, pp. 49-74.

33 See Belissa, Marc, *Fraternité universelle et intérêt national (1713-1795) Les cosmopoliques du droit des gens*, Paris, Kimé, 1998.

34 For this theme in Montesquieu, see Spector, Céline, *Montesquieu. Pouvoirs, richesses et sociétés*, Paris, PUF, 2004.

"progress" as not merely a repetition of (the best of) the past but as the advent of something new and unprecedented.[35] Not merely to lay out rules to limit the cabinet wars but to create the conditions of freedom. Fear of violent conflict hampered the realisation of freedom inside republican States and made proposals for an "international state" seem altogether unrealistic, and perhaps even smacked of "the most fearful despotism".[36] Thus, Kant held that a confederation of sovereign nations would have to suffice – an institution, however, constantly poised towards its own transcendence; from a federal compact under international law to a *Weltbürgerrecht*.[37] But Kant was never really clear about why one should believe in such a transformation. His own reliance on the "unsocial sociability" that would force states to cooperate even against their will was never terribly plausible and also contradicted his own anti-empirism.[38]

The Kantian teleology – "universal history with a cosmopolitan purpose"– has continued to attract liberal minds from the nineteenth century to the present. But how to fit the experience of human diversity into a perspective on humanity united by progress? Ethnography and anthropology used to do this at the outset of their careers by postulating universal laws that made all societies traverse through determinate "stages" on their way to modernity.[39] They would begin as hunter-gatherers and agriculturalists and then, depending on the theorist's political inclinations, progress either to commercial society and contract or to "collectivist organisation" transcending national and political divisions.[40]

---

35 This break in historical consciousness as a key part of the Enlightenment itself is elaborated in Koselleck, Reinhart, *Futures Past. On the Semantics of Historical Time*, transl. and with an introduction by Keith Tribe, New York, Columbia University Press, 2004, especially pp. 26-40. On Kant's notion of the *Völkerbund*, Koselleck states that it "was a pure concept of expectation that had no correspondence with an empirical past", *ibid.*, p. 272.

36 Kant, "On the Common Saying. This may be True in Theory, but is does not Apply in Practice," in *Political Writings*, pp. 61-92, p. 90.

37 Kant's formulation of the federation of free states as a traditional international law compact is given the most elaborate form in the "Second Definitive Article of a Perpetual Peace", in "Perpetual Peace. A Philosophical Sketch," in *Political Writings*, pp. 102-105. The justification for this pragmatic adjustment of Kant's ideal theory is the subject of much specialist debate. See e.g. Franchescet, Antonio, *Kant and Liberal Internationalism. Sovereignty, Justice and Global Reform*, New York, Palgrave, 2002, pp. 53-57.

38 Kant, "Idea for Universal History", p. 47.

39 See Burrow, J.W., *Evolution and Society. A Study of Victorian Social Theory*, Cambridge, Cambridge University Press, 1966.

40 See especially Maine, Henry Sumner, Sir, *Ancient Law. Its Connection to the History of Early Society*, New York, Cosimo, 2005 [1861]; and for the latter view,

Plurality was to be dealt with in terms of the alien being at a different stage of development. The embarrassing fact about this was that one would usually find one's own local mores at the top of the evolutionary ladder. Even Kant, on the subject of universal history, prophesied that "Europe will probably legislate eventually for all other continents".[41]

Adherence to cosmopolitan projects in the twentieth century has reflected the terms of the century's political polemic. Among the terms offered to us has been the call to *choose* between sovereignty and community, one's tribe and the world. As if there were such a choice to be made! Whatever cosmopolitanism has been taken to mean, or to lead up to, at least it has meant sharing a commitment against state sovereignty in its different registers: nationalism, the primacy of the national over the international, a preference for independence over integration, and so on.[42] Notwithstanding cosmopolitanism's historical alliance with nationalism (the "nation" as the representative of the universal), and the fact that political debates up until the early twenty first century have all been about some form of pluralism or multiculturalism, the two terms are still taken as opposites. Politically pressing matters are still conceived in terms of making a choice: which side are you on?

The question is impossible to answer. There is no choice to be made because the two are not opposite entities. They demarcate an intellectual situation that exists with respect to every social institution. The call for independent nationhood and community, the embrace of one's own historicity and social location and the emotional attachment to that which surrounds one is as "natural" or "artificial", as defensible or indefensible as its opposite – the call to unite with humankind by embracing the individuality that joins everyone on this earth. The need to be part of one's immediate community, family and traditions is as natural as the need to achieve distance from it. Each situation has a bright side and a dark side, and they always come together, by deriving their attraction from their mutual criticisms and by the identification in the world of some negative aspect that each proposes to correct.[43] The cosmopolitan situation is also always a situation of alienation. For those closest to oneself it translates as unfettered egoism, to choose the love of an abstract humanity over the concrete responsibility that one has for those who are closest. And yet lifting the boundary between oneself and one's community means

---

Vinogradoff, Paul, Sir, "Historical Types of International Law," 1 *Bibliotheca Visseriana*, Leiden, Brill, 1923, p. 69.

41 Kant, "Idea for a Universal History", p. 52.

42 For a discussion of the anti-sovereignty theme in the twentieth century, see Bartelson, Jens, *The Critique of the State*, Cambridge, Cambridge University Press, 2001.

43 See further my *From Apology to Utopia. The Structure of International Legal Argument*, Reissued with a new epilogue, Cambridge, Cambridge University Press, 2005.

loss of autonomy and being left at the mercy of one's rules and hierarchies of tradition; to be deprived of the sense that one is one's own master. On both sides can be found identity and community, virtue and vice, wholeness and disassembly.

3. Conclusion

The broad theme of "cosmopolitanism" oscillates between questions of identity and institutional politics. Who does one want to be? What kind of a world does one want to live in? I have here wanted to suggest that the interminable debate about the institutional realisations proposed for the international world turn on contested and political interpretations of the available alternatives. The cosmopolitan may either appear attractive or off-putting as an identity or a political blueprint depending on the unstable and varying cultural and political associations that we link with it in particular situations. The urge to think of oneself and one's role in the world in terms broader than oneself or one's locality is the most natural of urges – and yet it is also fraught with danger to oneself and to others. This is not an argument for refraining from engaging with the cosmopolitan *problematique* but it is, I suppose, an argument against thinking about it in abstract, philosophical terms. Translated into a concrete situation, that vocabulary may express sentiments of spiritual and political significance that no other language can communicate, or can do so only with great difficulty. I am thinking of an experience some years ago at that section of Arlanda, Stockholm's airport, designated for travellers coming from or departing to areas not covered by the Schengen agreement. The inside walls of the terminal building were covered by a large artwork that consisted of pictures of faces of people from all over the world. Above them circulated a text, written in perhaps two dozen languages: "I am a citizen of the world. My homeland is everywhere, everywhere I am a stranger."

The cosmopolitan experience can only be a local experience. Here it was the experience of arriving in the very local world of Sweden, meeting a people (the Swedish people) who wanted to say, as the first thing to someone who entered their world: "Hello stranger, this is your homeland as much as mine – also, if you feel alien here, so do I." Those images stuck with me as I boarded the plane to Helsinki where, like almost everywhere, empty, non-committal walls greet the incoming stranger. I thought: I just might know how Kant felt at home in Königsberg reading the news of the storming of the Bastille.

Photo of work of art at Arlanda airport by courtesy of the artist, Marie Jo Lafontaine

Part II

European Cosmopolitanisms?

Is there a "European Law" of the Early Modern Period?

Jan SCHRÖDER

In this essay I would like to discuss, whether a "cosmopolitan", that is common European Law existed in the early modern period. This position has been consistently maintained or suggested. A little more than twenty years ago, Helmut Coing wrote a two-volume opus on "European Private Law" ("*Europäisches Privatrecht*")[1] which he understood as referring to the Roman common *private law* of the early modern period and the nineteenth century. In the seventeenth and eighteenth centuries, one finds several books on the subject of a *public law* of Europe; for example *Le droit public de l'Europe* by Gabriel Bonnot de Mably.[2] A "European natural law" is also envisaged, for instance, in the title of a collection of papers edited by Diethelm Klippel four years ago.[3] And perhaps one can even consider the law of the *Holy Roman Empire of the German Nation* as being a precursor to current European Law. Accordingly, there would be four candidates for a "European Law" of the early modern period, namely 1) the Roman common law (*jus commune*); 2) the so-called "European public law"; 3) natural law; and 4) the law of the German Empire.

I do not, at this time, intend to "substantively" inquire as to the contents of these laws or their effects on modern European law (that is about constitutional models, human rights, notions and terms of property, etc.). That would be an enormous subject, which could neither be dealt with exhaustively in a single essay, nor, indeed, in a single symposium. Rather, I would like to concentrate on the "formal" side of things and attempt to outline the scope of applicability and the mode of application of those four types of "European law". Modern European law applies in all Member States and takes precedence over their respective

---

1 Coing, Helmut, *Europäisches Privatrecht*, 2 Vols., Munich, 1985-1989. See also the critical remarks by Brauneder, Wilhelm, "Europäisches Privatrecht – aber was ist es?," 15 *Zeitschrift für Neuere Rechtsgeschichte* (1993), pp. 225-235.

2 De Mably, Gabriel Bonnôt, *Le droit public de l'Europe, fondé sur les traités*, 4th ed., 4 Vols., Genève, 1768.

3 Klippel, Diethelm (ed.), *Naturrecht und Staat. Politische Funktionen des europäischen Naturrechts* (17.-19. Jahrhundert), Munich, Oldenbourg, 2006.

national law. Is that also true for the "European" law of the early modern period? My conclusion will be that none of the four forms applied throughout all of Europe and that even those that can be designated as being supranational had, as a rule, a subsidiary validity only.

1. Scope of Application

1.1. "European Public Law"

I will begin with the so-called "European public law". As elucidated in the famous bibliography by Martin Lipenius, it was evidently the only law which, as early as the seventeenth century, was explicitly referred to as being "European". The first pertinent opus seems to be *Ius publicum Europaeum* by Jochen Hagemeier. It was published in nine small volumes between 1677 and 1681[4] and depicts the constitutional laws of the European States of the time in a comparative manner. Thereafter, public international law supervenes,[5] in particular in the form of Johann Jakob Moser's work from 1732: *Anfangs-Gründe der Wissenschaft von der heutigen Staats-Verfassung von Europa und dem unter denen Europäischen Potenzen üblichen Völcker- oder allgemeinen Staatsrecht.*[6] Finally, the previously mentioned and widely distributed *Droit public de l'Europe* by Abbot Gabriel Bonnot de Mably, which was first published in 1748, contained public international law only.

Mably uses the term *Droit public de l'Europe* to refer to the treaties concluded between European States since the Peace of Westphalia, which he describes in several volumes. In so doing, he does not omit the Ottoman Empire,[7] which at that time stretched far into the southeastern reaches of Europe, from Crete to Romania. By this account, his concept of *Droit public de l'Europe* is not concerned with a common European law, which applies in all States but only a series of distinct rules of public international law. The term "European" in *Droit public de l'Europe* refers only to the *geographic* region, and not to the scope of *applicability of the law*. It is comparable to the situation which would arise if one were to compile all rental contracts concluded in Finland.

---

4 Hagemeier, Joachim, *Juris publici Europaei ... epistola(e)*, 9 Vols., Frankfurt am Main, 1677-1681, continued by Heinrich Günter Thülemar, 3 Vols., Frankfurt am Main, 1681-1682.

5 Concerning the "droit public de l'Europe" (as international law) see Ziegler, Karl-Heinz, *Völkerrechtsgeschichte*, 2nd ed., Munich, C.H. Beck Verlag, 2007, pp. 155-163.

6 *Fundamental principles of the science of the European state's-constitution of today and of the peoples that are subjected to European powers and of general state law*, 1. Theil, Tübingen, 1732.

7 De Mably, *Le droit public de l'Europe, fondé sur les traités*, Vol. 1, p. 290.

One would then have an epitome of many different tenancy laws in existence in Finland, but not a single tenancy law applicable throughout all of Finland. Thus, for the purpose of our further deliberations, we can disregard considerations of "European public law".

1.2. Jus commune

The *jus commune* was somewhat more a common European law. As is well known, the term is drawn from the ancient Roman law, which was rediscovered in the Middle Ages, edited by Italian glossators and commentators and then adopted predominantly by the southern and western European countries.[8] Private law is the most important element of *jus commune*. As a result of the widely varying political conditions to be found in Europe during the Middle Ages and the early modern period, neither criminal law nor, more particularly, constitutional law gained much of a foundation in European legal systems.

The *jus commune* was, thus, a European, but in no way a pan-European law. It applied in the Romanic States and, beyond that, primarily in the German Empire and the Netherlands, as well as Scotland. England, however, had opted for the local common law as opposed to Roman law as early as the Middle Ages. Moreover, in Scandinavian countries and Eastern Europe *jus commune* applied only in an attenuated form.[9] Accordingly, the *jus commune* was not a legal order applicable throughout the entire European continent.

1.3. Natural law

In respect of natural law, the issue is somewhat more complicated. I will ignore the question of whether natural law enjoyed "validity" at all as a positive rule of law (this was, in any event, the case in Germany). However, there was ultimately no *one* natural law; rather there were many different forms of natural law which differed significantly from one another depending on place and time.

Therefore, I would like to restrict the question concerning the scope of application of natural law and refer not to the ancient divine natural law but only to the law of human reason, which became prevalent from about 1650 onwards.[10] In Germany, this law of reason, under the influ-

8 See Stein, Peter G., *Römisches Recht in Europa. Die Geschichte einer Rechtskultur*, Frankfurt am Main, Fisher, 1996, pp. 68, 137; Coing, *Europäisches Privatrecht*, Vol. I, pp. 7-15.

9 See Coing, *Europäisches Privatrecht*, Vol. I, pp. 13-15, 95-100; Stein, *Römisches Recht in Europa*, p. 137.

10 Cf. the summary in Schröder, Jan, *Recht als Wissenschaft. Geschichte der juristischen Methodenlehre vom Humanismus bis zur Historischen Schule* (1500-1850), Munich, C.H. Beck Verlag, 2001, pp. 9-12, 99-104.

ence of the thinking of Thomas Hobbes, initially bore absolutist tendencies. Later, in the Kantian period, liberalist tendencies became evident. In England, a liberal law of reason influenced by John Locke was active much earlier; in France from the middle of the eighteenth century at the latest. But this law of reason was also not a pan-European occurrence.[11] It was prevalent mainly in northern and central Europe, but only to a certain extent in the Mediterranean region. Italy has accepted the absolutist law of reason since the middle of the eighteenth century, but arguably the only liberal author, Cesare Beccaria, cannot actually assert his influence (at least not in Southern Italy).[12] Traces of the absolutist law of reason can be found in Spain, but attempts were made to combine it with the old theological, Catholic natural law.[13] The Ottoman Empire need not be mentioned in this context.

The law of reason or, in any event, its liberal version spread itself throughout Europe to a similarly small degree as the *jus commune*. Their respective scopes of application are, to put it somewhat simply, complementary: *Jus commune* was prevalent in Catholic, Romanic southern Europe, and the law of reason in the Protestant northern and central regions of Europe. Of course there are overlaps, especially in France, Germany and the Netherlands. But neither the law of reason nor the *jus commune* were pan-European law.

1.4. The Law of the Holy Roman Empire of the German Nation

Finally, the same is true for the law of the German Empire. The Holy Roman-German Empire comprised an enormous area. It extended far beyond today's Germany and Austria, and even in the eighteenth century extended from the Duchy of Holstein to the Archdiocese of Trent and from the Austrian Netherlands (which correspond approximately with modern-day Belgium) to Bohemia and Moravia.[14] But, of course, this was only a *part* of Europe and its law was thus not pan-European.

---

11 Cf. the instructive survey by Othmer, Sieglinde C., *Berlin und die Verbreitung des Naturrechts in Europa*, Berlin, De Gruyter, 1970, pp. 136-142, and the supplements by Luig, Klaus, "Zur Verbreitung des Naturrechts in Europa," 40 *Tijdschrift voor Rechtsgeschiedenis* (1972), pp. 539-557 (546, 548-557).

12 Dipper, Christof, "Die politische Funktionalität des italienischen Naturrechts in der zweiten Hälfte des 18. Jahrhunderts," in Vanda Fiorillo and Frank Grunert (eds.), *Das Naturrecht der Geselligkeit. Anthropologie, Recht und Politik im 18. Jahrhundert*, Berlin, Duncker & Humblot, 2009, pp. 135-157.

13 Rus Rufino, Salvador, "Die Entwicklung des Naturrechts in der spanischen Aufklärung," in Klippel, *Naturrecht und Staat*, pp. 59-88; Tómas y Valiente, Francisco, *Manual de historia del derecho español*, 4th ed., Technos, 1997 [1983], pp. 392-395.

14 See Conrad, Hermann, *Deutsche Rechtsgeschichte*, Vol. 2: *Neuzeit bis 1806*, Karlsruhe, C.F. Müller Verlag, 1966, pp. 106-113.

2. Mode of Application

The *jus commune*, natural law and the law of the German Empire, therefore, did not apply in all European states, but nonetheless did enjoy at least a supranational status, stretching as they did across several European states. Did they now at least enjoy supremacy over the individual national laws so that one can compare them to this extent with modern European law? As it is scarcely possible to answer that question in respect of each European state individually, I will limit myself to the solutions provided by *German* legal theory.

2.1. Jus commune

German theory has since the beginning of the early modern period accepted that the Roman common law only applied in a subsidiary fashion, meaning that divergent German laws, whether that by imperial, regional, or local law, took precedence over it. Nevertheless, if no such divergent German law could be proven to exist, a "fundata intention" (a founded presumption) ought to indicate the applicability of Roman law.[15] Such proof was in practice difficult to obtain, for no one had a complete overview over the entirety of regional and local German law and, furthermore, not all German laws had been recorded in writing. According to this concept, *jus commune* would have been theoretically subsidiary but would generally have taken precedence in practice.

For a long time this was the prevailing opinion among German legal historians. However, more recent research (particularly by Klaus Luig, Peter Oestmann, Frank Schäfer, and Anja Amend-Traut)[16] has shown that this view still overestimates the importance of Roman law. German law also quite often seems to have prevailed over Roman law in practice. For instance, the respective (German) law was considered to fall under the rule of judicial notice at the court's location and did not have to be proven in particular. German law, which was available in printed form, was considered to be established, at least at the Imperial Chamber Court (*Reichskammergericht*), even if it only amounted to recorded customary law. Only German law not recorded in written form had to be

---

15 Cf. the summary in Schröder, *Recht als Wissenschaft*, pp. 21, 115.

16 Luig, Klaus, "Universales und partikulares Recht in den 'Meditationes ad Pandectas' von Augustin Leyser," in *Diritto comune e diritti locali nella storia dell' Europa*, Milano, Giuffrè, 1980, pp. 27-48; Oestmann, Peter, *Rechtsvielfalt vor Gericht. Rechtsanwendung und Partikularrecht im Alten Reich*, Frankfurt am Main, Veröffentlichungen des Max-Planck-Instituts für Europäische Rechtsgeschichte, 2002; Schäfer, Frank L., *Juristische Germanistik. Eine Geschichte der Wissenschaft vom einheimischen Privatrecht*, Frankfurt am Main, Klostermann, 2008, p. 221; Amend-Traut, Anja, *Wechselverbindlichkeiten vor dem Reichskammergericht: praktiziertes Zivilrecht in der frühen Neuzeit*, Cologne [u.a.], Böhlau, 2009.

specifically proven. But this is not an indication of the shortcomings of German law, rather a general problem of customary law. One can, therefore, postulate, given the present state of research, that the supranational Roman common law was of subsidiary meaning not only theoretically but also to a large extent in practice.

2.2. Natural Law

Concerning natural law, just a few decades ago German legal historians maintained that it did not have a subsidiary application, but instead enjoyed precedence: "Natural Law overrides positive law." I have maintained for some considerable period of time that this view is incorrect,[17] and hope that I have managed to persuade most of my legal historian colleagues to share my opinion. It was no different in respect of the natural law than the *jus commune*: In any event, it applied subsidiarily since the eighteenth century. Only until the early seventeenth century did natural law take absolute precedence over positive law. "Law" was at that time regarded as a reasonable and just rule only to the extent that positive law which was contrary to the requirements of natural law could not be law at all. Positive law could only broaden natural law or restrict it in certain cases on an individual basis. It could not completely abrogate norms of natural law, e.g. make an order that all humans are to be slaves. Such an order would have been void and not "law".

Since the middle of the seventeenth century, the precedence of natural law has begun to be questioned. Under the influence of Bodin and Hobbes a positivistic notion of law developed – at least in Germany – according to which law is nothing more than a command, an expression of the legislator's will.[18] This occurrence reflects the scientific revolution of the seventeenth century, that is, the transition of science to that which can be positively granted, that which can be experienced; but it also embodies the growing claim to power by the state. Positive law no longer necessarily has to be reasonable and just – it could also, as Pufendorf explicitly writes, arise from the "naked arbitrariness" (*ex nudo arbitrio*) of the legislator.[19] Then its application would obviously not depend on considerations of natural law anymore and this would no longer necessarily take precedence. Hobbes and Pufendorf still conceal

---

17 Schröder, Jan, "'Naturrecht bricht positives Recht' in der Rechtstheorie des 18. Jahrhunderts?," in Dieter Schwab *et al.* (eds.), *Staat, Kirche, Wissenschaft in einer pluralistischen Gesellschaft. Festschrift zum 65. Geburtstag von Paul Mikat*, Berlin, Duncker & Humblot, 1989, pp. 419-433.

18 See Schröder, *Recht als Wissenschaft*, pp. 97-99.

19 Pufendorf, Samuel, *De jure naturae et gentium libri octo* (1672), in Samuel Pufendorf, *Gesammelte Werke*, Vol. 4, Frank Böhling (ed.), Berlin, Akademie Verlag, 1998, lib. 2, cap. 3, § 24, p. 163.

this to some extent: natural law is still intended to take precedence but positive law can "define" concepts of natural law. For example, according to Hobbes, theft is prohibited by natural law, but the law of a state can determine that asportation (the act of carrying away or removing property or a person) is not theft.[20] This peculiar solution to this problem can be explained by the fact that God was still considered to be the creator of natural law and it would accordingly be unimaginable to raise the human legislator above God. Only in the middle of the eighteenth century did a period of secularisation remove this connection between God and natural law.[21] In this era, the belief began to take hold that the origin of natural law deriving from God could not be proven. "How do I know that God wants this?" asks Joachim Georg Darjes, a student of Wolff in 1762.[22] So, in the conflict between natural law/law of reason and positive law, divine law was no longer juxtaposed with human law but only human reason (or rather the reason postulated by a few philosophers) and the law of a national legislator. Thus, all hurdles to positive national law taking precedence were finally removed. From the second half of the eighteenth century onwards this was openly declared. For example, in 1808, Gottlieb Hufeland, a professor from Jena, wrote: *Alle gültigen positive Gesetze gehen den natürlichen vor* ("All valid positive laws take precedence over natural laws").[23] Supranational law thus drops down to the level of being simply a subsidiary source of law.

2.3. German Imperial Law

Finally, I think that this tendency can also be seen in the relationship between German imperial law and local laws. In relation to the laws of the individual states, such as Austria, Prussia, Bavaria, etc., the law of the Empire was supranational. The hierarchy which prevailed between the regional laws and the law of the Empire is nonetheless rather unclear in the leading legal-historical literature.[24] Despite this, a number of

---

20 Hobbes, Thomas, *De cive* (1642), cap. 14, §§ 3, 10 = Hobbes, Thomas, *Opera philosophica quae latine scripsit omnia*, William Molesworth (eds.), (1839-1845), Vol. 2, pp. 315, 319; Pufendorf, *De jure naturae et gentium libri octo*, lib. 8, cap. 1, § 3, pp. 746-747.

21 See Schröder, Jan, "'Gesetz' und 'Naturgesetz' in der frühen Neuzeit," *Abhandlungen der Geistes- und sozialwissenschaftlichen Klasse*, Akademie der Wissenschaften und der Literatur Mainz 1 (2004), pp. 1-35, pp. 26-28.

22 Darjes, Joachim George, *Discours über sein Natur- und Völkerrecht*, 1 Teil, Jena, 1762, p. 259.

23 Hufeland, Gottlieb, *Lehrbuch des in den deutschen Ländern geltenden gemeinen oder subsidiarischen Civilrechts*, I Gießen, 1808, p. 29.

24 See Schröder, *Recht als Wissenschaft*, pp. 20-21, 114-115, and furthermore Schneider, Michael, *Das Verhältnis des Reichsrechts zum Landesrecht im alten Reich seit dem Beginn der Neuzeit*, Diss. Jur., Tübingen, 2002; Schennach, Martin Paul, *Gesetz*

unequivocal statements can be made. Imperial law took absolute precedence in matters of constitutional law, that is, matters concerning the basic laws of the Empire (*leges fundamentales*).[25] This seems sensible because if the states had been in a position to change the imperial constitution at their own discretion, the Holy Roman Empire would have collapsed.

The situation concerning the non-fundamental – as they were frequently dubbed – private imperial laws was, however, disputed. Often they only had subsidiary applicability, as the Empire permitted the states to deviate from them. This was the case, for example, with the *Constitutio criminalis Carolina*, the well-known criminal code of the Empire from 1532. It was often the case that the laws – as in public international law – had to be implemented, transformed into state law.[26] In that case, it was in the state sovereign's power to decide whether to introduce imperial law or not. If he opted not to do so, he was indeed in breach of his obligations towards the Empire, but the Empire was rarely in a position to punish such breach. Thus, the precedence of imperial law only came into consideration if the Empire issued a compulsory ordinance which did not have to be implemented. It is noteworthy that even in this event the precedence of imperial law was contested. Thus, the leading jurists of Brandenburg-Prussia maintained that even compulsory "private" imperial laws applied only subsidiarily.

Here is an example of a well-known controversial issue in this area. The *Jüngste Reichsabschied*, an imperial law from 1654, allowed for the first time for the levying of interest on loans, but limited the interest rate to 5%. Prior to this, there was already a law in existence in Brandenburg which allowed for the imposition of an interest rate of 6%. The question, therefore, was whether in Brandenburg interest rates of 6% were still allowed or whether only 5% rates were permitted? The Prussian jurists Heinrich Cocceji, Samuel Stryk, Christian Thomasius, and Justus Henning Böhmer were of the opinion that the law of Brandenburg, permitting the higher interest rate of 6%, remained in force despite the new imperial law which imposed a 5% limit. Böhmer expressed the rationale of this opinion by saying that it could not be doubted that the state sovereigns were "also allowed to enact provincial leges contra recessus

---

und Herrschaft. Zur Entstehung des Gesetzgebungsstaates am Beispiel Tirols, Cologne [u.a.], Böhlau, 2010, p. 753.

25 See Schneider, *Das Verhältnis des Reichsrechts zum Landesrecht im alten Reich seit dem Beginn der Neuzeit*, p. 127.

26 Schennach, *Gesetz und Herrschaft*, p. 756.

imperii and introduce them within their States."[27] According to this view, imperial law would only have applied with subsidiary effect in respect of "private" matters. This opinion was not, however, the general opinion outside of Prussia. Nonetheless, in the late eighteenth century the important idea of (as I should like to call it) "material subsidiarity" comes to the fore and may be formulated thus: In areas of law which do not require a uniform regulation throughout the Empire, imperial law may not take precedence.[28] The continuing development of the law brought about the relegation of imperial law to a subsidiary position since the major states wished to achieve more and more independence from the restrictions it sought to impose.

In summary, one can establish that, according to the German theory, the *jus commune*, natural law and even German imperial law – at least according to the view held by Prussia and excepting the "basic laws of the Empire" – applied only with subsidiary effect. Even where it could be found to exist, "European law" or, to put it more precisely, "supranational law" did not have a particularly strong position. The two main reasons for this were the process of secularisation and the tendency towards a national legislative monopoly. Secularisation took away the former claim to validity of natural law/law of reason, and the national legislative monopoly led to the relegation to a subsidiary position of all law not created by the state.

3. Conclusions

My conclusion therefore is, first, that there was no "cosmopolitan" European law common to all of Europe in the early modern period. Diplomatic relations between European states, including the Ottoman Empire, did not establish a common law; the so-called "droit public de l'Europe" was law *throughout* all of Europe but not *for* Europe as a whole. Indeed *jus commune* and natural law were both common, supranational laws, but were only able to coexist in continental Western Europe; i.e. in France, the Netherlands and the German Empire. Secondly and most notably, the effects of these supranational laws must not be overestimated. They applied, at least in Germany, only subsidiarily; the particular law of the state took precedence.

Do these historical situations have any relevance whatsoever for modern-day Europe? Such questions have to be answered cautiously.

---

27 Böhmer, Justus Henning, *Consultationes et Decisiones iuris*, tomus 2, pars 1, Carl August Böhmer (ed.), Halle, 1734, Resp. 437, No. 23 (29, p. 663). Cf. Schröder, *Recht als Wissenschaft*, p. 114.

28 See Schneider, *Das Verhältnis des Reichsrechts zum Landesrecht im alten Reich seit dem Beginn der Neuzeit*, pp. 116, 118.

But within the concept of a "Core Europe", the common legal aspects of the early modern period obviously persist. The concept of subsidiarity is of particular interest and importance. A principle of subsidiarity also exists in modern European law (Article 5(3) of the Treaty on European Union). However, this provision is not about subsidiarity of *law*, as in the early modern period, but about subsidiarity of *competences*. Nevertheless, the basic idea is the same as the one phrased in the German Empire of the late eighteenth century: if the objective in question cannot be better achieved by the entire state on a federal level than by the individual state on the local level, then the rule of the individual state applies. So certain continuities and similarities may be seen. Our politicians may not be aware of these continuities, but we learned jurists and historians should not completely forget about them.

Universalistic but Not Discriminatory

Rousseau's *Principles of the Rights of War*

Gabriella SILVESTRINI

> The first thing I note when considering the position of the human species is a manifest contradiction in its constitution, rendering it forever unstable. From one man to the next, we live in a civil state and subject to laws. From one people to the next, each enjoys natural liberty. But this basically makes our situation worse than if these distinctions were unknown. For, living at once in social order and a state of nature, we are subjected to the disadvantages of both without finding safety in either.[1]

From the *Discourse on the Origin and Foundations of Inequality Among Men* Rousseau was very perceptive in shedding light on the perverse and contradictory effect that is produced with the birth of the political society and the division of the human race into numerous states: war is the deadly consequence of the creation of the political relationship: "since each of us is in the civil state with his fellow citizens and in the state of nature with all the rest of the world, we have forestalled private wars only to ignite general ones, which are a thousand times more terrible; and that by uniting ourselves to several men, we really become the enemies of the human race".[2] As Victor Goldschmidt has written, the realisation and exposition of this manifest contradiction is one of "Rousseau's great discoveries", which made him the first to

1 Rousseau, Jean-Jacques, "Principles of the Right of War," in Jean-Jacques Rousseau, *Of the Social Contract and Other Political Writings*, Christopher Bertram (ed.), Quintin Hoare (transl.), London, Penguin Books, 2012, p. 154; the English translation is based on the reconstruction of Rousseau's manuscripts on war edited by Bruno Bernardi and Gabriella Silvestrini in Rousseau, Jean-Jacques, *Principes du droit de la guerre. Écrits sur la paix perpétuelle*, Bruno Bernardi and Gabriella Silvestrini (eds.), Blaise Bachofen, Céline Spector (dir.), Paris, Vrin, 2008, pp. 43-81; for a first version of Rousseau's text see Bernardi, Bruno and Silvestrini, Gabriella, *Principes du droit de la guerre*, 46 *Annales de la Société Jean-Jacques Rousseau* (2005), pp. 201-280. See also the German translation by Michael Bloch, 58 *Deutsche Zeitschrift für Philosophie* (2010), pp. 307-317.

2 Rousseau, Jean-Jacques, "Abstract of Monsieur Abbé de Saint-Pierre's Plan for Perpetual Peace," in Jean-Jacques Rousseau, *The Plan for Perpetual Peace, on the Government of Poland, And Other Writings on History and Politics*, Christopher Kelly (ed.), Lebanon, Dartmouth College Press, 2005, p. 28.

establish, if not to invent, the terms of the problem of the conflict between patriotism and cosmopolitanism.[3]

However, knowledge of a problem does not necessarily require any faith in a possible solution of it. Indeed, while having found in this very "partial and imperfect association" the cause of tyranny and war, "the greatest plagues of humanity",[4] Rousseau did not envisage a global solution to this contradiction, unlike Kant, who instead believed it would be possible to set out a cosmopolitan law capable of slowly bringing the human race closer to a "cosmopolitan constitution".[5]

Rousseau's unambiguous scepticism towards international law as a means with which to regulate and pacify the relations between states has led some interpreters of his work to detect a radical break from cosmopolitanism in favour of a patriotism that, in his late writings on Corsica and Poland, appeared to be out-and-out nationalism, and by others as a shift towards federalism, made possible by the theory of legitimate societies of *The Social Contract*. However, a seemingly more convincing position is that of those who, keeping intact the declaration on the impossibility of transcending on a global level the underlying conflict inherent in relations between states, see Rousseau as having attempted to offer solutions to this problem that varied according to circumstances, and of having wedded moral cosmopolitanism with non-aggressive forms of patriotism.[6]

Nevertheless, the theoretical basis he assumed in his thought on the right of war, and in particular the "principles of the right of war", which he began to set out systematically in 1756 and he would define, in

3 Goldschmidt, Victor, *Anthropologie et politique. Les principes du système de Rousseau* (1974), Paris, Vrin, 1983, p. 631.

4 Rousseau, Jean-Jacques, *Emile, or on Education*, Christopher Kelly and Allan Bloom (eds.), Lebanon, Dartmouth College Press, 2010, p. 659.

5 Kant, Immanuel, *Toward Perpetual Peace and Other Writings on Politics, Peace, and History*, Pauline Kleingeld (ed.), New Haven, Yale University Press, 2006, p. 82.

6 See Hoffmann, Stanley, "Rousseau, la guerre et la paix," 5 *Annales de Philosophie politique* (1965), pp. 195-240; Lalatta Costerbosa, Marina, "Guerra e libertà in Jean-Jacques Rousseau. L'impossibilità di un progetto per la pace internazionale," 15 *Teoria politica* (1999), pp. 125-141; Ramel, Frédérick and Joubert, Jean-Paul, *Rousseau et les relations internationales*, Paris, Harmattan, 2000; Cavallar, Georg, "'La société générale du genre humain': Rousseau on Cosmopolitanism, International Relations, and Republican Patriotism," in Paschalis M. Kitromilides (ed.), *From Republican Polity to National Community. Reconsiderations of Enlightenment Political Thought*, Oxford, Voltaire Foundation, 2003, pp. 89-109; Bachofen, Blaise, "La nation, la patrie, le pays. La question de l'appartenance politique chez Rousseau," 50 *Annales de la Société Jean-Jacques Rousseau* (2012), pp. 267-298.

Emile, "the true principles of the right of war",[7] appears to be problematic. In effect, in Rousseau's construction the deduction of the principles of the right of war does not seem to fit, in contrast to what occurred in the case of treatises on natural and international law, into a wider treatment of the "law of nations", whether this be conceived as an application of the law of nature to relations between states, or as a positive law derived from the tacit or explicit consensus of nations.[8] In Rousseau's works, rather than being placed within the framework of the law of nations, the principles of the right of war seemingly emerge only after the critique that invalidates this rule: "the law of nations has no guarantee apart from its usefulness to the person who submits to it, its decisions are respected only insofar as interest confirms them".[9] This is a criticism that does not herald any alternative approach: in contrast to natural right, political right and the right of war, Rousseau never mentions the possibility of establishing the principles, or even less, the "true principles" of the law of nations.[10] In the summary of *The Social Contract* included in *Emile*, Rousseau states that the exposition of the "principles of political rights" should be followed by the analysis of relations between states and the problems of the "mixed condition", then to the study of federal associations and the right to federate and finally to the "true principles" of the right of war, and the right of nations is not mentioned. In the final chapter of *The Social Contract*, on the other hand, the "true principles of political right" are not followed by further "true principles", and in the list of what Rousseau includes in the "ex-

---

7 Rousseau, *Emile, or on Education*, p. 659. It is worth noting that Rousseau used the expression "Principes du droit de la guerre" in a letter to Marc-Michel Rey, 9 March 1758, where he wrote: "Mes principes du Droit de la guerre ne sont point prets", Jean-Jacques Rousseau, *Correspondance Complète de Jean-Jacques Rousseau*, Ralph A. Leigh (ed.), Ginevra/Oxford, The Voltaire Foundation, 1965-1998, V, No. 626, p. 51. On the contrary, the expression is absent from the manuscript recently reconstructed; for the dating of the manuscript see Bernardi, Bruno, Silvestrini, Gabriella, "Principes du droit de la guerre," 46 *Annales de la Société Jean-Jacques Rousseau* (2005), pp. 229-232.

8 See Haggenmacher, Peter, *Grotius et la doctrine de la guerre juste*, Paris, PUF, 1983; Jouannet, Emmanuelle, *Emer de Vattel et l'émergence doctrinale du droit international classique*, Paris, Pedone, 1998.

9 Rousseau, "Principles of the Right of War", p. 154.

10 On Rousseau's doctrine of the law of nations the most illuminating observations are still in Goldschmidt, *Anthropologie et politique*, pp. 614-632, who however does not tackle the problem of the "principles of the right of war"; see also Lassudrie-Duchêne, Georges, *Jean-Jacques Rousseau et le Droit des Gens*, Paris, H. Jouve, 1906; Nys, Ernest, "Le droit des gens et les écrits de Jean-Jacques Rousseau," *Revue de droit international et de législation comparée* IX (1907), pp. 77-89; and more recently Fleury, Thibaut, "Le droit des gens dans la pensée de Jean-Jacques Rousseau," *Annales de Philosophie du Droit*, Institut Michel Villey (2006), pp. 295-335.

ternal relations" of the state, the "right of nations" simply precede, but does not include, "the right of war and conquest".[11]

The aim of my contribution is to reconsider Rousseau's doctrine of war in order to have a better understanding of the "principles of the right of war" and their place in his political thought. Moreover, I aim to highlight and to interpret the apparent paradox inherent in his ideas, an apparent contradiction which helps to explain why he has often been read in such different and conflicting ways. This paradox can be found in the persistence of the concept of the *agresseur injuste*, or of *guerre injuste*, within the context of a doctrine which at first glance ought to imply the elimination of the problem of just cause and the neutralisation of natural law.

Rousseau, Legitimate War and Unjust War

Rousseau set out his doctrine of war in its definitive form in the *Social Contract* (published in 1762), but had already elaborated it in the *Second Discourse* and in the manuscript on the *Principles of the Right of War* written in 1756.[12] In the latter text he unambiguously uses the term *légitime* in relation to war, a term that recalls Grotius's doctrine of solemn war, which Barbeyrac had translated as "guerre légitime, ou dans les formes".[13] The same words were taken up by Emer de Vattel's *Law of Nations* published in 1758. This continuity of terminology allows one to ask whether Rousseau's theory of war could be better understood by reflecting not only on the explicit criticism he directed at earlier writers – the "scholars and jurisconsults" who justify and distort the "public institutions" – but also on the way in which, when criticising them, he reworks their language and appropriates it in an original way.

11 Rousseau, *Emile, or on Education*, p. 659; Rousseau, *Of the Social Contract and Other Political Writings*, IV, 9, p. 133.

12 The reconstruction of the manuscripts has permitted to better show the coherence and the autonomy of Rousseau's reflections on war and interstate relations, see particularly Bernardi, Bruno, *La fabrique des concepts. Recherches sur l'invention conceptuelle chez Rousseau*, Paris, Champion, 2006, pp. 225-268; Bachofen, Blaise, *Les raisons de la guerre, la raison dans la guerre*, in Rousseau, *Principes du droit de la guerre*, pp. 131-192. Nonetheless, the complexity of Rousseau's thought may make it legitimate to speak of an "Aporetik des Krieges", see Bloch, Michael, "Möglichkeit und Unmöglichkeit internationaler Politik. Rousseaus Auffassung des Krieges," 58 *Deutsche Zeitschrift für Philosophie* (2010), pp. 288-306, p. 304.

13 Grotius, Hugo, *Le droit de la guerre et de la paix*, nouvelle traduction par Jean Barbeyrac, Amsterdam, Pierre du Coup, 1724, III, III, t. II, p. 750. In the *Principes du droit de la guerre* (Paris, Vrin, 2008), p. 80, we read: "Je prie les lecteurs de ne point oublier que je ne cherche pas ce qui rend la guerre avantageuse à celui qui la fait mais ce qui la rend légitime."

To begin with, we can observe similarities in the deduction of the law carried out by Vattel and Rousseau, both of whom had read Barbeyrac and knew the way in which he had led Grotius' law of nations back to natural law. In keeping with Hobbes and Pufendorf, Barbeyrac had defined the law of nations as natural law applied to the nature of the states. Vattel had explained that "the maxims of the necessary law of nations are founded immediately on the nature of things and particularly on that of man, and of political society".[14] The reference to the "nature of things", "nature of man" and "of political society" as the foundations of law or right was fairly widespread, but it is not possible to survey this well-studied debate here. I limit myself to observing that Rousseau declared that he had followed this method in the *Discourse on Inequality*, citing Burlamaqui's doctrine that the idea of right and natural right "are manifestly ideas relative to the Nature of man".[15] In the passages of *The Social Contract* which discuss the right of war, Rousseau explains how to understand this in very clear terms: "war gives no right that is not necessary to its aim. These principles are not those of Grotius; they are not based on the authority of poets, but derive from the nature of things and are based on reason."[16]

At first glance one might think that this sentence involves a radical opposition between "these principles" and Grotius' system. Yet in reality, the principle according to which there is a right to do whatever is necessary in order to fulfil an aim imposed by nature was a maxim that Grotius used frequently. This was the criterion that made it possible not only to take a law or right and deduce what specific actions and rights they permitted, but also to establish what is or is not permissible (or

---

14 de Vattel, Emer, *The Law of Nations*, Béla Kapossy and Richard Whatmore (eds.), Indianapolis, Liberty Fund, 2008, p. 593; for the French original see de Vattel, Emer, *Le droit des gens ou principes de la loi naturelle*, London, 1758, III, XII, § 192, t. II, p. 169. I have investigated Vattel's argument on this subject in Silvestrini, Gabriella, "Vattel, Rousseau et la question de la justice de la guerre," in Vincent Chetail & Peter Haggenmacher (eds.), *Vattel's International Law from a XXIst Century Perspective*, Boston, Brill, 2011, pp. 99-127. In the following I will take up and develop the second part of this article.

15 Rousseau, Jean-Jacques, "Discourse on the Origin and the Foundations of Inequality among Men," in Jean-Jacques Rousseau, *The Discourses and Other Early Political Writings*, Victor Gourevitch (ed.), Cambridge, Cambridge University Press, 1997, pp. 111-231, p. 126; for the French edition see *Œuvres complètes de Jean-Jacques Rousseau*, Bernard Gagnebin & Marcel Raymond (eds.), Paris, Gallimard, 1959-1995, 5 Vols.; in the following: *OC* III, p. 124.

16 Rousseau, *Of the Social Contract and Other Political Writings*, p. 16 (English translation slightly modified). See also the French version: "Or la guerre ne donne aucun droit qui ne soit nécessaire à sa fin. Ces principes ne sont pas ceux de Grotius, ils ne sont pas fondés sur des autorités de poètes, mais dérivent de la nature des choses, et sont fondés sur la raison", *Du Contrat Social*, I, IV, *OC* III, pp. 357-358.

what is a right) by extrapolating it from the aim of society itself. This maxim was also the fundamental standard, established at the beginning of book III of the *Rights of War and Peace*, which fixed the right of war by reference to natural law: "And here we must observe, first, that in things of a moral nature, as we have often said before, those means which conduce to a certain end, do assume the very nature of that end: And therefore we are supposed to be authorised to employ those things, which are (in a moral, not a physical sense) necessary to obtain our just rights."[17] As Grotius himself underlined, this is a principle which he had already used before[18] and which became the essential criterion in establishing what – according to natural law – is permissible in war, and how far this permission extends. In effect, it is the aim of war defined as the reestablishment of law that guides the just actions of war against those who have committed a crime, by causing damage in proportion to the damage suffered, and justifying means by the ends.

I do not intend to deal with the question of the origin and history of this principle and the original use that Grotius made of it,[19] although I do

17 Grotius, Hugo, *The Rights of War and Peace*, edited and with an Introduction by Richard Tuck, from the edition by Jean Barbeyrac, Indianapolis, Liberty Fund, 2005, III, I, § II, 1, Vol. 3 p. 1186. I also quote the original Latin: "Primum, ut iam ante diximus aliquoties, ea quae ad finem ducunt in morali materia aestimationem intrinsecam accipiunt ab ipso fine: quare quae ad finem iuris consequendi sunt necessaria, necessitate sumpta non secundum Physicam subtilitatem sed moraliter, ad ea ius habere intelligimur: Ius dico illud quod stricte ita dicitur et facultatem agendi in solo societatis respectu significat", Grotius, Hugo, *De iure belli ac pacis libri tres* Aalen, Scientia Verlag, 1993, III, I, § 1, p. 612.

18 In note 1 (*Le droit de la guerre et de la paix*, t. II, at 714), Barbeyrac mentions another two earlier passages from *De iure belli*, in which Grotius states this principle: *De iure belli ac pacis*, II, V, § 24, pp. 254-255: "Et sane gregatim discedi non posse satis expeditum est ex necessitate finis, quae ius facit in moralibus. nam id si liceat, iam civilis societas subsistere non possit" [tr. fr. t. I, p. 306: "Or que l'on ne puisse sortir de l'Etat en troupes, cela paroit assez par le but de la Société Civile, laquelle ne sauroit subsister, si on accorde une telle permission: et en matiére de Choses Morales, ce qui est nécessaire pour arriver à une fin, tient lieu de Loi"]; II, VII, § 2, p. 269: "Dominium autem hoc modo transferri probatur a fine, quae in moralibus optima est probatio" ["cela se prouve par la liaison nécessaire de ce transport avec une fin légitime; qui est le meilleur argument en fait de Choses Morales"]. However, there are passages that are very important because they connect this principle to natural law in a more explicit way. For example, II, V, § 5, p. 233: "Censetur quippe ipsa natura ius dare ad id omne sine quo obtineri non potest quod ipsa imperat" [tr. fr. t. I, at 281: "En effet, la Nature même est censée donner droit de faire tout ce sans quoi on ne peut obtenir une fin qu'elle prescrit"].

19 I limit myself to signalling its explicit use by Juan Gines de Sepúlveda, *Democrates alter*, 16, 1, who cites St. Thomas Aquinas, *Summa Theologiae*, II, IIae, q. 40, ar. 2, ad. 3, as a source, along with Popes Alexander III and Celestine III, *Decretales*, L. I, Titulus 29, cap. 5 (*cui causa committitur*), pp. 21 and 39; see also F. Suarez, *De censuris in communi*, II, 5. I take these quotations from Juan Ginés de Sepúlveda,

wish to underline the fact that in the eighteenth century it was treated, so to speak, as a general legal principle which was sanctioned by Grotius' authority.[20] It is also important to make clear that in this case "necessity" does not imply the suspension of a rule: here it is not related to the "state of necessity" and does not refer to an exception, as is often thought.[21] On the contrary, it is a principle which permits the establishment of a universally applicable general rule. Consequently, Rousseau's conceptual move in *The Social Contract* is not really that of criticising Grotius' doctrine in the name of this principle but is an attempt to free it from Grotius' authority and, above all, to contrast it, citing the "authority of poets", with everything that does not derive from the nature of things and is not founded on reason. Like Barbeyrac and Vattel, Rousseau refused to look for the "right of war" in the consensual or positive law of nations and deduces it from reason and from the "nature of things". In order to establish the right of war, the "things" whose nature are under consideration are war, men and political societies. This is the method that Rousseau follows in the manuscript on the principles of the right of war, which leaves out any reference to the society of the human race and the society of nations.

In this manuscript, Rousseau tackles the definition of war beginning with, to use the language of the *Discourse on Inequality*, the "physical" aspects of things, from nature itself, from the "constitution of this universe". Running through the different levels of sensory beings that make up the universe, he searches for the precise point in which peace gives way to war. Peace and war, he asserts, despite being mutually related terms, do not have the same conceptual range. Peace can be disturbed "in a number of ways without going so far as war". The image of the universe that Rousseau presents is not at all peaceful. There is no harmonious relationship between the different things that constitute the

---

Democrate secondo, ovvero sulle giuste cause di guerra, Domenico Taranto (ed.), with the original Latin text, Macerata, Quodlibet, 2009, pp. 100-101.

20 For example, Micheli du Crest, writing a pamphlet against the government of Geneva between 1731 and 1735, justifies the request for the introduction in Geneva of the right to appeal in the General Council by referring to this principle of Grotius, quoting with accuracy from Barbeyrac's translation. See Micheli du Crest, Jacques-Bathélémy, *Discours en forme de Lettres sur le Gouvernement de Genève* (1735), Kenneth Godwin, Guillaume Poisson, Gabriella Silvestrini and Richard Whatmore (eds.), Genève, Slatkine, 2011, second Letter, pp. 28-29. Barbeyrac does not fail to underline that the ends and the means must be *légitimes*, Grotius, *Le droit de la guerre et de la paix*, III, I, § 2, note 1, t. II, 715. See also Vattel, *Le Droit des Gens*, III, VIII, § 137, t. II, p. 105: "La fin légitime ne donne un véritable droit qu'aux seuls moyens nécessaires pour obtenir cette fin."

21 On the "Janus-faced" character of necessity in natural law tradition, see Neff, Stephen C., *War and the Law of Nations. A General History*, Cambridge University Press, 2005, pp. 64-65.

universe and in fact the opposite is true – the principle of survival derived from the law of nature often implies the advantage of one party to the detriment of another. The intensity of conflict gradually increases with the passing from the domain of sensibility to the domain of reason: when there is a reciprocal recognition and the intentional nature of the harm suffered is perceived, there is an effort to turn it back on the instigator, thus giving rise to "discord and disputes, sometime conflicts, but not yet war".[22]

War is not therefore a limited conflict or an occasional outbreak of violence. In the first instance it implies the passage from intelligence to reason, because it is based on an evaluation of the situation that calls for reasoning. Secondly, even though it may be evaluated subjectively, it is an "objective" situation, in other words an incompatibility between the desire for self-preservation and the continuing lives of others. Thirdly, it is a form of reciprocity which makes the relation of war perfectly bilateral: war takes place only when whoever is attacked, seeing that his survival is incompatible with the survival of the enemy, chooses to attack the life of the enemy with all his might. War therefore contains a sort of consensual bilateralism. The combination of these three aspects makes it possible to formulate a definition of war: "This demonstrated will to mutual destruction, and all the acts that flow from it, produce a relationship between the two enemies that we call war". In other words, war consists "in the steady, well-considered and manifest will to destroy our enemy" ["dans la volonté constante réfléchie et manifestée de détruire son ennemi"].[23]

Thus we see that in attempting to define war Rousseau begins by observing the nature of perceptible things and concludes that war cannot exist except between reasoning beings. Although this is a troubled peace, which exists on the level of sentient and animated beings, the universe does not know war. In opposition to a tradition that stretches from Cicero to Grotius, Pufendorf "and the others", Rousseau denies the existence of war in the animal kingdom: animals do not make war; only reasoning beings do, and there is therefore no war between animals or between animals and man.[24] Furthermore, it is clear that because war is

22 Rousseau, "Principles of the right of war", p. 155.

23 *Ibid.*, p. 156.

24 We should remember Cicero's famous phrase in *De officiis*, I, XI: "Nam cum sint duo genera decertandi, unum per disceptationem, alterum per vim, cumque illud proprium sit hominis, hoc beluarum [...]". Cicero, *De officiis*, with an English translation by Walter Miller, London, Heinemann, 1913. Samuel Pufendorf traces war back to animality ("cum bellum ex principio surgat, quod hominis et brutis commune est", *De jure naturae et gentium*, in Pufendorf, Samuel, *Gesammelte Werke*, Vol. 4.1-2, F. Böhling (ed.), Berlin, Akademie Verlag, 1998, VIII, VI, § 2, p. 843) and founds a

not part of the order of nature, it must, like public law, have a conventional origin. It derives from a voluntary, reasoned act and can thus be distinguished analytically from mere violence. Violence is not a voluntary act, but comes from passions, from instinct. However, war and rights belong to two different orders, because war is above all a relation that pertains to the realm of facts. Rousseau therefore rejected the juridical definition of war as an instrument of law as "that state in which we prosecute our right by force".[25]

Rousseau's definition of war, despite having much in common with the Hobbesian definition, differs from it in at least two ways that I believe are decisive. Firstly, in *De Cive*, Hobbes derives war from the "right to all things", which is essentially a *reductio ad absurdum* of the principle of the "aim" that, in Grotius's treatise, governs just war based on natural law.[26] As we have already seen, Rousseau remains faithful to this principle as a criterion from which a rational right could be deduced. Moreover, he did not believe that the desire for self-preservation is unlimited: in his definition, war does not depend on a completely subjective decision that opens the door to a sort of spiral of potential, imaginary violence. Instead there is a subjective judgment concerning an "objective" incompatibility between two existences: war can arise only if there is a certain "relationship between things".[27] Furthermore, it is true that in the manuscript on the *Principles of the Right of War* Rousseau delivers a frontal attack on the Hobbesian doctrine of the "state of

---

sort of right of subservient on this war between animal and man, much like the right to eat the flesh of animals. Rousseau, by contrast, in his second *Discourse*, derives mankind's obligation to avoid needlessly mistreating any sentient being from the "commiseration", *OC* III, p. 126.

25 de Vattel, *The Law of Nations*, III, I, § 1, p. 469. This is Grotius' definition and can also be found in the article "Guerre' from the *Encyclopédie, ou Dictionnaire raisonné des sciences, des arts et des métiers*, Paris, Briasson, 1751-1780, 35 Vols., t. VII, p. 905.

26 Hobbes, Thomas, *Le Citoyen*, I, VIII, French translation by Samuel de Sorbière, Paris, Flammarion, 1982, p. 96: "Or, parce que ce serait en vain qu'on aurait droit de tendre à une fin, si on n'avait aussi le droit d'employer tous les moyens nécessaires pour y parvenir, il s'ensuit que, puisque chacun a droit de travailler à sa conservation, il a pareillement droit d'*user tous les moyens, et de faire toutes les choses sans lesquelles il ne se pourrait point conserver*". In the original Latin: "Quoniam autem *jus* ad finem frustra habet cui *jus* ad media necessaria denegatur, consequens est, cum unusquisque se conservandi *jus* habeat, ut unusquisque *jus* etiam habeat *utendi omnibus mediis, et agendi omnem actionem, sine qua conservare se non potest*", *Elementa philosophica de Cive*, Amsterdam, Apud Henr. Et Viduam Th., 1696, p. 11. See also Hobbes, Thomas, *Le corps politique*, French translation by Samuel de Sorbière (1652), with an Introduction by Roux, Louis, Saint-Etienne, Publications de l'Université de Saint-Etienne, 1977, I, VII, p. 4.

27 Rousseau, *Of the Social Contract and Other Political Writings*, I, 4, p. 15.

war". At the anthropological level Hobbes is criticised for having imagined "the senseless system of a natural war of all against all" and for having depicted man as a "strange" animal, "that would believe its well-being depended on the destruction of its entire species"[28] – a sentence that recalls the "strange" doctrine of the *Leviathan* "that nature should thus dissociate, and render men apt to invade, and destroy one another".[29] However, the Hobbesian definition of war is not focused primarily on the concept of "destruction", but on "the Will to contend by Battle", on "the known disposition" to turn to force.[30] On the other hand, Rousseau himself underlines the inherently unreal nature of the "universal war of each against all, the odious image of which Hobbes dares to outline". In Hobbes, man is animated by the desire to put "everyone in irons", which rules out the desire of "massacring everyone".[31] As Michel Foucault correctly observed, no blood flows in Hobbes' war, and there are no bodies.[32]

Rather than in Hobbes's own texts, the language of destruction appears more clearly and frequently in the writings of his critics.[33] Particularly, we find it in the Lockean definition of war: "The State of War is a State of Enmity and Destruction; and therefore declaring by Word or Action, not a passionate and hasty, but a sedate settled Design, upon another Mans Life, *puts him in a State of War* with him against whom

28 Rousseau, "Principles of the right of war", p. 157.

29 Hobbes, Thomas, *Leviathan*, Richard Tuck (ed.), Cambridge, Cambridge University Press, 2003, ch. XIII, p. 89. This sentence of *Leviathan* is quoted by Richard Cumberland, *Traité philosophique des lois naturelles*, Jean Barbeyrac (transl.), Amsterdam, Pierre Mortier, 1744, I, § XXXII, p. 92, footnotes 1-2. Comparing Hobbes' texts, Cumberland accuses Hobbes of being inconsistent: while in *De Cive* he derives "la guerre de tous contre tous" from "le droit de tous à toutes choses", in the *Leviathan* "il prétend, que la Guerre ne peut que naître de la nature même des Passions Humaines". Therefore, even if it is not sure that Rousseau had read Hobbes' *Leviathan*, he could surely find quotations drawn out from it in the polemical texts of Hobbes' readers and critics. See also Pufendorf, Samuel, *Le droit de nature et des gens*, trad. par Jean Barbeyrac, Bâle, E. & J.R., Thourneisen, 1732, II, II, § V, pp. 159-160.

30 *Ibid*., ch. XIII, pp. 88-89.

31 Rousseau, "Principles of the right of war", p. 159.

32 Foucault, Michel, *Il faut défendre la société*, Paris, Gallimard, 1997, p. 79.

33 See for example Filmer, Robert, "Observations on MR Hobbes' Leviathan: or his Artificial Man a Commonwealth," in Johann P. Sommerville (ed.), *Patriarcha and Other Writings*, Cambridge, Cambridge University Press, 1991, p. 188: "It is not to be thought that God would create man in a condition worse than any beast, as if he made men to no other end by nature but to destroy one another"; Abbé de Saint-Pierre, *Projet pour rendre perpétuelle la paix en Europe*, Paris, Fayard, 1986, p. 493: "Dans l'état de Guerre, ou de non Arbitrage, chaque Chef de famille, chaque Chef de nation, ne peut avoir de sûreté entiere ou suffisante de sa conservation, que par la destruction entiere de son voisin, qui est son ennemi".

he has declared such an Intention, and so has exposed his Life to the others Power to be taken away by him."[34] Here we find a number of elements, partly drawn from Hobbesian doctrine, that also feature in Rousseau's concept of war: design implies elements of intentionality and temporality, and life itself is at stake so that one's very existence is threatened with destruction. Even the way that the argument progresses is the same: first there is the definition of the state of war, followed by the application of this concept to the actors in the different situations that they might find themselves in, namely the state of nature and the civil state. However, there is an essential difference between Locke's definition and Rousseau's. First of all, for Locke whoever declares the intention to destroy another violates the law of nature, whereas anyone who defends himself not only obeys this law, but obtains a "right to destroy" the aggressor. In Rousseau, on the other hand, both the aggressor and the defender obey natural law. Thus there is none of the inequality and unilateral nature that characterises the Lockean state of war.[35] Moreover, there is absolutely no mention of the right to kill.

As is well known, Rousseau drew a celebrated conclusion from this definition of war, namely that war does not exist except between states.[36] The incompatibility of existences presupposes stable conditions that do not hold true among individuals. Individual people cannot be involved in a relation of war either in a state of nature or in a civil state. On the other hand states, given their contiguity and the difference in their sizes (factors that imply the impossibility of any analogy between states and

34 Locke, John, *Two Treatises of Government*, II, III, § 16, Peter Laslett (ed.), Cambridge, Cambridge University Press, 2003, p. 278. The French translation by David Mazel slightly alters Locke's text: "L'état de guerre est un état d'*inimitié* et de *destruction*. Celui qui déclare à un autre, soit par parole, soit par actions, qu'il en veut à sa vie, doit faire cette déclaration, non avec passion et précipitamment, mais avec un esprit tranquille: et alors cette déclaration met celui qui l'a faite, dans l'*état de guerre* avec celui à qui il l'a faite", *Traité du gouvernement civil*, Simone Goyard-Fabre (ed.), Paris, Garnier Flammarion, 1992, p. 154.

35 On the state of war in Locke, I permit myself to guide the reader towards Silvestrini, Gabriella, "Guerre juste et droit de résistance dans la tradition protestante du droit naturel," *Genève et la Suisse dans la pensée politique. Actes du Colloque de Genève (Septembre 2006)*, Aix-en-Provence, Presses Universitaires d'Aix-Marseille, 2007, pp. 103-116; "Diritti naturali e diritto di uccidere. Teorie moderne della guerra fra modelli teorici e tradizioni di pensiero," 21 *Filosofia politica* (2007), pp. 425-452.

36 In the manuscript on *Principes du droit de la guerre* Rousseau had written in a note at the foot of the page: "Fin du chapitre: il n'y a point de guerre entre les hommes il n'y en a qu'entre les États", p. 53, note 2; a second formulation can be found in *Manuscrit de Genève*, *OC* III, p. 263: "La guerre n'est pas une relation entre les hommes mais entre les puissances". The third, and definitive version is the celebrated phrase from the *Contrat social*: "La guerre n'est donc point une relation d'homme à homme, mais une relation d'État à État", *OC* III, p. 357.

individuals), inevitably find themselves in a relationship much like that of a zero sum game. I cannot follow Rousseau's arguments on this matter here, but it is worth offering a reminder of his conclusion that among states there exists a "general relationship tending towards their mutual destruction".[37] Applying this notion of war to states leads to a change in its definition: "I call war between one power and another, therefore, the effect of a constant, demonstrated, mutual disposition to destroy the enemy State, or at least to weaken it, by all possible means. This disposition reduced to actions is war properly speaking; so long as it remains without effect it is merely the state of war."[38]

The originality of Rousseau's doctrine should not be sought in his definition of war as a relation between states and as a consequence of the birth of political societies. As a result of his polemic against the Hobbesian idea of a natural state of war between men, Pufendorf had denied that the origin of political societies can be explained by reference to war as this requires a unified command that is produced only after the birth of societies.[39] Because of this, he developed the doctrine of the "legitimate defence of oneself" without making any mention of a right of war. However, when he confronts the problem of war, which he logically placed at the end of his treatise as war occurs after the birth of political societies, self-defence is implicitly linked to war and the state's right to war is derived from that of single individuals.[40] In much the same way, Montesquieu had denied the existence of a natural state of war between individuals and had attributed the origin of war to the birth of societies. He had also established with greater clarity the difference between individual defence as a right to kill, and the right of war which states need in order to survive.[41] However, Montesquieu did not offer any specific fundamental arguments in support of this distinction. Rousseau's innovation was to formulate a definition of war that makes it possible to distinguish analytically between war and violence and between aggression and individual self-defence and state warfare. A

37 Rousseau, "Principles of the right of war", p. 164.

38 *Ibid.*, p. 167.

39 Pufendorf, *De jure naturae et gentium*, VII, III, § 5, p. 665: "Imperium civile non fuit productum per bella".

40 "Cum non minus singuli in libertate naturali viventes, quam civitates à natura concessam habeant facultatem sese contra vim injuste defendendi, ac jura sibi ab aliis laesa aut denegata per vim asserendi; conveniens puto fuerit prius dispicere, quae bella singulorum et civitatum habeant communia; dein, quae hisce sua natura aut moribus gentius sint propria", Pufendorf, *De jure naturae et gentium*, VIII, VI, § 1, p. 842.

41 Montesquieu, Charles de Secondat, *De l'esprit des lois*, X, II, Paris, Garnier Flammarion, 1979, Vol. 1, p. 273. For a comparison between Rousseau and Montesquieu on this point, see Hoffmann, "Rousseau, la guerre et la paix", pp. 198-199.

general relation of reciprocal destruction exists only between states and it is thus impossible to attribute to them a right that derives from an individual right to war.[42] Thus war is no longer to be thought of as an action taken by the "prince" or "master" in the traditional sense, as a phenomenon which emerges from "single" or "private" combat, and should be understood instead as a specifically "political" phenomenon: if the goal of war is the destruction of the enemy, the enemy is the *polis*, the moral person.

From this point of view, the reading of Rousseau as a theorist with a structural explanation of war is incontestable.[43] Nonetheless, after having established the "General Idea of War between State and State" with considerable realism, he did not fail to move from the factual to the legal level, from "the natural state" to "the legitimate state".[44] This shift is made possible by the declaration of war which brings into play the right of war; in other words, the right to do whatever is necessary to destroy the enemy state. From this perspective, such a declaration is comparable to the purely formal moment of declaration contained in Grotius' consensual law of nations and in Vattel's voluntary law of nations. It is a formal act that permits us to distinguish war from simple violence and brigandage, and which gives war its public character. Nonetheless, for Rousseau, this activation of the right of war does not denote the passage from a state of peace to one of war or from the right of peace to the right of war, as the state of war and the right of war are not the same thing, but oppose one another just as facts are opposed to law. Instead, this declaration marks the passage from a factual war to a legitimate one, from the sphere of facts to that of law.

---

42 From this point of view I do not believe that, according to Rousseau, states have a natural right of war, as stated by Asbach, Olaf, *Die Zähmung der Leviathane. Die Idee einer Rechtsordnung zwischen Staaten bei Abbé de Saint-Pierre und Jean-Jacques Rousseau*, Berlin, Akademie Verlag, 2002, p. 255.

43 This is Rousseau the theorist of the "third image" that we find in Waltz, Kenneth, *Man, the State and War. A Theoretical Analysis*, New York, Columbia University Press, 1959, p. 160 onwards; on Waltz' interpretation and its limits see, among others, Williams, M.C., "Rousseau, Realism and Realpolitik," 18 *Millennium: Journal of International Studies* (1989), pp. 188-195; Ramel, Joubert, *Rousseau et les relations internationales*, pp. 165-167.

44 Rousseau, "Principles of the right of war", pp. 164-167. See also the French text: "Je prévois une objection: puisque selon moi l'état de guerre est naturel entre les puissances, pourquoi la disposition dont elle résulte a-t-elle besoin d'être manifestée? À cela je réponds que j'ai parlé ci-devant de l'état naturel, que je parle ici de l'état légitime, et que je ferai voir ci après comment pour le rendre tel la guerre a besoin d'une déclaration […] Je prie les lecteurs de ne point oublier que je ne cherche pas ce qui rend la guerre avantageuse à celui qui la fait mais ce qui la rend légitime. Il en coûte presque toujours pour être juste. Est-on pour cela dispensé de l'être?", *Principes du droit de la guerre*, p. 80.

Although it is the last and the worst of the evils unleashed in the process of forming social institutions, war can be "justified" and made legitimate just like property and political society. The normative discussion of war that Rousseau developed is much closer to the positions held by theorists of just war than to those of supporters of the idea of perpetual peace. It presupposes the possibility of "justifying" and limiting war, not of eliminating it altogether. What is more, like Vattel, but in a more rigorous way, the "right of war" activated by the declaration is not a conventional right to war established consensually by two belligerents. The "principles of the right of war" are universal principles because, as we have already observed, they "derive from the nature of things and are based on reason". It is precisely at the moment that he affirmed this universal character that Rousseau felt the need to clarify that his doctrine on this point was not entirely original. Despite the polemic with "Grotius and the others", he says that the principles he was outlining conformed "to the maxims established in every age and with the constant practice of all civilized peoples".[45]

This does not mean that the principles of the right of war are founded in positive law, whether this be in custom, political law or convention. On the contrary, their origin, as we have seen, lies in the nature of things and their foundation is reason itself, a reason whose normativity is not directed toward the future – as later in Kant – but is already embodied in history, in the laws and "the constant practice of all civilized peoples". As with the principles of political law and social contract theory, Rousseau did not think that this was a normative theory exclusively aimed at the future, but presents it as a criterion with which to separate, in the present as in the past, legitimate institutions from illegitimate ones, and "good" laws from "bad" ones. It is no coincidence that Rome, which Rousseau defined as the nation that had "the best Government to have existed",[46] was also cited, in an explanatory note of *The Social Contract* added to the 1782 edition, as the people "who understood better and respected more the right of war than any other nation in the world". Here we see that the right of war can be "understood" and "respected". This understanding refers to the principles taken from the nature of things and based on reason, principles that the Romans learnt to translate into positive law. Thus Rousseau was well aware of the fact that for

[45] Rousseau, *Of the Social Contract and Other Political Writings*, I, 4, p. 16. Here Rousseau refers to the principle according to which "chaque Etat ne peut avoir pour ennemis que d'autres Etats", and to the need for the declaration to distinguish between an enemy and a bandit, *OC* III, p. 357. On the collective and public character of war for the Greeks and Romans see Neff, *War and the Law of Nations*, pp. 15-20.

[46] Rousseau, *Letters from the Mountains*, VI, in Rousseau, *Of the Social Contract and Other Political Writings*, p. 180.

the Romans the right of war was part of the political law, a positive law that was a "good law", which kept to the principles, as we can infer from the note's final sentence: "The Romans are the people who least often infringed their laws, and they are the only people to have had such fine ones".[47]

As for the contents of the principles of the right of war, *The Social Contract* contains a single terse and illuminating sentence which sums up the juridical effects that war has on things and on people: "Even in the thick of war, a just prince may indeed seize all that belongs to the public in an enemy country; but he respects the person and the goods of individuals, he respects rights upon which his own are based".[48] Like earlier authors, Rousseau established the right of war using the principle of the aim of war: because this aim is the destruction of the enemy state, which is a moral being, it "gives no right that is not necessary to its aim". Therefore the right to kill applies only against combatants bearing arms, and this right is lost as soon as they surrender: "Sometimes you may kill the State without killing a single one of its members". The criticism levelled against the doctrine which derives the right to slavery from the right to kill prisoners stems from this principle, as does the idea that the right of combatants to appropriate goods from their enemies extends only to items belonging to the state and its assets.[49]

In relation to their content and extent, the principles of the right of war do not appear to be particularly new. As has been noted several times, Montesquieu had already deduced a rigorous limitation of the right to kill from the idea of war as a moral and political relation: "The State is the association of men, and not the men themselves; the citizen may perish, and the man remains."[50] In the same way, he had criticised the way that the *jurisconsultes* had used the right of war to provide justification for the right of slavery: "It is false that killing in war is lawful, unless in a case of absolute necessity: but when a man has made another his slave, he cannot been said to have been under a necessity of taking away his life, since he actually did not take it away."[51] In relation

47 *Ibid.*, p. 16.

48 Rousseau, *Of the Social Contract and Other Political Writings*, I, 4, p. 16.

49 *Ibid.*, pp. 357-358. I do not agree with the judgement of Neff (*War and the Law of Nations*, p. 148) on this point: "Rousseau expressed the same view [than Bynkershoek], holding that war conferred a right onto the belligerents to commit whatever destruction was necessary in order to bring about victory."

50 Montesquieu, Charles de Secondat, *The Spirit of Law*, X, III, Thomas Nugent (transl.), New York, Cosimo Classics, 2011, p. 135; see also *De l'esprit des lois*, cit. Vol. 1, p. 275.

51 Montesquieu, *The Spirit of Law*, XV, II, p. 236; see also French original, cit. Vol. 1, p. 390. Robert Derathé refers to these texts by Montesquieu in note 358 of the *Con-*

to the juridical effect on things, it is also enough to remember Vattel's words on the subject: "one sovereign makes war against another sovereign, and not against the unarmed citizens. The conqueror seizes on the possession of the state, the public property, while private individuals are permitted to retain theirs. They suffer but indirectly by the war; and the conquest only subjects them to a new master".[52]

Up to a certain point, Montesquieu and Rousseau did little except resume a discussion that had developed from Locke to Barbeyrac, and had even been taken up by Vattel, but which had encountered an insurmountable theoretical obstacle in the idea of a just war that includes the power to punish. While denying the possible existence of voluntary slavery, Locke had defined slavery as an on-going state of war between the just winner and the unjust loser. The doctrine of the power to punish provided a justification for slavery, as he believed that the act of committing a crime led to the surrender of all rights, including the right to life and the right of liberty. The same justification can be traced in Barbeyrac's notes and in Wolff and Vattel's work.[53] Montesquieu and

---

trat social, *OC* III, p. 1442. See also Derathé, Robert, *Jean-Jacques Rousseau et la science politique de son temps*, Paris, PUF, 1950, pp. 202-207; Larrère, Catherine, "L'état de guerre et la guerre entre les États: Jean-Jacques Rousseau et la critique du Droit naturel," *La Bataille, l'Armée, la Gloire*, Actes du Colloque de Clermont-Ferrand, 1983, Clermont-Ferrand, Association des Publications de Clermont II, 1985, pp. 135-148.

52 Vattel, *The Law of Nations*, III, XIII, § 200, p. 598; see also the French text in Emer de Vattel, *Le Droit des gens*, cit., t. II, p. 177. This rule is founded, on the one hand, on the distinction between the private domain of the citizens and the eminent dominion of the sovereign, see *Le droit des gens*, II, VII, § 79, t. I, p. 314; and on the other, on the theory according to which war is made by the Sovereign, who is the only one responsible for it, III, XI, § 187, t. II, p. 161. These two elements are also found in Rousseau. Thus it seems that on this point, Vattel is closer to Rousseau than to Grotius, in contrast to what Christine Jane Carter, *Rousseau and the Problem of War*, New York/London, Garland Publishing, 1987, pp. 114-116 argues, taking up the analysis by Georges Lassudrie-Duchêne, *Jean-Jacques Rousseau et le Droit des Gens*, Paris, H. Jouve, 1906, pp. 247-252. It is true that, according to Vattel, all the subjects of a nation "sont ennemis de tous les sujets de l'autre" (Vattel, *Le droit des gens*, III, V, § 70, t. II, p. 59), but he does not deduce the right of war from this definition of the enemy. It is not possible to go into detail here, but it suffices to remember that, for Vattel, war only takes place between nations and that he establishes a clear discrimination between the civilian population and the combatants: "l'on n'a pas les mêmes droits contre toute sorte d'ennemis" (§ 72, t. II, p. 59).

53 "Peut-on réduire en esclavage les prisonniers de guerre? Oui, dans les cas où l'on est en droit de les tuer; lorsqu'ils se sont rendus personnellement coupables de quelque attentat digne de mort", Vattel, *Le Droit des gens*, III, VIII, § 152, t. II, p. 122. In another passage, Vattel had stated that the right of war "ne s'étend jamais jusqu'à ôter la vie à un Ennemi qui pose les armes, à moins qu'il ne se soit rendu coupable de quelque crime envers le Vainqueur", III, VIII, § 141, t. II, p. 111. On Locke and slavery see Farr, James, ""So Vile and Miserable an Estate": The Problem of Slavery in

Rousseau, on the other hand, having ruled out a punitive right of war, were able to put together a coherent and rigorous set of arguments that established the impossibility and illegitimacy of any right of slavery, and they thus removed any final exception to the rule stating that the right to kill ends once the danger or necessity has passed.

However, Rousseau's argument appears to be more coherent and radical than Montesquieu's.[54] His originality lies in the clarity and rigour with which he deduced the right of war, starting from a non-juridical definition of its aim; namely the destruction of the enemy state. In his conception, the right of war as a limit placed on war obtains an unconditional validity that is not present in the work of earlier authors, who remained anchored to an understanding of war which is in principle asymmetric. In accordance with the law of nations, Grotius effectively presented the declaration of war as an agreement to suspend the unilateral nature of the juridical effects of war. However, in so doing he left war unconstrained by any rule. Vattel, on the other hand, saw the declaration in terms of the voluntary rights of nations as a sort of consensual and reciprocal submission to the laws of war. In this way the bilateralism of war brings about a consensual limitation, but this very reciprocity presupposes the inequality of those who are not willing to be constrained by the laws of war and the inequality of the unjust enemy.[55] In Rousseau, war is by definition bilateral and consensual in its factual dimension. Consequently, the declaration presents itself as an act which activates the right of war unilaterally and does not depend on the behaviour or the nature of the enemy: "Declarations of war are warnings less to powers than to their subjects."[56] The emergence of the "moral" dimension of war, and the move away from the mere fact of war to "legitimate" war, comes about as a consequence of a unilateral voluntary act. It is the unilateralism of the declaration that makes "discriminatory"

Locke's Political Thought," 14 *Political Theory* (1986), pp. 263-289; Glauser, Wayne, "Three Approaches to Locke and the Slave Trade," 51 *Journal of the History of Ideas* (1990), pp. 199-216; Armitage, David, "John Locke, Carolina, and the Two Treatises of Government," 32 *Political Theory* (2004), pp. 602-627.

54 Montesquieu effectively admits a right to enslave as a necessary means of safeguarding the conquest, Montesquieu, *De l'esprit des lois*, X, III, p. 275. On the theoretical audacity of Montesquieu's anti-slavery stance, which is, however, accompanied by a "reformist timidity" see Ehrard, Jean, *Lumières et esclavage. L'esclavage colonial et l'opinion publique en France au XVIIIe siècle*, Brussels, André Versaille, 2008, and in particular from p. 157 onwards.

55 See Silvestrini, Gabriella, "Justice, War and Inequality. The Unjust Aggressor and the Enemy of the Human Race in Vattel's Theory of the Law of Nations," in Béla Kapossy (ed.), *Rival Histories of Emer de Vattel's Law of Nations*, 31 *Grotiana* (2010), pp. 44-68.

56 Rousseau, *Of the Social Contract and Other Political Writings*, p. 16; *OC* III, p. 357.

activation of the right of war impossible. Furthermore, no appeal to the good of human society or the society of nations can intervene to minimise or modify the application of the principles of the right of war. Finally, if destruction relates only to a moral being and its rights, the right of war allows the natural rights of man, which are the basis of political society, to remain completely intact. Despite deriving from the "nature of things", the principles of the right of war no longer retain anything that is "natural", as they relate to "artificial" beings that do not exist in nature and their roots lie in "reason". Yet it would be wrong to think that this conclusion renders natural law invalid. On the one hand, as we have seen, its assumption presupposes the acceptance of a fundamental deductive criterion which earlier authors identified with natural law; in other words, if one is obliged to pursue an aim, one automatically has the natural right to use any means necessary to reach it. On the other hand, these principles hold natural rights to be inviolable limits on the actions permissible in war: the rights of men as men cannot be violated. What is absent in Rousseau, in contrast with Vattel and the other theorists of natural law, are the natural rights of states. This is one of the most important consequences of the rejection of the domestic analogy.

Because of its moral dimension, legitimate war is, for Rousseau, both limited and total. It is limited by the natural rights of man and total in so far as states and public entities are concerned, making it very different to Vattel's war in due form. For Vattel, war is above all an instrument used to enforce law within the society of nations and the survival of the enemy is desirable as it helps to conserve the plurality of nations. The reciprocal recognition of enemies is also the guarantee of the possibility of an equitable peace. In Rousseau, on the other hand, the very idea of a natural state of war between states appears to destroy the possibility of a society of nations and of any recognition that is not tied to a fight to the death.

From this perspective, one could ask if his ideas on war led Rousseau to abandon the presuppositions that had allowed him to argue, in *Political Economy*, that "it is not impossible that a well-governed republic might wage an unjust war".[57] Do the conclusions of the manuscript on the principles of the right of war not rule out the possibility of "just war"? This supposition appears unfounded when one considers Rousseau's *Emile*, which makes explicit reference to the notion of an "unjust aggressor" taking up arms against smaller states and specifically pro-

57 Rousseau, Jean-Jacques, "Discourse on Political Economy," in Jean-Jacques Rousseau, *The Social Contract and other later Political Writings*, Victor Gourevitch (ed.), Cambridge/New York, Cambridge University Press, 1997, pp. 3-38, p. 8; see also *OC* III, p. 256.

poses the formation of confederations as a means of defence.[58] Rousseau's doctrine not only foresees the application of limits to the conduct of war, or the *jus in bello*, but also a limitation on the objectives of war.[59] However, this limitation does not derive from the principles of the right of war, but instead comes from the principles of political right.

Firstly, permanent troops, which are needed for an offensive war and a war of conquest, are above all an instrument of enslavement at the domestic level, being the means by which the government subjugates its citizens. As Rousseau told the Poles, an offensive power "is incompatible with your form of government. Whosoever seeks to be free must not seek to be a conqueror."[60] Once again the Romans are presented as a military paragon, in that they originally availed themselves of a military system that was purely defensive, like the Swiss. Yet nevertheless, even when interpreting Roman expansionism as the outcome of defensive wars, and opposing attack and defence, attacking system and defensive system, Rousseau did not use the language of "just" war. War for the sake of conquest is therefore criticised above all because it is a source of injustice on the level of domestic politics: there is an intrinsic link between offensive war and despotism. This aspect is the basis for the "republican" interpretations of Rousseau's international politics.[61]

---

58 Rousseau, *Emile, or on Education*, p. 659; see also *OC* IV, p. 848. It is true that Rousseau employs the expression "la justice de leur cause" in relation to the war of the Israelites against the Benjaminites, see *Le Lévite d'Éphraïm*, *OC* II, p. 1218. However, the context and the source of this text, which is a retelling of the story narrated in the last three chapters of the *Judges*, do not, in my opinion, permit of the possibility, to see here a proof of the existence of a just war theory in Rousseau's thought. In another perspective, the importance of this text for the understanding of Rousseau's international theory has been signalled by Bloch, Michael, "Is Rousseau really a Realist? On the Political Theory of Peace and War," Paper presented at the Annual Congress of the Swiss Political Science Association, 7-8 January, 2010, Geneva (December 2009) p. 25 onwards. On this poem and its importance for the understanding of Rousseau's thought, see Kavanagh, Thomas, "Rousseau's *The Levite of Ephraim*: Synthesis within a "Minor" Work," in Patrick Riley (ed.), *The Cambridge Companion to Rousseau*, Cambridge, Cambridge University Press, 2001, pp. 397-417; Menin, Marco, "La fin de l'innocence: une lecture du "Lévite d'Éphraïm" de Jean-Jacques Rousseau," 18 *Les Études Rousseau* (2009-2010), pp. 203-225.

59 As is underlined by Hoffmann, Stanley and Fidler, David P., *Rousseau on International Relations*, Oxford, Clarendon Press, 1991, p. XX.

60 Rousseau, Jean-Jacques, *Considerations on the government of Poland*, in *Of the Social Contract*, p. 305; see also *OC* III, p. 1013.

61 Apart from the previously cited works dealing with the solidarity between democracy and the confederation of small states, which is opposed to the link between war and tyranny, see Windenberger, Joseph-Lucien, *Essai sur le système de politique étrangère de J.-J. Rousseau. La République confédérative des petits Etats*, Paris, Picard et fils, 1899; Fetscher, Iring, *Rousseaus politische Philosophie. Zur Geschichte*

Yet there is another element that makes the notion of unjust war possible, one which is tied to rules of property. Before the constitution of civil societies property had no juridical foundation, as the right of first occupancy was no more legitimate than the right of the strongest. After the foundation of civil societies, however, the right of property is valid only inside the borders of the state: for foreigners public possession involves title no more certain than that accorded to individual possessions in the state of nature. In relation to other powers, the state's mastery of its own territory is built solely on the basis of the law of first occupancy and it could therefore be concluded that – for Rousseau as for Hobbes – a sovereign wishing to take over the rights that another sovereign enjoys over the lands of his subjects – the *droit éminent* – would be doing nothing wrong.[62]

Nevertheless, the introduction of property has modified the statute of the right of first occupancy: it "becomes a true right only after establishment of the right of property". The act that assigns ownership to something implies the renunciation of everything else. The original community is abolished and there is no longer "any right to common property"; therefore "the right of the first occupant, so weak in the state of nature, is respected by every civil man". Clearly these pages show that Rousseau was not thinking only about common land inside the borders of one state, but also of land not belonging to the *possession publique* lying outside the territories of the state. Three conditions are necessary to justify the right of first occupancy: "First, that this land not yet be inhabited by anyone; secondly, that you occupy only so much of it as you need to subsist; in the third place, that you take possession of it not through some vain ceremony, but by labour and cultivation, the only sign of ownership that, in the absence of legal titles, should be respected by others".[63] These norms do not apply solely to "men", but also to any people that wishes to "seize hold of an immense territory". Here Rousseau explicitly attacks Spanish conquest and, while speaking of "usurpation deserving punishment", he seems to approve the position taken up by Locke or Vattel: according to them the "Protestant" work ethic

des demokratischen Freiheitsbegriffs, 2nd ed., Neuwied am Rhein, Luchterhand, 1968, pp. 178-183; Roggerone, Giuseppe Agostino, *Saint-Pierre et Rousseau. Confederazione, democrazia, utopia*, Milan, Franco Angeli, 1985, p. 14 onwards; Nabulsi, Karma, "Guerre et inégalité dans la pensée politique de Rousseau," *Les études philosophiques* (October 2007), pp. 413-424.

62 Rousseau, *Contrat social*, I, IX, *OC* III, p. 365. The term "droit éminent" can be found in the summary of the *Contrat social* included in book V of *Emile*, *OC* IV, p. 841.

63 Rousseau, *Of the Social Contract and Other Political Writings*, I, 9, pp. 25-26 (translation slightly modified); see also *OC* III, pp. 555-566.

justifies the right to occupy habited but unfarmed land, thus legitimising the appropriation of North America by Protestant countries.[64]

But there is an undeniable distance from Locke and Vattel. As we have seen, for Rousseau the right of first occupancy, even if it is legitimised by work, does not permit the seizure of "inhabited" land. Thus the possibility of recognising – from an external point of view – the earlier rights of inhabitants even if they do not cultivate land emerges. We could therefore ask if these rules should not apply only to private individuals, but also, and even more strongly to any state that has established the right of property internally. From this point of view, even if the right of the strongest is the most inviolable rule between states, there could be also the possibility of recognise a minimal core of mutual rights and duties between states, whose condition is therefore very different to that of single individuals in a state of nature, who cannot inflict "injury" on each other because property does not exist. We could ask if these passages of *The Social Contract* show the emergence of a duty of abstention among *puissances* with regard to the land that they occupy – a duty not limited to respecting the private property of individuals, but one which also applies to the *droit éminent* of sovereigns and to public property. It is in this duty of abstention that we could find the conceptual basis for the possibility of a reciprocal recognition among states and of the concept of unjust war.[65] A war is unjust if it is started to acquire a territory that is already legitimately occupied by other states, populations or individuals. The exception is the state of necessity, in which concern for one's own survival authorises individuals, populations and states to disregard the right to property. Yet such a situation is not related to just war, because necessity leads once again to the arena of facts and

---

64 Arneil, Barbara, *John Locke and America. The Defence of English Colonialism*, Oxford, Clarendon Press, 1996; Armitage, David, *The Ideological Origins of the British Empire*, Cambridge, Cambridge University Press, 2000, and in particular pp. 96-97. On the continuity between Locke and Vattel regarding the legitimisation of the North American conquest, see Tully, James, *An Approach to Political Philosophy. Locke in contexts*, Cambridge, Cambridge University Press, 1993, pp. 168-169; Pagden, Anthony, *Lords of all the World. Ideologies of Empire in Spain, Britain and France c. 1500-c. 1800*, New Haven/London, Yale University Press, 1995, pp. 78-79.

65 Victor Goldschmidt has rightly emphasised that the "formation d'une société politique est conçue, quant à son territoire, comme une *prise de possession*, limitée par le travail et le besoin […] et limitée, par là même, contre d'autres Etats", Goldschmidt, *Anthropologie et politique*, p. 593. Furthermore, the potential for peace is based on that of a reciprocal recognition between the states, which dismisse following the path of mutual destruction: "l'état de guerre étant établi par le libre consentement des parties, ce libre et mutuel consentement est aussi nécessaire pour rétablir la paix […] à moins que l'un des adversaires ne soit anéanti la guerre ne peut finir entre eux qu'à l'instant où tous deux en liberté déclarent qu'ils y renoncent", Rousseau, *Fragments sur la guerre* in *Principes du droit de la guerre*, p. 62.

of *la loi de la nature* in other words to the right of the strongest.[66] In the same way, the defence against an unjust aggressor cannot be defined – in the logic of Rousseau's argument – as a just war, since the aggression sits within the rule of the strongest and in a certain sense authorises an opposite and equal reaction by recourse to force and therefore from the juridical point of view there is once again a perfectly bilateral and egalitarian relationship. Everyone has the right to use force and any inequality is found purely on the factual level of relative force and power.

Conclusion

My provisional conclusions are as follows. It is difficult and perhaps impossible to treat Rousseau's ideas as perfectly coherent and complete in certain areas – for instance, the external relations of states – where the author himself admitted their incompleteness. Perhaps the incompleteness of the system in fact reflects the fundamental contradiction that Rousseau denounced and – as he has shown – which makes it difficult to separate perfectly internal and international politics and to draw a line between order and disorder, justice and injustice. On the one hand, by rejecting the assumption of equality between states and the "society of nations", Rousseau compromised the possibility of founding a general right of nations that could have gone beyond the law of the strongest, or of a positive law – consensual or based on customary law – the realisation of which would also depend on relationships of strength, and on the interests of the strongest. However, at the same time Rousseau did not apparently refuse to confront the problem of justice in the contest of relations between states, which was inextricably intertwined with that of justice and freedom on an internal level. From that point of view there appears to emerge a justification only for defensive war, which however seems to be difficult to identify with an out-and-out theory of just war. On the other hand, Rousseau believed it is possible to develop a rational code, the principles of the right of war, in order to limit the *jus in bello* and the *jus post bellum*. These principles have a universal validity but their realisation is problematic: they cannot be effectuated by an international community who guarantees their respect, or by virtue of a reciprocal consent between states. In a certain sense, the principles of the right of war appear to be the mirror image of the principles of political right. The latter can be affirmed only on the basis of reciprocity, which is embodied by the social contract. On the contrary, the right of war can

66 On this point, and on the way to understand the notion of the just war, I do not agree with the positions taken by Nabulsi, "Guerre et inégalité dans la pensée politique de Rousseau", and those who take up the ideas of Windenberger, *Essai sur le système de politique étrangère de J.-J. Rousseau*, p. 131 onwards.

be applied only unilaterally. Thus Rousseau seems to overturn the typical dilemma of just war theories, or the problem of realising justice with force in a world in which he who has justice on his side does not always win. Rousseau implicitly recognises that only the winner can choose to be just and unilaterally effectuating the right of war, as Romans did.

I am not sure that this perspective can help us to find a third way, described with clarity by Jürgen Habermas between a "legalisation of international relations" and an "ethicisation of world politics" on the part of a superpower.[67] However, it can certainly help to give useful indications as to how an "ethical" unilateralism can be thought out in a different way to those proposed today. The "strong", the superpower, is not presented as both judge and executioner in relation to others on the basis of his own vision of global justice; on the contrary, justice can be realized only if the winner is just, having submitted himself to "good laws". The limits of this solution did not escape Rousseau. But for this very reason he suggested that the weak should protect themselves against the cupidity of "unjust aggressors", for example by creating federations. Perhaps, rather than providing indications on the practical solutions for contemporary problems, the Rousseauian perspective allows us to shed light on the limits of both realism and ethical universalism.

67 Habermas, Jürgen, *Der gespaltene Westen. Kleine Politische Schriften X*, Frankfurt a.M., Suhrkamp, 2004, pp. 114-117.

When Liberalism Meets the World

A Lesson from Alexis de Tocqueville

Demin DUAN

In Europe, in the eighteenth and nineteenth century, the age-old doctrine of cosmopolitanism, descending from Diogenes of Sinope and the Stoics, found a new shape. Liberal thinkers, ranging from John Locke to Immanuel Kant, started to envisage a certain kind of "natural" human beings, deserving to be treated "equally" and "indiscriminately". A world order conforming to this set of "liberal" values thus began to be conceived. One might plausibly suggest that, since then, our world politics is largely shaped by the discourse of liberalism and its critics. But apparently it has long been forgotten that liberalism was once only confined to domestic politics; and when it expanded to the world, it went together with imperialism. The event of liberalism meeting the world could thus function as a focal point from which we can observe how liberalism conceives the world politics from the beginning, liberalism's inner contradictions and its weakness. This essay will use the nineteenth century Western imperialist expansion as background, taking Alexis de Tocqueville's vocal support of French imperialism as an example, to shed some light on the curious relationship between liberalism and imperialism.

If the idea of freedom in liberalism is in a certain sense intimately connected with the tendency of imperialism, it may prove to be anti-imperialistic and conducive to a better world order under another definition. It is this "another definition" that I will try to unearth in Tocqueville's theory of freedom, using his imperialism as a starting point. Firstly, I will introduce the problem of Tocqueville's involvement in the French imperialist expansion and its meaning to his overall theory of freedom. Secondly, I will interpret Tocqueville's notion of freedom differently from classical liberalism so as to separate it from the discourse of liberal imperialism. Thirdly, I will compare Tocqueville's support of imperialism with the so-called "imperial turn" of liberal thinkers in nineteenth century Europe. In conclusion, I will show that the two different "liberalisms" are visions for different orders of world politics. However, which one is superior should be left to the readers of this article to judge.

1. Tocqueville and Liberal Imperialism

Alexis de Tocqueville has long been considered a liberal thinker who has greatly influenced the way we look at politics. Being the first serious thinker of democracy,[1] he teaches us how to preserve freedom in a democratic age.[2] But what has escaped many interpreters of Tocqueville's thought is that he is also a full-fledged imperialist. In 1833, when Tocqueville was preparing his famous book *Democracy in America*, he wrote an essay "How to have good colonies". In 1837, in the middle of writing the second *Democracy in America*, he published two letters on Algeria in which he analysed the situations in Algeria and made suggestions concerning how to best amplify French power there. In order to better serve his country's cause in taking over North Africa, he studied various materials, including government documents, travel diaries, religious scriptures, etc. As a deputy of Chamber, Tocqueville was among those who strongly supported the French expansion in North Africa. His eagerness and enthusiasm was strong enough for him to personally travel to Algeria twice in order to see the place himself. There, as in America, he took notes, interviewed various kinds of people, observed the structure of the society, grasped the mores. In 1841, two years after he had been elected to the Chamber, he made his first trip to Algeria and came back with an "Essay on Algeria". In 1846, he was charged with examining the financial requests from French colonial authorities in Algeria and made his second trip there. On returning, he wrote two lengthy reports in which he not only fulfilled his original mission, but also had serious discussions about Algerian society and how to turn it into a French territory.[3]

Indeed, Tocqueville is an imperialist who ardently supports French empire building. In his two "Letters on Algeria" first published in 1837, he states: "I have no doubt that we shall be able to raise a great monu-

1 John Stuart Mill says in his "M. De Tocqueville on Democracy in America" that Tocqueville's book is "the first book ever written on Democracy." See Cohen, Marshall (ed.), *The Philosophy of John Stuart Mill. Ethical, Political and Religious*. New York, Random House Inc., 1961, p. 123.

2 See Manent, Pierre, *Tocqueville and the Nature of Democracy*, transl. by John Waggoner, Lanham, Rowman & Littlefield Publishers Inc., 1996; Siedentop, Larry, *Tocqueville*, Oxford, Oxford University Press, 1994.

3 Tocqueville's writings on Algeria is well documented in Jardin, André & Chevallier, Jean-Jacques (eds.), *Oeuvres complètes. Oeuvres, Papiers et Correspondances d'Alexis de Tocqueville*, Paris, Gallimard, 1962, volume 3, part I; and André Jardin & J.-P. Mayer (eds.), *Oeuvres complètes. Oeuvres, Papiers et Correspondances d'Alexis de Tocqueville*, Paris, Gallimard, 1958, volume 5, part II. A good English translation and collection of Tocqueville's writings on empire and slavery is Tocqueville, Alexis de, *Writings on Empire and Slavery*, ed. and transl. by Jennifer Pitts, Baltimore/London, The John Hopkins University Press, 2001.

ment to our country's glory on the African coast."[4] In the 1841 "Essay on Algeria," Tocqueville begins with a firm rejection of the stance that France should withdraw from the imperialist expansion in North Africa. He states:

> I do not think France can think seriously of leaving Algeria. In the eyes of the world, such abandonment would be the clear indication of our decline. [...] If France shrank from an enterprise in which she faced nothing but the natural difficulties of the terrain and the opposition of little barbarous tribes, she would seem in the eyes of the world to be yielding to her own impotence and succumbing to her own lack of courage. Any people that easily gives up what it has taken and chooses to retire peacefully to its original borders proclaims that its age of greatness is over. It visibly enters the period of its decline.[5]

Even in *Democracy in America*, in a side note to the colonial issues in North America, Tocqueville betrayed his regret that, in comparison with the British, France had failed to build a strong colonial presence there. He says:

> There was a time when we as well could have created a great French nation in the American wilderness and, with the English, held the balance of the destinies of the New World. [...] But a concurrence of circumstances that would be too long to list deprived us of this magnificent inheritance.[6]

Thus, there is no doubt that, deep in his mind, Tocqueville believes a powerful French empire is desirable and worthy of struggle. However, a question quickly comes up: is this compatible with his well-known image of a moderate liberal thinker? Is this in coherence with his liberal thought? Some commentators obviously think it is not. For instance, Melvin Richter argues that, on the issue of imperialism, Tocqueville failed to apply the sociological insight he developed in *Democracy in America*.[7] The main reason appears to be that, according to Richter, when things forced him to choose, Tocqueville "placed nationalism above liberalism; the interests of 'progressive' Christian countries above the rights of those that were not."[8] Richter banishes Tocqueville so hard on the imperialism issue that he even states "the time has passed when Tocqueville needed to be praised."[9] Cheryl Welch similarly believes that

4 Tocqueville, *Writings on Empire and Slavery*, p. 24.

5 *Ibid.*, p. 59.

6 Tocqueville, Alexis de, *Democracy in America*, ed. and transl. by Harvey C. Mansfield & Delba Winthrop, Chicago, The University of Chicago Press, 2000, p. 391.

7 Richter, Melvin, "Tocqueville on Algeria," 25 *The Review of Politics* (1963), pp. 362-398.

8 *Ibid.*, p. 364.

9 *Ibid.*

Tocqueville's support of imperialism is a breach of his own liberal doctrines. The imperialist stance betrays Tocqueville's inner moral tensions, according to Welch, by allowing national interests override the "universally acknowledged 'human axioms'" implied by his own liberal theory.[10]

Jennifer Pitts, on the other hand, puts Tocqueville in a broader line of the so-called "liberal imperialism." Her view of liberalism and its relationship with imperialism is more nuanced than Richter and Welch in the sense that she situates liberalism in a historical perspective. She points out that previous interpretations of liberal imperialism have been too simplistic in rejecting imperialistic tendencies as merely illiberal moments in the otherwise righteous liberal doctrine. As a matter of fact, Pitts states, "liberalism as such has never produced a definitive position on conquest or empire."[11] Rather, liberalism should be considered as a historical phenomenon which is constantly entangled with the issue of imperialism. To put it another way, for Pitts, liberalism is always in the "making" and imperialism is an integral part of this never-ending process. Liberalism has produced various positions towards conquest and empire; these positions have essentially shaped liberalism as a strand of political theory. For instance, Pitts notices that during the period between the late eighteenth and early nineteenth century, there was a "sudden" sea change with regard to intellectuals' attitudes towards empire building. She states:

> Skepticism about both particular imperial ventures and the general project of unlimited expansion was, by the 1780s, almost received wisdom among liberal intellectuals. Just fifty years later, however, we find no prominent thinkers in Europe criticizing the European imperial project. Indeed, the greatest liberals of the nineteenth century, including J.S. Mill and Tocqueville, were avid imperialists.[12]

For Pitts, there are moments when liberalism is connected with imperialism and there are moments when it is not. For instance, while nineteenth thinkers like Tocqueville and John Stuart Mill support imperial expansion, there are a lot of thinkers in the eighteenth century who clearly believe conquest and empire building at the cost of other peoples are categorically wrong. Pitts cites Denis Diderot to make a point on the potential "antithesis" between freedom and empire. Diderot says, as quoted by Pitts:

---

10 Welch, Cheryl B., "Colonial Violence and the Rhetoric of Evasion. Tocqueville on Algeria," 31 *Political Theory* (2003), pp. 235-264.

11 Pitts, Jennifer, "Empire and Democracy. Tocqueville and the Algeria Question," 8 *The Journal of political Philosophy* (2000), pp. 295-318.

12 *Ibid.*, p. 296.

> [European explorers] arrive in a region of the New World unoccupied by anyone from the Old World, and immediately bury a small strip of metal on which they have engraved these words: This country belongs to us. And why does it belong to you? [...] You have no right to the natural products of the country where you land, and you claim a right over your fellow men. Instead of recognizing this man as a brother, you only see him as a slave, a beast of burden. Oh my fellow citizens![13]

While it is enlightening to point out that liberalism is actually articulated alongside imperialism, the question remains as to how to interpret this proclaimed historical nature of liberalism. Specifically on this point, there seems to be an inner contradiction within Pitts' interpretation. On the one hand, Pitts puts liberalism in a certain relativistic view, as if there are radically different "versions" of liberalism; but on the other hand, particularly on the issue of imperialism, intentionally or not, she tries to establish an essentialist view in which liberalism is good and imperialism is portrayed as intrinsically evil. In this regard, although Pitts rejects the view that imperialism is only an "irrational" part of otherwise liberal thinkers' thought, she herself resorts to the usage of irrationality to explain why there are fluctuations in liberal attitudes towards empire throughout the history of liberalism. We can spot this apparent contradiction in the following quote from her:

> It is clear that the arguments and resources of liberal political theory do not lead ineluctably either to an imperialist or to an anti-imperialist position. Given the astonishing diversity of views on empire that we find in thinkers who are often classed as liberal, we must pay greater attention to how these thinkers' understandings of their historical and national contexts drove them to reinterpret the imperatives of their liberalism. The domestic political pressures of democratization and nation-building, in particular, play a central and hitherto under-examined role in this history.[14]

Given the explicit moral tone exhibited throughout Pitts' text regarding the evil of empire,[15] her initial historical or relativistic reading of liberalism in its relationship with imperialism is almost rendered meaningless. For, in the end, Pitts has to resort to the "political pressures" in history to give a "rational" explanation to liberal thinkers' turn towards empire. The ultimate "rationality," as Pitts' text reads, resides in history, in the fact that history will teach the correct lesson with regard to how liberals *should have* related to imperialism. We could almost draw the

---

13 Quoted by Pitts, *ibid.*, p. 295. Originally this quote is from Diderot, Denis, *Political Writings*, John Hope Manson & Robert Wokler (eds.), Cambridge, Cambridge University Press, 1992, p. 177.

14 Pitts, "Empire and Democracy", pp. 317-318.

15 See *ibid.*, pp. 316, 395.

conclusion that a "superior" type of liberalism is Pitts' ultimate aim, one which transcends all the historical wrongness. Thus, actually there isn't much difference between Pitts and those "simplistic" commentators of liberal imperialism with whom she argued. Both camps believe that liberalism should maintain a certain moral integrity – typically in the form of universal individual rights and humanism; imperialism is basically a breach of this liberal integrity. The only slight difference perhaps is that Pitts adds much more nuance and a (greater) sense of history to this consistent narrative.

In interpreting Tocqueville's stance on imperialism, Pitts strictly follows this line. Pitts generally puts Tocqueville together with other liberal thinkers such as Jeremy Bentham and John Stuart Mill, by indicating that all of them hold "a commitment to the supreme value of freedom, equal human dignity, the rule of law, and representative democracy."[16] But what distinguishes Tocqueville, Pitts argues, is that he has a strong sensitivity towards the sense of community in enhancing (individual) freedom.

Pitts rightly points out that a major worry of Tocqueville concerning the democratic age is individualism, a term Tocqueville is usually credited for coining.[17] The individualisation of society, prompted by the new trend of egalitarianism in democracy, leads to the stifling of public virtue. It deadens the will of people to participate and sacrifice. By indulging in private business and enjoyment, people leave political affairs to the state. Politics become mere centralized administration; individuals are dictated by the state agents as to how to run their own affairs. This development, as Pitts and many other commentators point out, is the biggest threat to freedom and rights in democratic society.[18] And what Tocqueville does in his theoretical works is to find ways to avoid this scenario.

Thus, according to Pitts, Tocqueville is highly sensitive to what contributes to and what diminishes people's sense of community. In this regard, war and empire building is a perfect moment when this communal sense could be drummed up. External war and empire building bring people together as a nation. There is much invested in this common project: national glory, common memory, a sense of solidarity, etc. France has experienced a lot of divisive revolutions ever since the late eighteenth century. The gap between classes, between revolutionaries and conservatives, between intellectuals and peasants has never been

---

16 *Ibid.*, p. 296.

17 Tocqueville, *Democracy in America*, p. 482.

18 See Pitts, Jennifer, *A Turn to Empire. The Rise of Imperial Liberalism in Britain and France*, Princeton/Oxford, Princeton University Press, 2005, p. 234.

bigger. As Pitts sees it, Tocqueville deems this a good opportunity for France to demonstrate that the French people can still act together. Pitts quotes a letter by Tocqueville to John Stuart Mill:

> I do not have to tell you, my dear Mill, that the greatest malady that threatens a people organized as we are is the gradual softening of mores, the abasement of the mind, the mediocrity of tastes; [...] One cannot let this nation take up easily the habit of sacrificing what it believes to be in grandeur to its repose, great matters to petty ones; it is not healthy to allow such a nation to believe that its place in the world is smaller, that it is fallen from the level on which its ancestors had put it, but that it must console itself by making railroads and by making prosper in the bosom of this peace, under whatever condition this peace is obtained, the well-being of each private individual.[19]

Tocqueville sees the post-revolutionary French society particularly vulnerable to centralized rule. The public spirit has largely been lost. People have been driven to their own private sphere and enjoy their petty happiness. The supposedly inspirational revolutions haven't been very helpful in rebuilding that lost sense of community. The symptom of this disease is centralisation, which stubbornly persists before and after the Revolution. It reflects the situation in France that people no longer have the habit of associating with one another. Tocqueville says in *L'Ancien Régime et la Révolution*: "When the Revolution happened, one would have searched most of France in vain for ten men who had the habit of acting in common in an orderly way, and taking care of their own defence themselves."[20] For Tocqueville, what results is that freedom is in danger. In this regard, Pitts is correct in pointing out that a sense of urgency in rebuilding the sense of community runs deep in Tocqueville's thought.

However, Pitts further stretches this point to argue that it is this sense of urgency that drives Tocqueville to opt for imperial war and conquest. Pitts says: "Tocqueville's position that the Algerian conquests could help France avoid the threat of future dictatorships by uniting the French people behind a national cause and drawing them out of their narrow private interests was, after all, a rather Napoleonic strategy."[21] According to Pitts, the problem here is that this imperialist stance is obviously in contradiction with liberal norms such as individual rights and freedom. On this point, Pitts admits: there is no way to "find a neat *theoreti-*

---

19 Tocqueville, Alexis de, *Selected Letters on Politics and Society*, Roger Boesche (ed.), transl. by James Toupin and Roger Boesche, Berkeley, University of California Press, 1985, pp. 150-151.

20 Tocqueville, Alexis de, *The Old Regime and the Revolution*, François Furet and Françoise Mélonio (eds.), transl. by Alan S. Kahan, Chicago, University of Chicago Press, 1988, p. 243.

21 Pitts, "Empire and Democracy", pp. 309-310.

cal resolution to the contradictions in his [Tocqueville's] thought" (Pitts's italics). Rather, Pitts continues,

> [W]e must look to the demands that the unsettling social and political situation placed on thinkers, such as Tocqueville, who sought both internal stability and an honorable international politics, in an effort to understand how a perceptive sociologist with a deeply moral understanding of politics could have produced such an implacable defense of empire.[22]

Or, to put it another way, Pitts adds, "Tocqueville's anxieties about the difficulty of maintaining political engagement in France in an age of democratisation led him to approve of the exercise of French power in Algeria and elsewhere (India, if possible) and largely to ignore the claims of those France sought to dominate."[23]

Therefore, in the end, Pitts still believes that Tocqueville's support of French imperialism fundamentally contradicts his commitment to liberal ideals. This contradiction may find some consolation in its specific historical background. But nevertheless, it is a betrayal of what Tocqueville should have held up – universal liberal rights and freedom.

2. Tocqueville and the Other Notion of Freedom

Is this the right picture of Tocqueville's engagement with imperialism? On top of everything else, there are some technical problems with this approach of explanation that we should deal with. Pitts blames Tocqueville's imperialist tendency on the so-called "anxieties" caused by specific historical situations. It is as if some formidable pressure has derailed his otherwise decent liberal thought. Although Pitts has repeatedly warned against the wrongness of discarding Tocqueville's imperialist stance as a merely "irrational" part of his overall works, her argument nevertheless leads to the conclusion that there are two distinct parts of his works: a good part and an evil part. If this strongly insinuated Manichean dichotomy is indeed true, we might ask: why Tocqueville himself does not see it as a problem? And how should we interpret this apparent inner contradiction in Tocqueville in the first place?

It should be reiterated that there is no way Tocqueville conceives his conduct and writings on the issue of imperialism as so much deviant from his own doctrine of freedom. As we have already mentioned, Tocqueville supported France's expansion overseas early on. He had shown interest in the issue before he took to study America's democracy. His major writings on imperial and colonial issues were finished in the 1840s and early 1850s, exactly the time period when he was writing his

22 *Ibid.*, p. 314.

23 Pitts, *A Turn to Empire*, p. 207.

most famous books, i.e. *Democracy in America*. Regarding this, we should assume that, from the beginning, Tocqueville himself sees little or no contradiction between his imperialist stance and his support for empire and war. As a matter of fact, I would argue that the latter is an integral part of his overall theory of freedom, which has not been adequately emphasized so far by Tocqueville studies.

Tocqueville supports France's imperialist project, not only for what Pitts calls the boosting of public virtue, but for other reasons as well. We could even say these other reasons are more correct and in a sense "greater" reasons. These reasons initially have to do with the consciousness of international competition among European powers for overseas territory and influence in the eighteenth and nineteenth century.

This consciousness is apparently at work in Tocqueville's appetite for imperial power. The nineteenth century is usually called the "age of imperialism," in which many European countries were expanding overseas for territory, raw materials, markets, and above all, influence and power. Tocqueville feels that France should not back down from this competition. Otherwise France's place on the international stage would diminish in the foreseeable future. "Too much is at stake for France to lose this battle," this is the real thought that dominates Tocqueville's mind in his support of French imperialism. France should actively engage in it and become a strong imperial power itself, even if this means war and conquest. In his "Essay on Algeria," Tocqueville states:

> I do not think France can think seriously of leaving Algeria. In the eyes of the world, such abandonment would be the clear indication of our decline. […] if France shrank from an enterprise in which she faces nothing but the natural difficulties of the terrain and opposition of little barbarous tribes, she would seem in the eyes of the world to be yielding to her own impotence and succumbing to her own lack of courage. Any people that easily gives up what it has taken and chooses to retire peacefully to its original borders proclaims that its age of greatness is over. It visibly enters the period of its decline.[24]

A realist concern is obviously present in Tocqueville's concern for international power struggle. Tocqueville believes that France cannot afford to be reduced to a second-place country in the international arena. Instead, she has a duty to stand up for its people and become a great power. This stance is much like Max Webber's support for German imperialist policy in early twentieth century almost a century later. Weber is also a well-known liberal sociologist for whom individual autonomy is an unsaid value for modern politics. But as Weberian

---

[24] Tocqueville, *Writings on Empire and Slavery*, p. 59.

scholar Wolfgang Mommsen points out, this does not prevent Weber from adopting an imperialist stance for the German Reich. The reason, which could be used on Tocqueville's France as well, is that "he [Weber] thought that in an age of imperial power conflicts it was simply the duty of the German Reich to assert itself as a world power if only in order to assure a place on earth for German culture in the centuries to come."[25] What we need here is simply to substitute "Weber" with "Tocqueville" and "German Reich" with "France". For both Tocqueville and Weber, an international order in which a balance of powers exists is much better than one that is structured by a single dominant power. This check-and-balance among powers is crucial for freedom to exist in international politics. In other words, for them, freedom involves power structure and requires struggles and conflicts.

To further qualify this point, this logic of conflicts could also be found in Tocqueville's writings on domestic politics. To begin with, the notion of freedom in Tocqueville is not based on a natural sense of human rights. Rather, it primarily has to do with the fact that there are dynamic conflicts and struggles in society. According to Larry Siedentop, Tocqueville's theory of freedom starts with a debate on whether the democratic revolution would lead to freedom or slavery.[26] While many enlightenment thinkers applaud the revolution for its liberating function in breaking the hierarchical chains, Tocqueville observes that this revolution signals a fundamental transformation of society whose future is illusory rather than assured.

After traditional aristocratic bodies are eliminated by revolution in the name of equality, individuals are left bare and isolated. The result is that, they are not more free, but more vulnerable to slavery instead. For the intermediary bodies that once separated the Monarchy and ordinary people no longer exist. Centralisation and bureaucratisation become inevitable in this process. The habit of civil and political association could not be found anymore. The whole country falls under the centralized administration of the state, as has happened both before and after the Revolution in France. For Tocqueville, this is the end of freedom instead of its realisation. He states: in democratic society, "it is therefore never effortless for these men to tear themselves away from their particular affairs to occupy themselves with common affairs; their natural inclination is to abandon the care of the latter to the sole visible and permanent representative of collective interests, which is the state."[27]

---

25 Mommsen, Wolfgang J., *The Political and Social Theory of Max Weber*, Cambridge UK, Polity Press, 1989, p. 28.

26 Siedentop, Larry, *Tocqueville*, Oxford, Oxford University Press, 1994, pp. 20-30.

27 Tocqueville, *Democracy in America*, p. 643.

The way to avoid this fate of democracy, Tocqueville sees, is to increase conflicts within society. Tocqueville thinks that the reason why America has largely preserved freedom in democracy is that it successfully maintains the unity of the whole country while magnifying the dynamism within it. In contrast to the absolute centralisation in Europe, especially in France, the Unites States preserves the beautifully constructed decentralized political system: while the federal government unifies the whole country politically, administrative affairs are largely left to local bodies. Local governments in the US have significant control over their own affairs. It could be said that the sovereignty is divided between central and local governing bodies. As long as this decentralized system stays, the space for political initiation is maximized. Also very important for Tocqueville is the association among people. While aristocratic bodies no longer exist, it is up to the individuals themselves to create new artificial bodies with similar political functions. These associations – which are called new "aristocratic" bodies by Tocqueville – create dynamism within society and diminish the state's administrative control. By uniting together as associations, individuals gain the habit of acting together, which reduces the chance that the state monopolizes the whole of affairs that concern the nation. Tocqueville hasn't reached the point of appreciating the party system in the United States, as he largely agrees with the Federalists in viewing parties as factious elements. Nevertheless, Tocqueville represents the sort of thinker who highlights the necessities of conflicts and struggle in avoiding the prospect of a closed society in the democratic era. He states:

> If one chooses a certain moment in the existence of a nation, it is easy to prove that political associations trouble the state and paralyze industry; but should one take the whole life of a people, it will perhaps be easy to demonstrate that freedom of association in political matters is favorable to the well-being and even to the tranquility of citizens.[28]

In comparison with America, France largely represents the downside of the story of democracy. In *L'Ancien Régime et la Révolution*, Tocqueville powerfully points out that, despite the Revolution claims to radically erase the old customs and institutions in the *ancien régime*, there is one thing that has never changed, namely the system of centralisation. Tocqueville argues that the real democratic revolution has actually long begun since before the 1789 Revolution. The relationships among people had gradually been shaped by the principle of equality; individuals had increasingly been isolated from traditional social networks. Along with this development the states' or Monarch's power gradually increases. The state increasingly tends to centralize local affairs in its direct con-

[28] *Ibid.*, p. 499.

trol. Local initiatives, once taken care of by local people themselves, gives place to state administration. Further, Tocqueville observes that the Revolution not only did not change this situation, but also aggravates it by formally sweeping away all aristocratic bodies. The conclusion of Tocqueville's analysis is clear: the Revolution has not brought freedom to France, but freedom has been put further away.

Along this vein, Tocqueville also criticizes socialism, which was a new and seemingly attractive ideology in the aftermath of the French Revolution. He sees in socialism a dangerous tendency of bringing everything under control, eliminating the possibility of people's own initiatives and conflicts. The main danger he detects in socialism is its tendency to abolish private property and bring everything under the state's control. If private property is to be questioned, in Tocqueville's eyes, nothing could be immune from being questioned. The space for free movement by citizens is fundamentally restrained. Tocqueville states:

> [Socialists] hold that the State must not only act as the director of society, but must further be master of each man, and not only master, but keeper and trainer. For fear of allowing him to err, the State must place itself forever by his side, above him, around him, better to guide him, to maintain him, in a word, to confine him. They call, in fact, for the forfeiture, to a greater or less degree, of human liberty, to the point where, were I to attempt to sum up what socialism is, I would say that it was simply a new system of serfdom.[29]

Again this early criticism of socialism finds renovation in Max Weber, who attacks the domination of capitalism but nevertheless rejects the prospect of socialism as its alternative. And as with Weber, Tocqueville also believes that the democratic system offers a better chance for freedom. For in this form of society, people can more freely organize themselves into political powers and keep a dominant power from emerging. As long as this space for social conflict and struggle is open, there is hope for freedom. Otherwise, the society is not free no matter what kind of ideology applies itself.

Therefore, we could conclude that Tocqueville's notion of freedom is not so much of the classical liberal notion. The classical definition is that freedom largely means individuals' private sphere is exempt from external interference. This definition is fundamentally concerned with the autonomous status of individuals, putting exclusive emphasis on individual rights and freedom. However, as we have demonstrated, Tocqueville's notion of freedom is clearly not in that tradition, with its emphasis not on individual rights but on the absence of a dominating power. We could say that this notion of freedom is akin to what Quentin

---

[29] See "Tocqueville on Socialism," transl. by Ronald Hamowy, 1 *New Individualist Review* (1961), pp. 18-23.

Skinner calls "liberty before liberalism," or the "neo-roman" notion of freedom. It is a freedom which requires a free state rather than merely free individuals.[30] It is more in the old republican tradition of freedom than the modern liberal tradition.

3. Liberal Imperialism and Republican Imperialism

From the above, we can say that what we see in Tocqueville is not really a "liberal imperialism" that Jennifer Pitts claims. Rather, it could more properly be called "republican imperialism" as has been proposed by Duncan Bell.[31] This kind of imperialism does not intend to justify itself by a universalistic sense of human values, or try to apologize for its self-interested motives by vaguely alluding to a kind of domestic emergency. Rather, it should be seen more as an effort to intervene in the international order and seek to shape that order. Tocqueville clearly realises that European countries' competition for colonial power has tremendous consequences for the international order in the future. There is no doubt that France would be much affected by this competition. As we have shown, for Tocqueville, it is simply too important for France to shy away. Certainly we do not have to condone the tendency of war and conquests as such in either Tocqueville or other liberal imperialists. But their curiously different ways of engaging international affairs, supported by their respective theories of freedom, deserve our attention.

If Pitts has misjudged Tocqueville's imperialism, she is absolutely correct in depicting a large part of the liberal imperialists. Under her pen, the so-called "liberal imperialists" either do not have many formal reasons for their support of empire except a nationalistic impulse, such as that of Tocqueville; or they tend to justify their imperialist stance on some "liberal" norms. John Stuart Mill, for instance, is a thinker of the latter kind. Like Tocqueville, Mill is an ardent supporter of his country's imperialist policy and he actively participated in imperialist undertakings.

But a major difference between Mill and Tocqueville is: Mill believes that there are perfectly legitimate causes for Britain's imperialist rule over its overseas subjects. For instance, in *On Liberty*, Mill states: "despotism is a legitimate mode of government in dealing with barbarians, provided the end be their improvement, and the means justified by actually effecting that end."[32] As with many other liberal thinkers in the

---

30 Skinner, Quentin, *Liberty before Liberalism*, Cambridge, Cambridge University Press, 1998, p. 60.

31 Bell, Duncan, "Republican Imperialism. J.A. Froude and the Virtue of Empire," XXX *History of Political Thought* (2009), pp. 166-191, p. 178.

32 Mill, John Stuart, *The Spirit of the Age, On Liberty, The Subjection of Women*, New York, W.W. Norton & Company, Inc., 1996, p. 48.

nineteenth century, Mill holds a hierarchical view of the degree of civilisation throughout the world. He believes that the West has been on the upper scale of the development of human civilisation while non-Western places are generally lagging behind. Thus, the "advanced norms" that govern societies in the West could be legitimate reasons to bring other people under rule. The aim, it proclaims, is to help them realise the same "universal" values. Mill further says in his *Considerations on Representative Government*:

> As it is already a common, and is rapidly tending to become the universal, condition of the more backward populations, to be either held in direct subjection by the more advanced, or to be under their complete political ascendancy.[33]

It has to be noted that Mill is certainly not alone in this genre of liberal imperialism. *Mission civilisatrice*, for example, had been a very popular mode of justification for colonisation in the West in the nineteenth century. According to this view, it is the "mission" of the superior western countries to spread civilisation to underdeveloped places. Actually, this principle had guided French policy of colonialism right until the First World War. French statesman Jules Ferry once said in a speech: "it is our right *vis-à-vis* inferior races (to colonize); it is also an exercise of duty. [...] If we have the right to go with the barbarians, then we have the obligation to civilize them."[34]

This curious combination of liberalism and imperialism has prompted Pitts to state that, "liberalism has always contained an imperialist core: that a liberal insistence on progress and establishing the rule of law at any cost has led liberals over and over again to support imperialist projects."[35] However, Pitts also seems to be perplexed by another phenomenon that puts liberalism against imperialism. "Another argument might be that," she adds, "liberalism is inherently anti-imperialist, given its commitment to human equality and self-government: in this account, otherwise liberal thinkers who support empire merely reveal an illiberal side or smuggle illiberal ideas into their arguments."[36]

As we have already discussed, this perplexity primarily has to do with the fact that Pitts herself is obsessed with finding a more authentic, truly humble and moderate liberalism. And she tends to believe that it is under this kind of liberalism that the international order could be proper-

---

33 Mill, John Stuart, *On Liberty and Considerations on Representative Government*, R.B. McCallum (ed.), Oxford, Basil Blackwell, 1946, p. 314.

34 Ferry, Jules François Camille, *Discours et opinions de Jules Ferry*, Tome 5, Paul Robiquet (ed.), Paris, Armand Colin & Cie, 1897, p. 156.

35 Pitts, "Empire and Democracy", p. 296.

36 *Ibid.*

ly regulated. Though definitely anti-imperialist, Pitts nevertheless shares with many liberal imperialists the view that a rationally conceived internationally order is possible. While Pitts rejects those thinkers' suggestion that this rationality should be advanced in an imperialist way, the very universal tendency in her own narrative still carries an imperialist germ. Considering the more hidden structure of power and the more invisible relationship of domination in the post-colonial era, this "germ" of imperialism is all the more important to point out.

In this regard, Tocqueville's theory of freedom and its apprehension of the world politics may provide us with another angle of understanding. Unlike classical liberalism, Tocqueville's notion of freedom does not hinge upon an abstract notion of human rights.[37] Rather, he deploys "freedom" in a specific power structure, where authority is recognized as crucial in the constitution of society and where the space for human initiative is open. In *Democracy in America*, he states the following:

> I think, therefore, that one must always place somewhere one social power superior to all the others, but I believe freedom to be in peril when that power finds no obstacle before it that can restrain its advance and give it time to moderate itself.[38]

In the arena of international politics, likewise, what Tocqueville sees as critical is the power relationship among nations. It is inevitable that there would be power structures when nations engage in international politics. And Tocqueville acutely understands that in order for France to have a space in this scenario, it would have no choice but to become a world power itself.

In this regard, what is telling is that Tocqueville never tries to justify French imperialism on the basis of universal values, or on a discourse of *mission civilisatrice*. Although we find in him the similar "European" pride towards other civilisations or cultures, which is displayed in many other eighteenth and nineteenth intellectuals as well, he never draws the conclusion that the Europeans are as such "entitled" to rule over other peoples. In a letter to his former secretary Arthur de Gobineau, addressing the latter's book *Essai sur l'Inégalité des Races Humaines*, Tocqueville says that the idea of racial inequality proclaimed in the book is "very probably wrong and very certainly pernicious." For Tocqueville, the theory that one race is naturally superior to another and thus has the

---

[37] In *L'Ancien Régime et la Révolution* Tocqueville criticizes the so-called "men of letters's obsession with the 'origin of societies,' the 'essential nature of government,' and the 'primordial rights of the human species." See Tocqueville, *The Old Regime and the Revolution*, p. 197.

[38] Tocqueville, *Democracy in America*, p. 241.

right to rule is "a great contraction, if not a complete abolition, of human liberty."[39]

Moreover, unlike many liberal imperialists, Tocqueville harshly criticizes Western colonialism, especially for the inherent hypocrisy in the so-called *mission civilisatrice*. In sharp contrast to those supporters of the *mission civilisatrice* narrative, Tocqueville blatantly exposes that the western colonists not only fail to bring "light" to local indigenous people, but also tend to destroy the culture and civilisation these people already have. For instance, in his 1847 report on Algeria, Tocqueville says that the French colonists actually do more than physical violence to the people there: they do cultural and spiritual violence as well. He states the following:

> Civilized peoples often oppress and dispirit barbarous people by their mere contact, without intending to and, so to speak, without knowing it: the same rules of administration and justice that seem to the European to be guarantees of liberty and property, seem an intolerable oppression to the barbarian.[40]

This is hardly surprising if we look at Tocqueville's earlier writings such as *Democracy in America*. There he devoted lengthy chapters to analysing the racial relationships in North America where the white colonists, the black, and the Indians live together. In one passage on the contact between the white settlers and the Indians, Tocqueville acutely points out the demeaning effect on the indigenous people by the invasion of the supposedly "superior" culture. Tocqueville says:

> Living within the freedom of the woods, the Indian of North America was miserable, but he did not feel himself inferior to anyone; from the moment that he wants to enter into the social hierarchy of the whites, he can occupy only the lowest rank in it; for he enters ignorant and poor into a society where science and wealth reign.[41]

In this vein, Tocqueville admits that the French empire in North Africa is nothing more than domination. Fairly speaking, Tocqueville's support of French imperialism is absolutely not a good message for the people in North Africa. Western domination in the non-western world has become a political reality. Tocqueville's realism tells that the only choice left for France is to aggressively participate in this game of building imperial power. If France loses the strategic points in North Africa, Tocqueville says, "they will pass into those of another European

---

39 Tocqueville, *Selected Letters on Politics and Society*, p. 298.

40 Tocqueville, *Writings on Empire and Slavery*, p. 144.

41 Tocqueville, *Democracy in America*, p. 317.

people."[42] If this happens, Tocqueville worries, France would be inevitably reduced to second rank and the control of European affairs would pass into other hands.[43] It is a kind of *realpolitik* that Tocqueville is presenting here. And as we have demonstrated, behind this *realpolitik*, it is a peculiar notion of freedom which gives understanding and guidance on both domestic and international political relationships. According to this version of freedom, the international order should not be submitted to the universalist standard of human rights and freedom as such, but has to be preserved by the dynamism of checks and balances among powers.

4. Conclusion

We do not have to agree with violence and imperialism as such. But we have to keep in mind that violence and imperialism often come together with values. These values, ethical as they are, could be used as legitimating tools for empire and domination, as is exemplified in liberal imperialism. Freedom and rights are usually the language to be used in this case. And those overseas empire-buildings are supposed to follow one direction: the universal progress of human beings. This language can hardly be said to be out of date today, as various wars are still being waged in the name of universal values. However, there are other ways to perceive this relationship between power and values. The other language of freedom, as we have found in Tocqueville's political thought, persuades us to see that freedom is better considered in a relationship with power and power structure. This language sees power and domination as largely inevitable; but it objects to the effort to legitimate it with moral values. Rather, it tells us that freedom exists in this very structure of power, in bringing the dominating power in check and making it more moderate. It is with this aim in mind that we here bring up the problem of Tocqueville's imperialism, and, hopefully it could serve as a lesson for our contemporary reflection on world politics.

---

42 Tocqueville, *Writings on Empire and Slavery*, p. 60.

43 *Ibid.*, p. 59.

Part III

Different Cosmopolitanisms and their Practices

We either Invent or We Err

Post-Colonial Critical Cosmopolitanism in the Nineteenth Century?

Francisco A. ORTEGA

> Since he [Simón Rodríguez] is a cosmopolitan philosopher, he has neither country nor home, nor family, nothing.
>
> Bolívar to Cayetano Carreño, uncle of Simón Rodríguez, June 27, 1825

1. Introduction

In recent years cosmopolitanism – the belief that human beings, regardless of their origin, faith or race are fundamentally the same and constitute a single moral community – has gained prestige and has become a contemporary intellectual reference to those interested in critically engaging the democratic and emancipatory possibilities present but not realised in the process of globalisation that has ensued since the Enlightenment. Though cosmopolitanism enjoys a redoubtable philosophical tradition, going back at least to Diogenes and the Cynics and the Stoic tradition of Cicero and Seneca, those who argue for the critical potential of contemporary cosmopolitanism contend that it gained notoriety during the second half of the eighteenth century as an ideal that could, as Emer de Vattel stated, bring lasting peace on earth and produce desired human happiness.[1] According to Vattel a cosmopolitan view would allow:

> [...] the nations of the world to communicate their goods and their understanding. A profound peace would reign over the earth, and would enrich it with its precious fruits. Industry, science and the arts also would be as much concerned with our well-being as with our needs. There would be no more violent means for resolving such differences which might arise. They would all be solved by moderation, justice and equity. The world would seem like

1 See Venturi, Franco, *Italy and the Enlightenment. Studies in a Cosmopolitan Century*, transl. by Susan Corsi, London, Longman, 1972.

> one great republic. Men would live everywhere as brothers, and each one would be a citizen of the universe.[2]

Immanuel Kant most eloquently elaborated modern cosmopolitanism in his well-known essay *On Perpetual Peace* (1795). For Kant the desired peace between nations would be the outcome of a federated system of Free states, with each state internally organised around republican principles and adhering to the tenet of universal hospitality to foreigners, hospitality based on "the right to the *earth's surface*, which belongs to the human race in common". For Kant, observing these principles would "finally bring the human race ever closer to a cosmopolitan constitution".[3]

These cosmopolitan tenets find philosophical, political and even methodological resonance in our century. Martha Nussbaum, for example, proposes a cosmopolitan understanding of politics "[...] based upon reason rather than patriotism or group sentiment, a politics that [is] truly universal rather than communitarian [...]."[4] Anthony Appiah argues that in the midst of a post-colonial age when we are forced to coexist intimately with strangers on a daily basis, the Stoic tradition of cosmopolitanism helps us fulfil our responsibilities to others and appreciate the realm of cultural and political differences.[5] For his part, sociologist Ulrich Beck recently launched a manifesto urging a cosmopolitan approach to scientific research that might allow us to address through the generation of knowledge in the social sciences the urgent global

---

2 Translation of "Quel seroit le bonheur du genre-humain, si ces aimables préceptes de la nature étoient par-tout observés! Les Nations se communiqueroient leurs biens & leurs lumières; une paix profonde règneroit sur la terre & l'enrichiroit de ses fruits précieux; l'industrie, les sciences, les arts s'occuperoient de notre bonheur, autant que de nos besoins. Plus de moyens violens, pour décider les différends qui pourroient naître; ils seroient terminés par la modération, la justice & l'équité. Le monde paroîtroit comme une grande République; les hommes vivroient partout en frères, & chacun d'eux seroit Citoyen de l'Univers." Vattel, Emer de, *Le droit des gens ou principes de la loi naturelle*, London, 1758, Livre II, De la Nation considérée dans se rélations avec les autres, Chapitre I, "Des devoirs communs d'une nation envers les autres, ou des offices de l'humanité dans entre las nations", Num. 16, *Regle et mesure des Offices d'humanité*, pp. 452-453. English translation of this passage in Pagden, Anthony, "Stoicism, Cosmopolitanism, and the Legacy of European Imperialism," 7 *Constellations* (2002), p. 15.

3 Kant, Immanuel, "Towards Perpetual Peace (1795)," in *Practical Philosophy*, Mary J. Gregor (transl. & ed.), Cambridge, Cambridge University Press, 1999, pp. 311-351, p. 329 (Thesis 8: 358).

4 Nussbaum, Martha Craven, "Kant and Cosmopolitanism," in James Bohman and Marthias Lutz-Bachmann (eds.), *Perpetual Peace. Essays on Kant's Cosmopolitan Ideal*, Cambridge, MIT Press, 1997, pp. 25-58, p. 27.

5 Appiah, Kwame Anthony, *Cosmopolitanism. Ethics In a World of Strangers*, New York, W.W. Norton & Company, 2006.

challenges, challenges that will be impossible to even glimpse under the old nationalist framework.[6] And Jacques Derrida finds in the intellectual and moral legacies of cosmopolitanism a precarious platform from which to invoke, once again, the principle of friendship towards the foreigner, combat the wave of anti-immigration legislation, and promote a new sense of solidarity with the immigrant, the displaced, the outcast.[7]

However, it may be wiser to moderate such optimism. Anthony Pagden has argued that cosmopolitanism is much less cosmopolitan than we often think. For Pagden the cosmopolitan principle produces a stratifying effect distinguishing between those regarded worthy of consideration and those unworthy of it. Indeed, ever since the Stoics, those considered cosmopolitan are wise, esteemed and morally honourable, while the latter ignorant, despicable and objectionable. Moreover, Pagden argues, "cosmopolitanism is a distinctively European concept [...] whose fortunes have been linked, for far longer than has generally been supposed, with the history of European universalism".[8] Thus, contemporary to Kant's *On Perpetual Peace*, Friedrich Schiller claimed in "What is Universal History…?" (1789) that world history had reached a stage when "a cosmopolitan link now connects all thinkers" while observing that all around us, Europeans, savages live "like children of various ages [stand] around an adult, and through their example [remind] him of what he once was and of the place from which he came."[9] In this regard cosmopolitanism appears to be linked closely with the benevolent side of imperialism, in particular with its civilising mission.

It was Karl Marx who first developed the association of cosmopolitanism with the economic transformation brought about by the expansion of capital. For Marx and Engels: "The bourgeoisie has through its

---

6 Beck, Ulrich, "The Cosmopolitan Manifesto," in Ulrich Beck, *World Risk Society*, Cambridge UK, Polity Press, 1999, pp. 1-18. See also Ulrich Beck's more recent work, *Cosmopolitan Vision*, London, Polity Press, 2006. In the same direction, though ostensibly less rigorous, see Delanty, Gerard, *The Cosmopolitan Imagination. The Renewal of Critical Social Theory*, Cambridge, Cambridge University Press, 2009.

7 Derrida, Jacques, *On Cosmopolitanism and Forgiveness (Thinking in Action)*, New York, Routledge, 2001, pp. 1-24. For a particularly interesting development of this position, see Nyers, Peter, "Abject Cosmopolitanism. The Politics of Protection and the Anti-Deportation Movement," 24 *Third World Quarterly* 24 (2003), pp. 1069-1093.

8 Pagden, "Stoicism, Cosmopolitanism, and the Legacy of European Imperialism", p. 4. For Pagden, "The Stoics […] far from embracing all peoples seem to have looked only upon those they held wise or worthy of consideration". *Ibid.*, p. 5.

9 Friedrich Schiller, "What is Universal History, and to What End Does One Study It? An Academic Inaugural Address", 1789, in Rolf Saltzer (eds.), *German Essays on History*, New York, Continuum, 1991, pp. 24, 26.

exploitation of the world market given a cosmopolitan character to production and consumption in every country."[10] Far from being a harmonious and peaceful process, the universal character of the commodity appears, in the first instance, as a potently destructive force, wreaking havoc on local, traditional and corporatist societies:

> All old-established national industries have been destroyed or are daily being destroyed. They are dislodged by new industries, whose introduction becomes a life and death question for all civilised nations, by industries that no longer work up indigenous raw material, but raw material drawn from the remotest zones; industries whose products are consumed, not only at home, but in every quarter of the globe. In place of the old wants, satisfied by the production of the country, we find new wants, requiring for their satisfaction the products of distant lands and climes.[11]

Thus, emerges the double nature of the cosmopolitan character of commodities under industrial capitalism: on the one hand, it is responsible for the disintegration of local spaces while, on the other, it contains the elements of civilisation that bring about a new universal cosmopolitan culture.

> In place of the old local and national seclusion and self-sufficiency, we have intercourse in every direction, universal inter-dependence of nations. And as in material, so also in intellectual production. The intellectual creations of individual nations become common property. National one-sidedness and narrow-mindedness become more and more impossible, and from the numerous national and local literatures, there arises a world literature.[12]

Thus, far from being a critical tradition that seeks an emancipatory agenda, cosmopolitanism might best be viewed as simultaneously implicated in the destruction of communal modes of existence and providing an intellectual and ethical response to such violence; at once an ideology that perpetuates asymmetrical differences between groups, classes and nations and a philosophical tradition furnishing a critical platform from which to assess segregation and inequality.

If we now return to Pagden's argument it may be possible to see how the cosmopolitan claim often devolves into a new kind of parochialism:

---

10 Marx, Karl and Engels, Friedrich, "Chapter 1. Bourgeois and Proletarians," *The Communist Manifesto* (1848), Middlesex, The Echo Library, 2009, p. 9.

11 *Ibid.*

12 *Ibid.* A couple of paragraphs later Marx and Engels elaborate this idea by stating that, "The bourgeoisie, by the rapid improvement of all instruments of production, by the immensely facilitated means of communication, draws all, even the most barbarian, nations into civilization [...] It compels all nations, on pain of extinction, to adopt the bourgeois mode of production; it compels them to introduce what it calls civilization into their midst, i.e., to become bourgeoisie themselves. In one word, it creates a world after its own image." *Ibid.*, p. 10.

it is now easier to see why – despite the fact that cosmopolitanism has been "an attempt to transform the values formally associated with the European Empires". This is because it "preserves the idea of a single human destiny, a *telos* for all mankind and the conception of the future – and ineluctable – emergence of a single human culture."[13] As post-colonial criticism has argued such notion of *telos* coincided with and in some cases facilitated European colonial expansion in Africa, Asia and the Americas.[14]

2. Cosmopolitanism outside Europe: Uses and Meanings

Since the intersection of cosmopolitanism and imperialism has already been explored in some detail, let me examine instead how cosmopolitanism has travelled outside Europe. What were some of its meanings and local uses outside Europe? In what sort of political projects has it found itself committed?

When addressing these questions it is important to emphasise that cosmopolitanism, like any other philosophical stance, does not conduct a life in the abstract, independent of its material existence, but is always embodied in very specific contexts which provide the medium within which its semantic possibilities are realised. Thus, just as the emergence of modern European cosmopolitanism in the late eighteenth century must be understood in the context of the antagonisms destroying social cohesion – including but not limited to the clash of diverse modes of production, the heightening of dynastic and imperial conflicts, and the emergence of nationalism – those modes of cosmopolitanism that travelled outside of Europe settled in diverse environments, responded to different challenges and acquired new meanings.

Cosmopolitanism was never simply imposed on non-Europeans. Furthermore, it played important and diverse roles in the construction of colonial and post-colonial societies. Certainly, as noted above, the emergence of modern cosmopolitanism coincided with the rise of late imperialism and, it could also be argued, imperial enterprises acquired

---

13 Pagden, "Stoicism, Cosmopolitanism, and the Legacy of European Imperialism", p. 19. See also, the arguments developed by Dipesh Chakrabarty, Arjun Appadurai, Sheldon Pollock and Homi Bhabha in Breckenridge, Carol A. *et al.* (eds.), *Cosmopolitanism*, Chapel Hill, Duke University Press, 2002.

14 Mignolo, Walter, "The Many Faces of Cosmo-polis. Border Thinking and Critical Cosmopolitanism," 12 *Public Culture* (2000), pp. 721-748. See also, Breckenridge *et al.* (eds.), *Cosmopolitanism*. On the other hand, Sankar Muthu has stated his disagreement with this assessment and points that cosmopolitanism contributed decisively to the existence of an anti-imperialist thought in Diderot, Kant and Herder. See his *Enlightenment against Empire*, Princeton/Oxford, Princeton University Press, 2003, pp. 150-154, p. 172 and ff.

substance and were validated by a Christian cosmopolitanism first developed by Francisco de Vitoria and the School of Salamanca in the sixteenth century.[15] However, quite frequently colonial and post-colonial local elites described themselves as cosmopolites and drew on cosmopolitan views to argue for the equality of all nations, including those that had been subjected to European powers. Their active engagement with cosmopolitanism shaped it and gave it the weight and importance it enjoys today.

The birth of Ibero-American republics in the nineteenth century is a good case in point. From the perspective of the process of globalisation, the emergence of the new American republics at the beginning of the nineteenth century is a turning point in the development and dissemination of modern cosmopolitanism. On the one hand, there was a strong stoic component to eighteenth century Creole patriotism which – contrary to belief – did not view itself as opposing empire, but regarded itself as the driving force of a civic culture seeking to achieve the common good. As Italian historian Franco Venturi put it, a cosmopolitan in the eighteenth century could at once consider himself "to be [a] citizen of the world and [remain committed] to transform and enlighten that little corner of the world where one had been born or brought by destiny to work".[16] On the other hand, the struggles for independence attracted patriots from all over – Ireland, North American, France, Italy, even Spain – which saw in these American struggles the same republican conflicts that were taking place in Europe. Publicists for the new states appealed to cosmopolitan principles in the international order so that European nations recognise them as equals in commerce and law. Jeremy Bentham and Andrés Bello, two of the most respectable interna-

15 Unlike latter cosmopolitan thought, the sixteenth century did not constitute an independent philosophical tradition but rather a scattered set of ideas and arguments that infused humanist thought. It is not difficult to recognise in Erasmus's *Querela Pacis* (1517) and in the Christian universalism of the Salamanca School components of the classical stoic cosmopolitanism. Erasmus, Desiderius, *Querela pacis undique gentium ejectae profligataeque*, Basel, Joh. Froben, 1517. For a discussion of Stoic cosmopolitanism in Vitoria, see Cavallar, Georg, *The Rights of Strangers. Theories of International Hospitality, the Global Community, and Political Justice since Vitoria*, Burlington, Ashgate, 2002, pp. 80-119. Walter Mignolo has insisted that the civilisatory matrix changes from the eighteenth century on and it will be Kant who articulates for the first time the contemporary ideology of cosmopolitanism, Mignolo, "The Many Faces of Cosmo-polis".

16 Venturi, *Italy and the Enlightenment*, pp. xix-xx. Eighteenth century cosmopolites did not feel the contradiction between locality and universality that allegedly moved Diogenes Laërtius to reply "I am a citizen of the world" in order to reject identification with any specific locality.

tionalists of the early nineteenth century, called for an international order built around the "common and equal utility of all nations".[17]

More importantly, faced with vast social and racial diversity in the Americas, Creole Republicans turned the Stoic tradition of one moral community into a fundamental principle of American republicanism. This principle allowed Creole, or Euro-Americans, to conceive of non-Euro-Americans as members of the same political community, even though this did not mean recognition of their equality either politically, economically or socially.

Finally, there was another way in which cosmopolitanism became an essential component of the American nineteenth century political vocabulary. To be a cosmopolite signalled the modernity of political, economic and social agents by indicating that they were familiar and acted in accordance with modern European doctrines. As in José María Samper's accounts of his travels in Europe, the idea of cosmopolitanism is associated with the modernity imagined and aspired to by Americans; one which though hardly realised on European soil remained an ideal for most American elites.[18]

In that context, not being cosmopolitan designated not only parochialism or narrow patriotism but, more forcefully, a stance associated with traditionalism and backwardness, oscillating between ignorance and savagery. Such belligerent cosmopolitanism was at the base of nineteenth century Latin American liberalism and gives strength and direction to a dichotomy that was fundamental to the cultural and political history of the region – the antithesis between civilisation and barbarism. For the Argentinian historian and intellectual Domingo Faustino Sarmiento, the continent's destiny depended on the "struggle between European civilisation and Indian savagery, between intelligence and matter";[19] while Juan Bautista Alberdi, in his influential *Basis and Points of*

17 "Principles of International Law," in Jeremy Bentham, *The Works of Jeremy Bentham, Now First Collected; Under the Superintendence of His Executor, John Bowring*, Vol. VIII, Edinburgh, 1839, Essay I, p. 537. For Andrés Bello and his role in expanding International law to the American hemisphere, see Obregón, Liliana, "Construyendo la región americana. Andrés Bello y el derecho internacional," in Beatriz González Stephan and Juan Poblete (eds.), *Andrés Bello y los estudios latinoamericanos*, Pittsburgh PA, Universidad de Pittsburgh, 2009, pp. 189-218.

18 See Samper, José María, *Viajes de un colombiano en Europa*, 2 Vols., Paris, Impr. de E. Thunot, 1862. For instance, see Samper's comments on London in Vol. I, pp. 78, 84, 110, etc.

19 Sarmiento, Domingo Faustino, *Facundo. Civilization and Barbarism*, trans. by Kathleen Ross, Berkeley, University of California Press, 2003, p. 59. Earlier in the same book, Sarmiento had written that "the mystery of the obstinate struggle tearing the Republic to pieces would have been explained; the opposing, invincible elements crashing into one another would have been distinctly classified; the configuration of

Departure for the Political organization in the Republic of Argentina (1852) urged the import from Europe of the habits of industry and the practice of civilisation. Through such debates cosmopolitanism often became the guiding principle by which the substance of citizenship and nationhood were defined.[20]

In this sense, cosmopolitanism allowed small elite in Latin America to feel part of European culture and to conceive of themselves as agents of its civilising mission. Its social function, therefore, was to authorise the redesigning of the social body, generally by reference to liberal doctrines, if not always with liberal goals in mind. In other words, cosmopolitanism performed (and in many cases still does perform) a legitimising role in the construction of a controversial and often violent social order. It is in this sense that one can argue that liberalism became a form of cosmopolitanism and vice versa; that cosmopolitanism – or at least, hegemonic forms of cosmopolitanism – bore the cloak of a certain form of liberalism. It is not unwise, therefore, to characterise the cosmopolitanism of nineteenth century Latin America as the sweeping premise shared by most of the local elites and intermediate groups, that political participation, social cohesion and economic success could only take place within confines already established by European cultural experience. In this sense, cosmopolitanism must also be understood as a form of colonisation which established a system of mimicry; that is, a tool for managing the production and administration of social difference.

3. Critical Post-Colonial Cosmopolitanism

This approach to cosmopolitanism requires us to consider yet another question. Was cosmopolitanism always manipulated in favour of an anti-democratic agenda, or was it able, on some occasions, to offer a critical dimension and democratic potential? Was there room for a cosmopolitanism that did not result in mimicry in nineteenth century America? Can we identify critical voices that sought to imagine a cosmopolitanism in which it was possible to be global citizens and active participants in local emancipatory projects?

---

the land and the customs it engenders would have been assigned their proper part; the Spanish traditions and the iniquitous, plebeian national consciousness that the Inquisition and Hispanic absolutism have left, their part; the influence of the opposite ideas that have disturbed the political world, its part; indigenous barbarism, its part; European civilization, its part; and finally, the democracy consecrated by the 1810 revolution, and equality, whose dogma has penetrated down to the lowest levels of society, their part". *Ibid.*, p. 33.

20 Frédéric Martínez develops this idea in Martínez, Frédéric, *El nacionalismo cosmopólita. La referencia europea en la construcción nacional en Colombia*, Bogotá, Banco de la República, 1993.

Several candidates come to mind, ranging from Guillermo Prieto in Mexico and Jose Maria Torres Caicedo in Colombia, to Pedro Emilio Coll in Venezuela, José Martí in Cuba, and even Nicaraguan poet Ruben Dario, for whom the modernist ideal was "very eighteenth century, and very old, / and very modern; bold, cosmopolitan."[21] In this case, however, I will dwell on the cosmopolitan dimension present in the work of Venezuelan Simón Rodríguez (1771-1854) – teacher, philosopher, avid traveller and committed Republican – whose response to the challenges posed by the construction of the new American nations can be understood by its cosmopolitan dimension.

Simón Rodríguez was perceived by contemporaries both as a strange man and as an extraordinary one. Bolívar wrote to Santander that Rodríguez was "my teacher, my traveling companion, [...] [he] is a genius, a wonder of grace and talent."[22] The Irish born Venezuelan general and Bolívar's aide-de-camp, Daniel Florence O'Leary, described him as a man of varied and extensive knowledge but eccentric in character.[23] The Chilean jurist and historian José Victoriano Lastarria, who met him at Andrés Bello's home in Santiago de Chile, said that Rodríguez "was off centre" and "often times passed as extravagant and grotesque". And yet, Lastarria quickly added, Rodríguez was widely admired as a brilliant thinker, a "true reformer, whose place was next to Spence, Owen, Saint Simón and Fourier, and not in these American societies".[24]

21 Translation of "muy siglo diez y ocho, y muy antiguo, y muy moderno; audaz, cosmopolita". From the poem "Yo soy aquel que ayer no más decía", first published in Dario, Ruben, *Cantos de vida y esperanza* (Paris, 1904). For an overview of the Cosmopolitan avatars at the end of the nineteenth century, see Salomon, Noel, "Cosmopolitismo e internacionalismo (1880-1940)," in Leopoldo Zea (ed.), *América Latina en sus ideas*, México, Siglo XXI, 1986).

22 "Carta del Libertador al general Santander," in Alfonso Rumazo González, *Simón Rodríguez, maestro de América*, Caracas, Biblioteca Ayacucho, 2005, p. 107.

23 O'Leary, Daniel Florencio, *Bolívar and the War of Independence*, transl. and ed. by Robert F. McNerney, Austin TX, University of Texas Press, 1970, p. 11. O'Leary describes him with great detail: "En figura y modales no era Rodríguez el hombre que podía inspirar confianza y cariño a un niño. Severo e inflexible en su discurso, de facciones toscas e irregulares, tenía pocos amigos fuera de su discípulo, cuyo cariño y confianza se había captado aparentando grande interés en sus entretenimientos infantiles. Extravagantes en sumo grado eran las ideas religiosas de Rodríguez, en pugna completa con la fé cristiana [...] Si Rodríguez era culpable en sus deberes para con Dios, no lo era en sus relaciones con sus semejantes, pues con ellos se distinguía por la benevolencia." In O'Leary, Daniel Florencio, *Memorias del General O'Leary*, transl. by Simón B. O'Leary, 30 Vols., Caracas, El Monitor, 1883, Vol. I, pp. 5-6.

24 Lastarria, José Victoriano, *Recuerdos literarios*, Santiago de Chile, Ediciones LOM, 2001, p. 45. For a collection of portrayals of Rodríguez as bizarre and outlandish, see Cúneo, Dardo, "Aproximación a Simón Rodríguez," in Simón Rodríguez, *Inventamos o erramos*, Caracas, Monte Ávila, 2004, pp. ix-xli.

In our day, however, he is vaguely remembered as Bolívar's tutor, although recently the Venezuelan revolutionary government of Hugo Chávez has identified him as one of its ideological sources and his name is now often associated with literacy campaigns, academic research institutes and political activist groups. His most celebrated quotes appear frequently in meetings and other political activities, scattered between pamphlets and manifestos distributed in Venezuela.[25] Beyond these very recent and relatively superficial appraisals, verging always on anachronism, a rigorous close reading of his writings reveals a fascinating thinker who is difficult to classify; the author of an original and powerful oeuvre, whose understanding of the early nineteenth century Latin American revolutions and the challenges they faced is both extremely lucid and sober.

Rodríguez was born in Caracas in 1771 and spent his childhood in the house of a maternal uncle who took him in after the premature death of his father.[26] He attended one of the three public schools in Caracas, where he must have received a conventional education for a child of the time. Minutes of the City Council of Caracas describe the academic programme used in primary schools in 1786, which closely resembled the education received by Simón Rodríguez. The curricula was in charge of teaching

> [...] the Christian doctrine according to father Ripalda's catechism, to write and read with large and small print, the four main rules of arithmetic with their fractions, the rule of three with distinction of time, to multiply com-

---

25 For a succinct assessment of Simón Rodríguez' place in the Bolivarian revolution of Venezuela, see Gott, Richard, *Hugo Chávez and the Bolivarian Revolution*, London, Verso, 2005, pp. 102-109.

26 The biographical information was culled from the several texts edited by Pedro Grases, *Simón Rodríguez. Escritos sobre su vida y su obra*, Caracas, Concejo Municipal del Distrito Federal, 1954; the biographies by Amunátegui, Miguel Luis, *Ensayos biográficos*, 4 Vols., Santiago de Chile, Imprenta Nacional, 1896, Vol. III, pp. 227-303; and Rumazo González, *Simón Rodríguez, maestro de América*; and several shorter biographical studies, such as García Bacca, Juan David, *Simón Rodríguez, pensador para América*, Caracas, Editorial de la Presidencia de la República, 1978; Grases, Pedro, "Simón Rodríguez, pionero de la educación republicana," in Buenaventura Delgado Criado (ed.), *Historia de la educación en España y América. La educación en la España contemporánea (1789-1975)*, Madrid, Ediciones Morata, 1994; Miliani, Domingo, "Simón Rodríguez. El hombre entre la historia y la ficción," in Beatriz González Stephan (ed.), *Esplendores y miserias del siglo XIX. Cultura y sociedad en América Latina*, Caracas, Monte Avila Editores Latinoamericana, 1995, pp. 25-40; Andrés-Lasheras, Jesús, "Simón Rodríguez en sus cartas," in Simón Rodríguez, *Simón Rodríguez. Cartas*, Caracas, UNESR, 2001, pp. 17-106; and the just published, Briggs, Ronald, *Tropes of Enlightenment in the Age of Bolivar. Simon Rodriguez and the American Essay at Revolution*, Nashville, Vanderbilt University Press, 2010.

pounds, accounting for purchases and for companies, for shares or wills, and everything else that touches on the practice of virtue.[27]

Most likely, this was the same programme Rodríguez encountered when he became teacher at one of the three elementary schools in Caracas in 1791. However, the City Council quickly recognised in him a person of great insight and asked him to draw up recommendations to reform the system. By 1794 he handed in his "Reflections on the defects that vitiate the Primary School System of Caracas and the means to achieve its reform", which argued for the need to increase the number of schools, to adopt a teaching method based on practical activities, to recruit qualified and certified teachers and pay them an adequate salary, and for education to be public, universal and identical for every child, whether white, indigenous or black.[28] Though the project was approved by the City Council it was rejected by the Royal Court (Audiencia), which led to his resignation from his teaching post in frustration. He took on private students, among whom was the young Simón Bolívar. In 1797 he left Venezuela and, though several authors have seen a connection with the republican conspiracy led by Manuel Gual and José María España against the monarchy in July of that year and the harsh repression that followed, there is absolutely no evidence of his involvement in this movement.[29]

From Venezuela he went to Kingston, Jamaica, where he changed his name to "Samuel Robinson", a name which he would assume for the next twenty-five years. Undoubtedly, there is a gesture of affinity here with Daniel Defoe's iconic hero and perhaps even more a revealing allusion to Rousseau's recommendation of *Robinson Crusoe* as the first book Emile should read: "the most certain method for him [Emile]," writes Rousseau, "to raise himself above vulgar prejudice, and to form his judgement on the actual relations of things, is to take on himself the character of such a solitary adventurer, and to judge of everything about

27 Minutes from the City Council, December 22, 1786. Quoted from Rumazo González, Alfonso, "El pensamiento educador de Simón Rodríguez," in Rodríguez, Simón, *Obras Completas*, Caracas, 1975, p. 26. My translation.

28 Rumazo González insists, quite persuasively, that the "Reflections" already evinces a strong Rousseaunian influence. *Ibid.*, pp. 32-33. Gustavo Ruiz and Jesús Andrés-Lasheras remain sceptical. See Ruiz, Gustavo Adolfo, *Simón Rodríguez. Maestro de escuela de primeras letras*, Caracas, Academia Nacional de Historia, 1990; Andrés-Lasheras, "Simón Rodríguez en sus cartas", p. 17.

29 Picón Febrés, Gonzalo, *Don Simón Rodríguez. Maestro del libertador*, Caracas, Cooperativa de Artes Gráficas, 1939, p. 18; Uslar Pietri, Arturo, *La isla de Róbinsón*, Barcelona, Editorial Seix Barral, 1982, p. 55. The theory is accepted by Rumazo González, *Simón Rodríguez, maestro de América*. Andrés-Lasheras once again expresses his doubts, in "Simón Rodríguez en sus cartas", pp. 17-106.

him, as a man in such circumstances would, by its real utility."[30] From that perspective, Simón Rodríguez adoption of Defoe's hero turns the travel genre on its head as this American castaway in Europe – his intended destination – takes on the wilderness of civilisation in order to distinguish the good from the bad. It is a reading as plausible as the one he offered many years later to General O'Leary when he claimed to have "changed his name and assumed that of Samuel Robinson, so that, he said, he might not be reminded of his former servitude".[31] And it is certainly not incompatible with it.

He stayed in Kingston for a few months before heading to the United States. In Baltimore, and also Philadelphia, a meeting place for early Latin American revolutionaries, he worked as a typesetter in a printing shop until 1801, when he left for France. In Bayonne, he opened a school where he taught English and Spanish and, with the Mexican exile Fray Servando Teresa de Mier, undertook the translation and publication of Chateaubriand's *Atalá*, the same year the original was published (1801).[32] He moved to Lyon and then to Paris, where, in 1804, Bolívar joined him. Together they journeyed to Italy, witnessed along the way Napoleon's coronation as King of Italy in Milan (17 March), travelled through Lombardy and Tuscany, settled in Rome for a short while and climbed the city's Monte Sacro, where Bolívar made his famous vow to liberate Spanish America (1805). After a brief stop in London, Bolívar returned to Venezuela and Rodríguez set off on an extended journey that took him through Austria, Prussia, Poland, Russia and back to England. By 1821 he was living in London, where he was apparently under the protection of the French consul and had acquired a reputation as a teacher of French and mathematics.[33]

There is very little information on this period of his life and therefore we have to rely on his reluctant and late characterisation: "I stayed in Europe for over twenty years; worked in an industrial chemistry laboratory, where I learned some things; attended secret socialist meetings; I met father [Barthélemy Prosper] Enfantin, [Benjamin] Olinde Rodrigues, Pedro [Pierre] Leroux, and many others who functioned as

30 Rousseau, Jean Jacques, *Emilius; or, a Treatise of Education*, 3 Vols., Edinburgh, printed for J. Dickson and C. Elliot, 1773, Vol. 1, pp. 334-335.

31 O'Leary, *Bolívar and the War of Independence*, p. 11.

32 Andrea Pagni has approached Rodríguez' translations as sites of cultural negotiation between European referents and emerging American identities. See "Versiones y subversiones del canon Europeo en el siglo XIX. Simón Rodríguez, Andrés Bello y Juan Antonio Pérez Bonalde," in Carlos Pacheco, Luis Barrera Linares and Beatriz González Stephan (eds.), *Nación y literatura. Itinerarios de la palabra escrita en la cultura venezolana*, Caracas, Equinoccio, 2006, pp. 153-175.

33 Amunátegui, *Ensayos biográficos*, Vol. IV, p. 234.

apostles of the sect; studied a little literature; learned languages; and ran a primary school in a Russian village."[34] From the available information on his years in Europe it is impossible to know if he had already heard of Robert Owen's educational experiments at New Lanark during his early stay in London in 1806 or whether he ever visited Johann Heinrich Pestalozzi at Yverdon-les-Bains, though he most certainly was very familiar with their writings, even if he never quoted them directly.[35]

In 1823, Rodríguez returned to America. He arrived in Cartagena and travelled to Bogota, where he communicated with local and national authorities. Soon he obtained approval to establish a school for orphans and the poor in an old abandoned hospice. Just as before, we know very little about this first experience and much of what we do know derives from his later writings, when he expressed great frustration at the reluctant official response to his efforts. In 1824 Bolívar learned of his return to America and asked him to join him in Peru to help establish the educational system of the new republics. When they arrived in Chuquisaca (nowadays called Sucre, in Bolivia), Bolívar appointed him "Director of Public Education, Physical and Mathematical Sciences and Arts" and granted him exceptional powers to implement a nationwide popular school system. Bolívar soon headed back to Lima, leaving Venezuelan Marshal José Antonio Sucre as the president of the newly created Bolivia. Rodríguez set to work with enthusiasm and opened up a model school and workshop in Chuquisaca, with about 200 students, 50 of whom were poor and from diverse backgrounds, and close to 20 young instructors from different parts of the country, who intended on becoming the future principals of regional schools. Despite its promising start, the experience proved to be a complete fiasco. Sucre soon became impatient with Rodríguez' chaotic style, his ambitious reforms (which included a plan for the settlement or "colonisation" of the inland) and his lack of social skills in dealing with the wealthy and powerful. Disconcerted, Sucre protested that Rodríguez had "the head of a stunned Frenchman" and:

> [...] his head filled with wild ideas, and was [unable to] execute his job under the plan he claims to have and that I still do not know what it is; because

34 Colombian geographer Manuel Uribe Ángel interviewed him towards the end of his life in Quito in 1850. See "*El Libertador, su Ayo* y su Capellán," in Manuel Ezequiel Corrales (ed.), *Homenaje de Colombia al Libertador en su primer centenario, 1783-1883*, Bogotá, Medardo Rivas, 1884, p. 73. Barthélemy Prosper Enfantin, Benjamin Olinde Rodrigues and Pierre Leroux were still very young when Rodríguez met them during the second decade of the nineteenth century.

35 As distinct from the traditional convention of backing an argument by piling on established European authorities, Rodríguez hardly mentions other authors and almost never quotes directly from them. Rousseau is perhaps the most recurring author and his name must appear less than a dozen times throughout his entire works.

> I have asked him several times to bring me in writing the system he wants to adopt, so that it serves me as a guide, and in eight months he has not been able to produce it. Even in his talks, he says one thing today and another tomorrow.[36]

Soon, Rodríguez resigned and left for Oruro, where one year later he wrote to Bolívar:

> [...] two trials I have made in America and nobody has transpired the spirit of my plan. In Bogotá I did something and I was hardly understood: in Chuquisaca I made more and they understood less; when they see me collecting poor children, some think my intention is to secure heaven because of the orphans [...], and others think that I am conspiring to demoralize them so that they accompany me in hell.[37]

From that moment on Rodríguez never worked again as an educator for national governments and begun a never-ending journey without stable employment, which took him from Peru to Chile, Ecuador and Colombia, to return and die almost alone and in complete destitution in the small village of Amotape, Peru, in 1854. During those 27 years Rodríguez established several schools and taught at various others in order to survive, managed to publish several important works and collaborated in newspapers and, when nothing else seemed possible, he opened a candle factory so that – he slyly claimed – he could continue to enlighten America.

Despite his spectacular failure at the official level, his texts represent bold proposals that remain to be explored in great detail: *Sociedades Americanas* ("American Societies"), first published in Arequipa in 1828, and expanded and revised in several subsequent editions (Concepcion 1834, Valparaiso 1840, Lima 1842); *El Libertador del Mediodía de América y Sus compañeros de armas, defendidos Por Un amigo de la causa social* ("The Liberator of South of America's Midday and his Fellow Soldiers, Defended by a Friend of the Social Cause") (Arequipa 1830); *Luces y virtudes sociales* ("Lights and Social Virtues") (Concepción 1834, expanded in Valparaiso 1840); a series of six articles published as "Crítica de las providencias del Gobierno" ("Critique of the Government's Orders") (Lima 1843); and "Extracto sucinto de mi obra sobre la Educación Republicana" ("Brief Extract of my Work on Republican Education") published in the Colombian newspaper *Neo-Granadino* (Bogotá April-May 1849). All of Rodríguez' known intellectual output rehearsed more or less the same themes, albeit with significant variations: the insistence on the uniqueness of America, the eluci-

36 O'Leary, Daniel Florencio, *Cartas de Sucre al Libertador (1820-1830)*, 2 Vols., Madrid, Editorial-América, 1919, Vol. 2, p. 49. My translation.

37 "Carta a Simón Bolívar", Oruro, September 30, 1827, in Rodríguez, *Cartas*, p. 153.

dation of republican principles, the emphasis on popular education as a fundamental way to create a citizenry capable of sustaining the republican project, and the need for an economic and social revolution that would complement and give substance to the political revolutions of the early nineteenth century.

As we have said before Rodríguez' projects were not always well received and were rarely understood. His aphoristic writing, full of sarcasm, puns and oblique references provided little clarity for his mostly untrained readers. Well aware of the novelty of his style, he claimed in the preamble to the 1828 edition of *Sociedades Americanas* that:

So EXOTIC it must seem
the PROJECT here contained
as STRANGE
the orthography with which it is written.
In some readers it will excite, perhaps, LAUGHTER

In others .... CONTEMPT
THIS will be unfair:
because,
neither in the observations there are FALSEHOODS
or in the propositions... Nonsense

As for the LAUGTHER
The author will be able to say
(in French better than Latin)
Rira bien qui Rira le dernier[38]

[38] Rodríguez, Simón, *Sociedades Americanas en 1828: cómo serán y cómo podrian ser en los siglos venideros*, Arequipa, s.n. 1828. The quote preserves the visual arrangement disposed by Rodríguez. My translation of:

Tan EXÓTICO debe parecer
el PROYECTO de esta obra
como EXTRAÑA
la ortografía en que va escrito.

En unos Lectores excitará, tal vez, la RISA
En otros .... el DESPRECIO
ESTE será injusto:
porque,
ni en las observaciones hay FALSEDADES
ni en las proposiciones..... Disparates

De la RISA
podrá el autor decir
(en francés mejor que en latín)
Rira bien qui Rira le dernier

Not only did others consider Rodríguez as cosmopolitan; he described himself as such in several passages. But it was, he intended to note, a different cosmopolitanism. As he commented his travels were not the product of his fortune but the result of his curiosity and his passion for knowledge: "I have been so far the only South American to have gone to Europe not to squander a fortune, but to acquire it." Furthermore, Rodríguez's cosmopolitanism underwent a sustainable development in the revised edition of *Sociedades americanas* (1842). At the beginning of the book he presented himself as the Old Man, a favourite trope in philosophical Stoicism, who

> … is not interested in the *Americans* as a COMPATRIOT, because that would mean putting his self-love ON THE GROUND – he makes himself responsible for them (*se apersona por ellos*) as a MAN. He who is interested in the *Human Species*, knowing that it is scattered throughout earth and that the earth is round, thinks he FLIES around it (*le parece que VUELA al rededor*) – that is, it puts his self-love up in the CLOUDS: – and this is, clearly, what everybody thinks, when they speak of their *native place*… of their country… their FATHERLAND![39]

In *Sociedades Americanas* Rodríguez takes up a subject that seems to go in the opposite direction of cosmopolitanism: for Rodríguez, societies in the American continent were original and faced an original situation, and their challenges were different from those of Europe and the United States:

> Where shall we go and look for models? …
> – Spanish America is *original* = ORIGINALS must be
> its Institutions and its Government = and ORIGINALS the
> means to create one and the other[40]

But originality did not make for a nativist argument. He scoffed at those who blindly sought to impose European or Anglo-American

---

[39] Rodríguez, Simón, *Sociedades americanas en 1828*, Lima, Imprenta del Comercio por J. Monterola, 1842, p. 13. My translation of: "No se interesa por los *Americanos*, en calidad de COMPATRIOTA, porque sería poner su amor propio EN EL SUELO – se apersona por ellos en calidad de HOMBRE. El que se interesa por la *Especie Humana*, sabiendo que está dispersa en varios puntos de la tierra, i que ésta es redonda, le parece que VUELA al rededor – esto es poner su amor propio en las NUBES: – I esto es, justamente, lo que cada uno piensa, cuando habla de su *suelo natal* … de *su país*… de su PATRIA!"

[40] *Ibid.*, p. 47. My translation of:
Dónde irémos a buscar modelos?...
– La América Española es *orijinal* = ORIJINALES han de
ser sus Instituciones i su Gobierno = i ORIJINALES los
medios de fundar uno i otro.

models, but his attitude was equally critical of those who passed off and posed as devoted patriots. Mockingly, he wrote:

Be careful when saying that this land is barren, because I am
from there
(that *is Patriotism*)
'What do you have to do with what happens here, if you are not
from here'
(it is *Patriotic Zeal*)[41]

Patriotic zeal is an equivocal attitude that renders impossible communication since it subordinates reason to love for country. Before patriotism, deliberation and criticism becomes difficult if not impossible:

The Cosmopolitan remains silent because he *fears*, or because he cannot make
himself understand
but says to himself
'there is nothing more *patriotic* than a *fool…*'[42]

His insistence on originality should not be regarded as a prejudice against Europe or Europeans. On the contrary, according to Rodríguez, a citizen interested in the fate of their fellow citizens should have "practical knowledge of the People and for this reason he should have travelled widely in countries where there is much to learn, and with the intention of learning."[43]

But such a cosmopolitan attitude, which valued the history and contributions of other nations, also rejected the servile attitude which he encountered at every turn, particularly with those who were supposed to lead the new republican institutions. It is precisely this refusal to simply

---

41 *Ibid.*, p. 97. My translation of:
'Cuidado con decir que mi tierra es Estéril, porque yo soy
de allí'
(*es Patriotismo!*)
'¿Qué tiene Ud. que ver con lo que se hace aquí, si Ud. no es
de aquí'
(es *Celo Patriótico*!)

42 *Ibid.*, pp. 97-98. Translation of:
El Cosmopolita calla porque *teme*, o porque no puede ha-
cerse entender
pero dice, entre sí
'no hay cosa más *patriota* que un *tonto…*'.

43 My translation of: "Conocimiento práctico del Pueblo, y para est haber viajado por largo tiempo, en países donde hay que aprender, y con la intención de aprender"."Nota sobre el proyecto de educación popular," in *El Libertador del Mediodía de América y sus compañeros de armas, defendidos por un amigo de la causa social*, in Rodríguez, *Obras completas*, Vol. 2, p. 359.

follow what others regarded as the European dictum – and not patriotic chauvinism – that led him to argue that:

Europe's enlightenment
and the prosperity of the United-States
are the two enemies of freedom of thinking
... in America...[44]

Americans should know and assess the experience of Europe, but it was equally important to proceed according to two principles, critical discernment and creativity: "Take the good – leave the bad – imitate with discrimination – and for that, which remains, INVENT."[45] To do otherwise would condemn the republics to err.

The tone of the argument was certainly noteworthy even if the argument itself went back to the early days of the American republics. Indeed, it is not difficult to discover among the most experienced leaders of the early republic – Miranda, Nariño, Bolívar – the idea that it was necessary to produce local responses to specific needs rather than importing European constitutional models. It was Bolívar himself who gave the problem an unambiguous formulation in his celebrated "Letter from Jamaica" (1815) and, subsequently, in the "Address to the Congress of Angostura" (1819). Echoing Montesquieu, Bolívar professed in the "Address..." that

> ... the laws must be relative to the physical appearance of the country, to the climate, to the quality of the terrain, to its locations, to its size, to the way of life of the peoples [...]. That they reflect the degree of liberty the constitution can permit, the religion of the inhabitants, their tendencies, their wealth, their number, their commerce, their habits, their manners [...]. Here we have the code we must consult, not that of Washington!!![46]

Rodríguez knew these texts well and very likely had rehearsed some of their arguments with Bolívar during their stay in Europe between 1804 and 1806, well before they were delivered to their respective audiences.

---

44 "Luces y virtudes sociales," in Rodríguez, *Inventamos o erramos*, p. 65.
la sabiduría de la Europa
y la prosperidad de los Estados-Unidos
son dos enemigos de la libertad de pensar
... en América...

45 My translation of "Tomen lo bueno – dejen lo malo – imiten con juicio – y por los que le falte INVENTEN." "El Libertador del Mediodía de América [...]," in Rodríguez, *Obras completas*, Vol. 2, p. 293.

46 Bolívar, Simón, "Address to the Angostura Congress, February 15, 1819, the Day of the Installation," in Janet Burke and Ted Humphrey (eds.), *Nineteenth-Century Nation Building and the Latin American Intellectual Tradition. A Reader*, Indianapolis, Hackett Publishing Company, 2007, p. 8.

In 1828 – despite all the disappointment produced by his brief stint in government – it still seemed plausible for Rodríguez to imagine the new Spanish American republics, together with North America, as the last refuge of true republicans around the world. For once, much of Europe was still in the hands of dynastic monarchies. Even France, despite its earlier political revolution, writes Rodríguez, found its legacy destroyed by the crowning of Napoleon as Emperor and later by the restoration of Louis XVIII and Charles X. True, some European cities enjoyed the benefits of science and high levels of refinement and luxury, but workers remained in social and economic misery and marginalised from political life. For Rodríguez, European traditions and customs were deeply monarchical and this was the reason for the disconnection between the most advanced intellectual ideas and the daily life of the masses. The United States, meanwhile, depended largely on slavery and thus was unable to entirely fulfil its promises of freedom. In these places, despite the advanced state of industry, the accumulated knowledge and obvious sophistication, social life was a sham, undermined by moral crisis. In Spanish America, on the other hand, Rodríguez thought that it was still possible to carry out a plan.[47]

The achievement of independence by Spanish America thus appears as an event of great importance in the global arena. On the one hand, original and unique circumstances, not directly comparable with other places and histories, were at hand; solutions to the predicaments of these nations could not be deduced from already existing models, but had to be created anew from local circumstances. On the other hand, republicanism was clearly an important European contribution to the freedom and wellbeing of mankind, an inescapable language that had to be appropriated or run the risk of degrading into anarchy and tyranny. But Rodríguez' republicanism was not ideal to be imported, but a promise to be realised through those local circumstances.[48] It was, therefore, the challenging task of American republicans to extend and give substance to the promise of freedom under conditions and circumstances which were not favourable to its attainment. The tension between European history and American originality could only be resolved by the critical exercise of appropriation and discernment. The lesson proved so elusive to his contemporaries that Rodríguez was willing to shore up his argument by stating that if "the new republics do not want to admit anything

47 "Luces y virtudes sociales," in Rodríguez, *Inventamos o erramos*, p. 49.

48 For more on Rodríguez' republican credo, see Rosales Sánchez, Juan, *La república de Simón Rodríguez*, Caracas, Fundación Editorial El Perro y La Rana, 2007.

that does not bring the seal of approval from the East or the North. Mimick originality, since they try to imitate everything."[49]

What were the features that, according to Rodríguez, defined the originality of American societies? To begin with, the political revolutions of the early nineteenth century led to a new global scenario, with the appearance of twelve Latin American States, all of which broke from a European empire but found themselves in non-European territory and with a population made up mostly of non-Europeans. These new republics repudiated the monarchical principle and enthusiastically adopted popular sovereignty as the only basis of legitimacy. Furthermore, according to Rodríguez, Americans did not reflect the prejudices of people steeped in monarchical values and traditions. However, despite the widespread existence of republican institutions in America and the existence of some truly committed republican leaders (Rodríguez is clearly thinking of Bolívar here), there is not yet a "people" (*pueblo*) that endowed these republics with life through a bustling civic life. In short, if in Europe there was a "people" that however did not find republican institutions, in America there were popular institutions that lacked a "people".

But perhaps the most important factor accounting for American originality has to do with the nature of what was there instead of a people. For Rodríguez, in addition to the aristocratic and middle classes (typical of social formations in Europe and the United States), in South America there was a variegated populace, a mob composed of

Rustics, Chinese and Barbarians
Gauchos, Half-breeds and Huachinangos
Negroes, Blackish and Gentiles
Highlanders, Calentanos, Indians
People of Color and of Ponchos
Browns, Mulattoes and Knock-kneeds
Stubborn Whites and Yellow Feet
and a CREW of Crossbreds
Terceroons, Quadroons, Quintroons
and Throwbacks
that make, like in botany,
a family of CRYPTOGAMS.[50]

49 Translation of "nada quieren las nuevas Repúblicas admitir, que no traiga el pase del Oriente ó del Norte – Imiten la orijinalidad, ya que tratan de imitar todo". Rodríguez, *Inventamos o erramos*, p. 65.

50 Rodríguez, *Sociedades americanas en 1828*, 1842, p. 24.
Huasos, Chinos ¡Bárbaros
Gauchos, Cholos i Huachinangos
Negros, Prietos i Jentiles

For Rodríguez, this mixture of colours and shapes do not make a people. It is not just the degree of ethnic diversity, a widely recognised problem since the late colonial period.[51] More serious was the fact that this heterogeneity pointed to the fragmentation and atomisation of public life, the proliferation of corporations with diverse and divergent interests.

In the case of the republic such fragmentation precluded the existence of a subject capable of sustaining sovereignty and, therefore, of being an agent capable of exercising citizenship, even though most inhabitants of the new republics were nominally recognised as citizens and some might even formally enjoy the right to vote. Not being a subject or object of sovereignty, the aggregation of subjects did not constitute a republic and its social existence did not contribute to public welfare.

It is, as I have said, a problem that had already been remarked upon with much agony. Thus, for Bolívar it was evidently "impossible to determine with complete precision to which human family we belong".[52] This was no minor problem:

> All our moral strengths – says Bolivar in his Angostura speech (1819) – will not be enough to extract our nascent republics from this chaos if we do not fuse the mass of people into a whole, the make-up of the government into a whole, the legislation into a whole, and the national spirit into a whole. Our slogan must be 'unity, unity, unity'.[53]

Serranos, Calentanos, Indijenas
Jente de Color i de Ruana
Morenos, Mulatos i Zambos
Blancos porfiados i Patas amarillas
i una CHUSMA de Cruzados
Tercerones, Cuarterones, Quinterones
i Salta-atrás
que hace, como en botánica,
una familia de CRIPTOCAMOS.

For a definition of these terms, see Stephens, Thomas M., *Dictionary of Latin American Racial and Ethnic Terminology*, 2nd ed., Gainesville, University Press of Florida.

51 By the end of the eighteenth century American Creole reformers, such as Pedro Fermín de Vargas, advanced proposals in which they thought it "highly desirable that the Indians went extinct by mixing with whites, declaring them free of *tributo* [traditional service tax] and other dues, and giving them land in ownership. Desire for their inheritance would make many Whites and Mestizos married Indians, and vice versa, so that within a very short time there would be no land without being cultivated." de Vargas, Pedro Fermín, *Pensamientos políticos y memorias sobre la población del Nuevo Reino de Granada*, Manuel José Forero (ed.), Bogotá, Banco de la República, 1953, p. 83. My translation.

52 Bolívar, *Address to the Angostura Congress*, p. 9.

53 *Ibid.*, p. 17.

Like Bolívar, Rodríguez believed that the creation of a breed was the only way to avoid an otherwise inevitable disintegration: "The blood of our citizens is various, let us mix it to unify it."[54] However, for Rodríguez this solution by itself was insufficient and failed to produce a people capable of exercising sovereignty.

In Rodríguez one discovers the formulation of the problem and a programme of action to tackle the problem. If the problem is characterised as the legacy of originary violence, the programme is perceived as the republican fate of America and the American dimension of republicanism. Appreciating the magnitude of the task of realising republicanism in America meant keeping both dimensions in mind. Thus, although the origins of racial diversity (the problem) revealed the violence of colonisation and "the greed of Europeans", the programme of action started from the premise that, "it [colonialism] fated America to be the place where the three known races met, mixed and produced a new race".[55] The apparently originally negative character of diversity appears thus as a historic opportunity in which Republicanism can be realised even more fully.[56]

This formula does not seem very different from what Kant developed in the *Idea for a Universal History with a Cosmopolitan Purpose* (1784). There he expressed the hope "that after many transforming revolutions, in the end that which nature has as its aim, will finally come about – a universal cosmopolitan condition, as the womb in which all original predispositions of the human species will be developed."[57] But for Rodríguez, as for Kant, the realisation of this cosmopolitan condition potential requires the recognition of this fundamental sociability and a particular course of action.

In Rodríguez' extended quote social difference appears as an excess of aggregates: rustics, Chinese, Barbarians/Gauchos, half-breed and

---

54 *Ibid.*, p. 17-18.

55 Translation of "La codicia de los Europeos … destinó hace tiempo, la América á ser el lugar en que se han de reunir las tres razas de hombres conocidos – cruzarse – y producir una sola." In "El Libertador del Mediodía de América y sus compañeros de armas, defendidos por un amigo de la causa social" (1830), in Rodríguez, *Obras completas*, Vol. 2, p. 291.

56 Let us recall that this claim is not unique to Latin America. Ronald Briggs argues that it is a hemispheric claim. In that sense, Rodríguez' texts share sensibilities with North American classics such as Hector Crève cœur's *Letters from an American Farmer* (1782), for whom "Here individuals of all nations are melted into a new race." See Briggs, *Tropes of Enlightenment*, pp. 21-57.

57 Schmidt, James and Oksenberg Rorty, Amélie (eds.), *Kant's 'Idea for a Universal History with a Cosmopolitan Aim'. A Critical Guide*, Cambridge, Cambridge University Press, 2009, pp. 20-21.

Huachinangos, etc. – graphically arranged on the printed page – which evoked the American genre of *casta* paintings of the eighteenth century.

Fig. 1 *Casta painting*

Fig. 1, *Castas de Nueva España* painted by Ignacio María Barreda. Reproduced with permission by the *Real Academia Española*

Casta paintings were not intended to illustrate the diversity of a nation or people, but the diversity of *peoples* or *nations* within the monarchy.[58] They figured a corporate model in which stratified and isolated bodies connect among themselves by the king's embodiment of the monarchy. It is no accident that this accumulation of differences culminates in the cryptogam; a figure of sterility that symbolises the impossibility of social reproduction.[59] If such excess represents a "lack of peoplehood", which threatens the political community and nullifies the republican dimension, how then to build republics in this land of barren anarchy? Rodríguez' response is to appeal to what he calls the pre-existing political principle of social life, the principle of the absolute interdependence of human beings – an eminently cosmopolitan principle.

Indeed, Rodríguez' cosmopolitanism is much more than an openness to other cultures of the world and a critical distance towards local attachments; above all, the cosmopolitan tradition allows Rodríguez to elaborate theoretically the interdependence inherent in society, an interdependence which constitutes the republican grounds on which these new American societies can be built. Just as diverse human faculties and abilities depend on each other to perform any action, in the same way whatever success is accomplished by individual human beings it is never the result of his merit alone. Hence, all members of society depend on each other and the very existence of society depends on recognising and acting on this fundamental fact of radical interdependence. Since a republican government is precisely that which recognises that the overall wellbeing of the commonwealth depends on the active participation of everyone, then cosmopolitanism cannot be a trait or virtue of the few. "*Any member of a society,*" writes Rodríguez, "*is bound to watch after society*, because in it he sees himself – and he who sees *in each of his fellow humans* a *brother*, and sees his homeland *wherever he is*, because he can not be *everywhere*, is eminently sociable."[60] It is precisely because of this interdependence that

58 It should be noted that Casta paintings emerged in eighteenth century Mexico and never constituted a popular genre. Rather, it was a bureaucratic discourse and the represented figures appear organised by a taxonomic gaze classifying passive, apolitical subjects. For an in-depth discussion of Casta paintings, see Katzew, Ilona *et al.* (eds.), *New World Order. Casta Painting and Colonial Latin America*, New York, Americas Society, 1996.

59 In botany the term designated species such as fungus and moss that do not reproduce by seeds. Though it is not longer used as category for classifying, it was then – and still is – associated with sterility.

60 My translation of "*Todo miembro de una Sociedad está obligado a ver por ella*, porque en ella se ve a sí mismo – y es eminemente sociable el que, *en cada uno de sus semejantes* ve un *Hermano*, y su Patria *donde se halla*, porque no puede estar en *todas partes.*" Rodríguez, *Sociedades americanas en 1828*, p. 97.

In Republican Societies
it is neither permitted to say
I am not concerned with public affairs
nor to ask another
what business do you have for meddling with them.[61]

Contrary to the authoritarianism of monarchies and the disaggregation of social groups that characterise colonies, entering into republican society means communicating with each other and acting with a view towards the collective good. Only in this way can a society build a viable common space.

Rodríguez infers from such interdependence three maxims: freedom is constitutive of man because interdependence precludes slavery, natural subordination or the usurpation of other's labour: "There is neither agreement that gives one man to another – nor pact that allows him to own somebody else's industry." Such interdependence values collective well-being over individual privileges and describes property as always provisional, as "things in the social state, are only privately owned by consent from everyone else". Finally, the recognition of such radical interdependence defines the ethics of republicanism because: "The will of a person should not arouse another's if it is not destined for the utility of both and should not refrain it except when it is harmful to either."[62]

This is true even for those so-called "doctors" who feel entitled to a natural position of pre-eminence:

> American Doctors – chides Rodríguez with sarcasm – don't realize they owe their science to Indians and Blacks: for if the Doctors had had to plow, sow, harvest, load and make what they have eaten, dressed and played during their useful lifetime … they would not know that much…: they would stay in the fields, and be as stupid as their slaves.[63]

---

61 My translation of:
En la Sociedad Repúblicana
No es permitido decir
No me toca hablar de las cosas públicas
Ni preguntar á otro
Qué injerencia tiene en ellas

62 "Luces y virtudes sociales," in Rodríguez, *Inventamos o erramos*, p. 57.

63 Translation of "Los Doctores Americanos no advierten que deben su ciencia á los indios y á los negros: porque si los Señores Doctores hubieran tenido qué arar, sembrar, recoger, cargar y confeccionar lo que han comido, vestido y jugado durante su vida útil… no sabrían tanto: … estarían en los campos y serían tan brutos como sus esclavos – ejemplo los que se han quedado trabajando con ellos en las minas, en los sembrados detrás de los bueyes, en los caminos detrás de las mulas, en las canteras, y en muchas pobres tiendecillas haciendo manteos, casacas, borlas, zapatos y casu-

The passage is from his defence of republicanism, published in 1830 shortly after its disastrous experience in Bolivia. Rodríguez was responding to accusations made by "decent people" (*gente principal*) that he had depleted the public treasure in order "to keep whores and thieves, rather than procuring the lustre of decent people." He counter-argued that, "the real whores and thieves were the daughters and sons of the owners of the country". On the other hand, he implied that if his educational project had been allowed to prosper those "*cholitas* and *cholitos* [Hispanicised Andeans] who now live off the streets would be more decent than the sons and daughters" of those who accused him.[64]

It was precisely the inability or unwillingness to recognise the social ties that bind people together as equals that transformed liberalism into a system that undermines republican principles. Because in these American societies, says Rodríguez, where sentiments of natural entitlement abound, the

Personal freedom
and
the right to property
these [phrases] are heard, with frequency
by men of talent

The first
in order to avoid any sort of collaboration for the public good –
to demand services without retribution and work without compensation –
to justify inaction with custom, and their
procedures with the law – *all together…*
to live INDEPENDENT in the midst of society.

The second
in order to convert FORCEFUL SEIZURE into *possession* –
to convert possession into *property* – and, by any means,
in order to ENJOY at the expense of others (whoever those others might be)
under the title of LEGITIMACY
(and thus legitimacy is a tolerated abuse).[65]

---

llas.'"El Libertador del Mediodía de América y sus compañeros de armas, defendidos por un amigo de la causa social," in Rodríguez, *Obras completas*, Vol. 2, p. 359.

64 "Carta al General Francisco de P. Otero", Lima, March 10, 1832, in Rodríguez, *Cartas*, p. 161.

65 "Luces y virtudes sociales," in Rodríguez, *Inventamos o erramos*, p. 54. My translation of:

Libertad personal
y
derecho de propiedad

On the other hand, recognition of the principle of radical interdependence allows for the restoration of republicanism. Thus, interdependence is not just a social phenomenon but the grounds on which republican virtues, essential for the survival of democratic societies, survive and might be cultivated.

Finally, the cosmopolitan notion of interdependence allows him to argue that every citizen, in so far as he is an actor in the public sphere must develop the ability to scrutinise through deliberation and critique and accept similar scrutiny from his fellow citizens. Such a collective public performance sustains the republic and constitutes Rodríguez' bedrock for the argument that republicanism is a superior stage of human civilisation. Indeed, the difference between the republic and the monarchy is that if the latter construct the public character of society on authority, "in the republic, authority rests on public custom".[66] The republic is the historic realisation of the psycho-sociological fact of interdependence inherent to every society, though not always fully realised; it is its most suitable political form, one which starts from its recognition and thrives in its realisation. The republic, unlike the monarchy, demands "a people who know what a PUBLIC AFFAIR is". Since,

The habits formed by
a PUBLIC authority
produce
not
a Social Education
a PERSONAL authority
in the Republic

---

se oyen alegar, con frecuencia
por hombres de talento

La primera
para eximirse de toda especie de cooperación al bien jeneral –
para exijir servicios sin retribución y trabajos sin recompesa
para justificar su inacción con las costumbres, y sus
procedimientos con las leyes – *todo junto. . . .*
para vivir INDEPENDIENTES en medio de la sociedad

El segundo
para convertir la USURPACIÓN en *posesión* (natural ó civil) –
la posesión en *propiedad* – y, de cualquier modo,
GOZAR con perjuicio de tercero (sea quien fuere el tercero),
á título de LEJITIMIDAD (y la lejitimidad es un abuso
tolerado).

66 "Estracto sucinto de mi obra sobre la educación republicana," in Núm. 39 *Neo-Granadino*, Bogota, 28 April 1849, p. 132.

In the profession of political faith that precedes the 1828 edition of *Sociedades Americanas*, Rodríguez argued that "the public cause" has a historical opportunity in America to form "a TRULY REPUBLICAN GOVERNMENT. America is (today) the only place where it might be established."[67] As we have already noted the difficulty is that those American republics, which were forged in 1810, had still not been brought into being at the end of the third decade of the nineteenth century. In his diagnosis Rodríguez agreed with leaders across the political spectrum: "Only EDUCATION! imposes obligations on the WILL. These OBLIGATIONS are those we call HABIT."[68] But while many conservative governments were instituting educational programmes to create "obedient, moderate, respectful and docile" citizens,[69] Rodríguez offered his method of education as the fundamental way of remedying the lack of public political virtues through the active participation of every citizen. In this proposal we discover in Rodríguez a continuation of the democratic programme advanced by Condorcet in the late eighteenth century.[70]

4. Conclusion: Popular Education

Such recognition of the cosmopolitan principle of interdependence as the pre-eminent social fact, and of the deficit that characterises Latin American societies – republican institutions without sovereign people – "demands a new conception of popular education".

PUBLIC INSTRUCTION
in the 19th Century
demands MUCH PHILOSOPHY
...
the GENERAL INTEREST
is claiming for
a REFORM
and that
AMERICA is destined

67 *Ibid.*

68 *Ibid.*

69 de Paula Santander, Francisco, *Obra educativa de Santander*, Vol. 1, Luis Horacio López Domínguez (ed.), Bogotá, Fundación Francisco de Paula Santander, 1990, p. 365. Santander was the Vice-president of the Great Colombia (1821-1830) and developed and implemented a massive educational system based on Lancasterianism.

70 Condorcet, "Rapport et projet de décret sur l'organisation générale de l'instruction publique (1792)," in Célestin Hippeau (ed.), *L'instruction publique en France pendant la Révolution*, Paris, Klincksieck, 1990.

by circumstances to carry it,
might seem a bold paradox ...[71]

If we take into account that radical interdependence is at the root of society and thus that Americans are inextricably linked, the process of making a sovereign people out of a dissimilar populace requires popular education, the only process that, according to Rodríguez, can "[...] give being to the imaginary Republic that stumbles around in books and Congresses".[72] Contrary to the understanding of education espoused by the new American States and official programmes, popular education does not consist in merely teaching basic literacy, instructing or disseminating information. For Rodríguez:

To Teach .... is to make comprehensible.
It is to employ the discerning mind [*entendimiento*], not to make memory work.[73]

For Rodríguez, to teach in modern republics means to make available existing information to individual discernment because it is only through such appropriation that knowledge becomes habitual and is generalised. In other words, it becomes part of the public body and constitutes the social: "What is not general, without exception, is not truly public, and what is not public is not social."[74] A republic, argued Rodríguez, is only made possible through the production of a public, only in the shuttling back and forth between discernment and generalisation, individual and community, does the individual becomes the public, and the public become generalised so that it constitutes the people: the foundation of a

---

71 "Estracto sucinto de mi obra sobre la educación", p. 132. My translation of:
la INSTRUCCIÓN PÚBLICA
en el siglo 19
pide MUCHA FILOSOFÍA
que
el INTERÉS JENERAL
está clamando por
una REFORMA
y que
la AMÉRICA está llamada
por las circunstancias, á emprenderla
atrevida paradoja parecerá...

72 "Carta al General Francisco de P. Otero", March 10, 1832, in Rodríguez, *Cartas*, p. 161.

73 Translation of "Enseñar .... es hacer comprender. Es emplear el *entendimiento*, no hacer trabajar la memoria." *Sociedades americanas*, 1842, p. 104.

74 "Luces y virtudes sociales," in Rodríguez, *Inventamos o erramos*, p. 67.

popular republic, which is the only political form that can aspire to the title of democracy.

In principle, to constitute a people means eliminating the populace, the rabble, the mob, all differential forms of existence of the people. But the populace is not a descriptor for socio-economic status. The use of the word "populace" designates the ignorance or neglect of the constitutive principle of society in favour of private interests that fragment the social. According to Rodríguez, the first axiom should be made clear to the populace during its instruction: "the word Populace is taken from the Italian *popolazzo* or *popolaccio*, and means *frail people* or *little folk…* and by extension DESPICABLE PEOPLE." A second maxim, which should be read to them immediately after the first one, clarifies that: "Men are only truly despicable because of their ignorance."[75] Therefore, becoming a people is fundamentally a process of self-discipline. Rodríguez recommends,

> As everything progresses by degrees, each person must start by refraining from mentioning *color* and *ancestry* on the merits or demerits of others, and that person will have taken a step out of the populace – [subsequently] he or she should not appreciate or despise anyone because of their place of birth, their political or religious beliefs... and that person will have taken another great step.[76]

This example illustrates Rodríguez' faith in the corrective power of reason; the ability to destroy old prejudices and reform old habits. Only people in possession of discernment can build a republic

Because
everything that is good
in society
is due
to criticism
or better yet
society exists ….. due to
Criteria the same as *discernment*
to critique is *to judge* with rectitude

The faculty to critique, the capacity to discern and the ability to appropriate are what make it possible to convert crisis, the political lack, into a historical opportunity:

Crisis is the case or
the moment of judging with criteria

75 "Libertador del Mediodía," in Rodríguez, *Obras completas*, Vol. 2, p. 291.

76 *Ibid.*

or the decisive judgement
do not take critique for acrimony
nor … censure for detraction.[77]

A popular education aimed at promoting the critical faculties to discern and reform customs creates a cosmopolitan "social consciousness".[78]

> If instruction were provided to everyone… how many of those we despise because of their ignorance would be our advisors, our well doers, or our friends?! […] How many of those who force us to lock our doors would be trusted with our keys!? […] How many of those we are afraid when on the roads would be our traveling companions!?[79]

Thus, Rodríguez argued, only through the institutionalisation of education, by making it available and free for everyone (that is, the same education, in the same classroom, under the same conditions for everyone, from the sons and daughters of the patricians to the abandoned orphans of the war, and the children of Indians and former slaves), will it become possible to conclude the political revolutions that began in the early nineteenth century. A task that, during these bicentennial dates, still appears as yet unfinished.

---

77 "Luces y virtudes sociales," in Rodríguez, *Inventamos o erramos*, pp. 69-70. My translation of

Porque
todo lo bueno que
hay en sociedad
se debe á
la crítica
o mejor dicho
La sociedad existe ….. por
Criterio es lo mismo que discernimiento
Criticar es juzgar con rectitud

Crisis es el caso o
el momento de juzgar con acierto

o el jucio decisivo
no se tome critica por mordacidad
ni … censura por detracción.

78 Rodríguez, *Sociedades americanas en 1828*, p. 20.

79 My translation of "Si la Instrucción se proporcionara a TODOS… ¿¡cuántos de los que despreciamos, por Ignorantes, no sería nuestros consejeros, nuestros Bienhechores o nuestros Amigos?! …. ¿¡Cuántos de los que nos obligan a echar cerrojos a nuestras puertas, no serían Depositarios de las llaves?! …. ¿¡Cuántos de los que tememos en los caminos, no serían nuestros compañeros de viaje?!" In Rodríguez, *Sociedades americanas en 1828*, 1842, p. 31.

Empires without Cosmopolitanism?

Locating Cosmopolitanism in the Nineteenth Century Ottoman and Russian Empires

Adrian BRISKU

1. Introduction

Cosmopolitanism is not only about ethnic and religious diversity for if it were nineteenth century Ottoman and Russian empires would be just that, "cosmopolitan". In this brief historical comparison, the attempts are made to locate the notion of cosmopolitanism within the cultural and economic domains of the nineteenth century Russian and Ottoman Empires. The following questions are asked: to what extent is this notion reflected in the cultural and economic discourses of these empires during this time and can they be seen as cosmopolitan? These questions are posed in light of a paradox, particularly in cultural politics – that while, as multi-ethnic and multi-religious empires,[1] it is possible to view them as culturally cosmopolitan, there is little, or rather sporadic scholarly depiction of the two in this light. More importantly, contemporaries do not make direct use of cosmopolitanism as such.

The endeavour of locating cosmopolitanism within these two settings is marred by obvious conceptual difficulties. One is the many registers that this notion can operate in, while the other is how to conceptualise cosmopolitanism, if contemporaries do not make direct use of it. On the first issue, rather than being a term for describing the composition and relations of a political entity, such as an empire, one principal meaning associated with it, stemming from intellectual attitude of Cynic and Stoic philosophy, is that of disregarding politics and identification of the individual morally and ethically to a *universal community*. Seeing it as a negation of politics, it directly challenges the concept of empire as a political entity – a supra-national body politic engaged in the control of vast space and multi-ethnicity, entailing power in general and hard

1 There are countless books that offer direct or indirect accounts on the ethnic and religious diversity of the nineteenth Russian and Ottoman Empires. Hence, it is not necessary to provide here a list of the nationalities and religions.

power in the international context.[2] Meanwhile, Immanuel Kant, a key representative of Enlightenment thought, considered cosmopolitanism from a structural perspective which was legal and political, rather than from that of the ethical and moral individual. Hence, instead of seeing it as negation of politics, he advanced the notion of *cosmopolitan right* constituted by universal hospitality, which meant that under this principle people would have the right to visit and use the earth's surface because it belonged to all the human race.[3] He also considered cosmopolitanism as a political *goal* for institutional improvement of the enlightened, mainly republican, nations and governments in the European continent. Enlightened European nations carried the knowledge of Greek and Roman nations, as he put it, which had brought about "a regular process of improvement in the political constitutions of our continent (which will probably legislate for all other continents)."[4] While legislating for other continents appeared secondary, the primary focus remained the improvement of civil constitutions, laws and the mutual relations among the states of the European continent. But this goal was contingent. It depended on how these legal structures and relations were handled by political actors – if political actors were virtuous, their nations would flourish, but if they failed to address the inherent defects of these structures, revolutions could erupt.[5]

However, it seems reasonable to suggest that besides these layers of meanings – an intellectual attitude of withdrawing from politics and identifying morally and ethically with a universal community, a cosmopolitan right and a goal for politics to improve existing structures and relations – it is possible to approach cosmopolitanism from the perspectives of openness within and without cultural and economic spaces of a political entity, such as empires in this case. And this offers one way of dealing with the second difficulty described above – namely, how to conceptualise cosmopolitanism if contemporaries do not make direct use of it. So, a culturally open empire would be one premised upon the coexistence of multi-ethnic and multi-religious communities and this would be overtly reflected in the imperial cultural politics – which justifies the

---

2 Lieven, Dominic, "Empire on Europe's Periphery. Russian and Western Comparisons," in Alexei Miller and Alfred J. Reiber (eds.), *Imperial Rule*, Budapest, CEU Press, pp. 133-149, p. 133.

3 Kant, Immanuel, "Toward Perpetual Peace," in *Practical Philosophy*, The Cambridge edition of the works of Immanuel Kant, Mary J. Gregor (transl. & ed.), Cambridge, Cambridge University Press, 1999, pp. 311-351, p. 329.

4 Kant, Immanuel, "Idea for a Universal History with a Cosmopolitan Purpose," in Hans S. Reiss (ed.), *Kant. Political Writings*, 2nd ed., Cambridge, Cambridge University Press, 1991, pp. 41-53, p. 52.

5 *Ibid.*

usage of the term *cultural cosmopolitanism*. Such practice is juxtaposed with a type of politics that seeks to homogenise the cultural fabric of empires around dominant ethnic and/or religious markers. As for openness in the economic realm, this is linked to the advancement of a doctrine of liberal economy and free trade, as well as espousing to the idea of *laissez-faire* economics, largely conceived here as *economic cosmopolitanism*. Crucial in this conception is the doctrine of nineteenth-century Scottish political economist, Adam Smith, of free trade among nations of the world[6] and the physiocrat notion of *laissez-faire*, which enter Russian and Ottoman vocabularies of political economy.[7] Importantly, then, one of the means through which this doctrine was promoted in the nineteenth century was by the conclusion of free trade treaties between nations. Meanwhile, an opposing political economy doctrine emerged and gained currency from the middle of the century onwards – that of "national economics",[8] authored by the nineteenth-century German economist Friedrich List. In it, he argued for the establishment of trade barriers and tariffs in order to provide *economic protectionism* for weaker economic spaces.

---

6 Smith, Adam, *An Inquiry into the Nature and Causes of the Wealth of Nations*, Hamburg, Management Laboratory Press, 2008.

7 Smith's doctrine was premised upon similar principles as his contemporaries, the French *économistes* with their physiocrat notion of *laissez-faire*, namely "let nature alone to rule human affairs" but with a crucial distinction, nevertheless. Unlike the *économistes* who would advocate policies of intervention in order to create *laissez-faire* economic spaces, Smith considered these measures as unnatural and prone "to disturb nature in the course of her operations" and ultimately were "obliged" to turn into oppression and tyranny. Meanwhile, the idea of natural, especially as conceived in the framework of natural jurisprudence of the seventeenth century and most notably by German jurist Samuel Pufendorf, meant not what was "natural" in nature but rather in human history. See Hont, Istvan, *Jealousy of Trade. International Competition and the Nation-State in Historical Perspective*, Cambridge Mass./London, The Belknap Press of Harvard University Press, 2005, pp. 359-364.

8 This concept stipulates that the outcome of a general free trade would not be a universal republic but rather a universal subjugation of the less advanced to the stronger industrial, commercial and naval powers. While List did not discard the quest for the gradual and ultimately final union of nations, which implied the promotion of true free trade, he also suggested that the most effective way to achieve it was when less-advanced nations erect protective measures so that they stand on an equal footing with powerful nations. Only in this manner and through gradual union could he conceive a "universal republic […] i.e. a union of the nations of the earth whereby they recognise the same condition of right […] and a number of nationalities attain to as nearly the same degree as possible of industry and civilisation, political cultivation and power." List, Friedrich, *National System of Political Economy. The Systems and Politics*, 3 Vols., New York, Cosimo Classics, 2005, Vol. II, p. 103.

2. Cosmopolitanism as Universality and Openness: Multi-ethnicity, Nationalism, Pan-Islamism and Pan-Slavism

Probably there is no better starting point for locating cosmopolitanism than the cultural realm of an empire – it entails a plurality of nationalities, languages, religions, mores and traditions. But if *cultural cosmopolitanism* implies a recognition and co-existence of many cultures in their particularities, while cultural uniformity is a recipe for cultural impoverishment,[9] then imperial attempts to homogenise the cultural fabric of their populations around dominant religious or ethnic groups suggest an intervention that seeks to negate this plurality and diversity.

Scottish diplomat and writer David Urquhart – a close observer of the 1830s Ottoman affairs writing in 1838 – noted that in the context of the Ottoman state's attitude towards the many different languages of its populations, its policy was that of non-interference, unlike the attitude of some European governments with respect to their own populations. Seemingly, this Ottoman approach was informed by a practice of

> Turks, as other Orientals, [who] never start by laying down an abstract principle which is to rule their practical conduct. They do not adopt, for instance, as an axiom, that the language of the state is to be one, that the laws of the provinces are to be uniform; and then build or destroy to enforce the application of this abstraction: they, on the contrary, never interfere in any way unless forced, by some necessity, to do so. They have not laid down non-interference as a principle of government; for that idea could only come as a result of interference.[10]

This observation cuts both ways in that, on the one hand, until the mid-nineteenth century, it would be an historical absurdity to characterise the ideology of the Ottoman state as *cultural cosmopolitanism* as it did not interfere to achieve it. However, on the other hand, this non-intervention allowed for the existence of diversity in languages and religions.

The ostensible lack of a consistent portrayal of the Ottoman Empire as being culturally cosmopolitan by scholars can be seen as contingent to the historical reality of the empire. For some – like Ira M. Lapidus who takes a long view on Islamic societies, including the Ottoman one – there were some earlier moments, particularly within the imperial Ottoman court, which can be characterised as open and rich in diversity.

---

9 Kleingeld, Pauline, "Six Varieties of Cosmopolitanism in Late Eighteenth-Century Germany," 60 *Journal of the History of Ideas* (1999), pp. 505-524, p. 515.

10 Urquhart, David, *The Spirit of the East*, 2 Vols., London, Henry Colburn Publisher, 1838, p. 237.

But, certainly in the ensuing centuries, such characterisation could not be ascribed. He wrote that:

> The authority of Ottoman Sultans was also based upon a cosmopolitan culture, comprising Arab, Persian, Byzantine, and European elements. Mehmet II [ruled 1432-1481], a liberal patron of arts, cultivated Persian poetry and European painting. At his court, Arab and Persian literati, Italian painters, and Greek and Serbian poets were welcome. Later regimes, however, moved away from Christian and European influences toward a more Muslim and Turkish style.[11]

To Edhem Eldem, meanwhile, the use of cosmopolitanism as a descriptive notion for the multi-ethnic mosaic of Istanbul as well as the entire empire – especially during the nineteenth century – was a rather sentimental and nostalgic move. He regarded it as ultimately unhelpful, because such diversity failed to develop into a more supra-communal or supra-religious ideology capable of providing an overarching alliance for all the communities. Instead, the *millet system*, separation along confessional communities with their own legal courts applying "personal law" to community members, which had been in place, was a formula of coexistence based on systematic avoidance of potential frictions from excessive contact and intermingling.[12] Whilst, for scholar Donald Quataert, *cultural cosmopolitanism* could be applied to some fragmentary episodes related to the effects of migrants moving from the interior of the empire and Aegean islands into the Ottoman port cities. However, these episodes had a Mediterranean rather than an Ottoman flavour. "Thanks to them" he wrote, "the port cities developed a cosmopolitan, multilingual, 'Levantine' culture more a part of the general Mediterranean world as a whole than the Ottoman Empire in particular."[13]

Especially from the mid-nineteenth century, the Ottoman state increasingly came under pressure, from internal and external forces, to reform. This meant a push for centralisation of political power in the empire, a major consequence of which was the extension of the centralising drive not only to administrative, military, juridical, economic domains, but also to that of culture. The efforts of the state, for instance, through the promulgation of Hatt-ı Şarif of Gülhane (the Imperial De-

---

11 Lapidus, Ira M., *A History of Islamic Societies*, 2nd ed., Cambridge, Cambridge University Press, 2002, p. 261.

12 Eldem, Edhem, "Istanbul. From Imperial to Peripheralized Capital," in Edhem Eldem *et al.* (eds.), *The Ottoman City between East and West. Aleppo, Izmir, and Istanbul*, Cambridge, Cambridge University Press, 1999, pp. 135-206, p. 154.

13 Quataert, Donald, *The Ottoman Empire, 1700-1992*, 2nd ed., Cambridge, Cambridge University Press, 2005, p. 116.

cree of the Rose Garden) in 1839 – sanctioning equal civil rights[14] for all the ethnic and religious communities – and the promotion of "Ottoman" as a legal concept with the aim of unifying the empire's nationalities through the Ottoman Law of Nationality in 1869,[15] produced paradoxical outcomes that could be read as either homogenising empire's cultural fabric or giving life to a cosmopolitan outlook. For scholar Nyazy Berkes, it was the latter. He considered the measures taken by the Ottoman state in establishing secular schools in Istanbul and other cities as providing cosmopolitan outcomes. He pointed out that:

> While many of these [schools] concentrated in the cosmopolitan commercial centres the missionary schools in particular penetrated far beyond the foreign economic enterprises. A few of these were secular institutions, all were cosmopolitan, and while many expanded their curricula to cater to the national cultures of their polyglot student bodies, the absence of Ottoman, let alone Turkish [as the language of instruction was French], cultural influences was conspicuous.[16]

However, beyond the cultural cosmopolitanism of the secular schools, by the late 1860s, it was also becoming apparent that the ideology of Ottomanism, which was premised upon the promotion of coexistence of multi-ethnicity and multi-religious communities, was losing its content. When prominent contemporary intellectual Namik Kemal, in the light of the empire's loss of territories inhabited by the Christian population and growing nationalism among other European nations, wrote about the "Ottoman nation", he increasingly implied a Turkish Ottoman nation. And he did not consider internationalism, understood as loving humanity as a whole – the closest in meaning to cosmopolitanism as an intellectual attitude – applicable to the Ottoman context.[17] Again, for Eldem, there were two moments that illustrated the inability of Ottoman *cultural cosmopolitanism* to turn into a real possibility during this period. The first was the failure of the Ottoman state to create a trans-ethnic Ottoman identity, which Kemal as a contemporary was already pointing to. And second, the brief emergence of a cosmopolitan Levantine society, especially with regard to Istanbul, driven by economic integration of the empire into the Western economic system, weaved

14 Holland, Thomas Erskine, *The European Concert in the Eastern Question*, 2nd ed., Darmstadt, Scientia Verlag Aalen, 1979, p. 322.

15 Hanioğlu, M. Şükrü, *A Brief History of the Late Ottoman Empire*, Oxford/Princeton, Princeton University Press, 2008, p. 74.

16 Berkes, Nyazy, *The Development of Secularism in Turkey*, Montreal, McGill University Press, 1964, p. 192.

17 Mardin, Şerif, *The Genesis of Young Ottoman Thought. A Study in the Modernization of Turkish Political Ideas*, Syracuse NY, Syracuse University Press, 2000, p. 330.

around European networks and values, collapsed by the end of the nineteenth century. He wrote:

> The illusion of a cosmopolitan Levantine society was rapidly shattered by the hard realities of the 1878 war and the wave of migration from the Balkans, the Armenian massacres of the last decade of the century, and the Greco-Turkish conflict of 1898. Under the growing resentments of the period and the rise of Turkish nationalism with the Young Turk movement, the pluralist dream soon turned into the nightmare of World War I and the War of Independence.[18]

During the reign of Sultan Abdul-Hamid II (1876-1909), the state responded to these pressures by discarding any of Ottomanism's remaining multi-religious attributes, which, as mentioned, had become more a vessel for Turkish nationalism. Instead, it strongly promoted the rhetoric of homogeneity based on the predominant religion of Islam, and beyond its ever-changing borders the concept of Pan-Islamism – the unity of Muslims under one Islamic state. Mimicking measures were taken by Austro-Hungarian Empire, which promoted Catholicism, and by the Russian Empire which promoted Christian Orthodoxy, as unifying markers for their respective multi-ethnic populaces; while the Sultan used the religious law of Şeriat to legitimise his rule inside and muster support from outside by evoking the Muslim tradition of Caliphate. However, while advancing an interpretation of Pan-Islamism, which encapsulated a universal vision for all Muslims to rally around the sultan,[19] Sultan Abdul-Hamid's attempt came into conflict with other Islamic interpretations from other Muslim communities, most notably the Shiite communities inside the empire.

Similarly, a sporadic scholarly description in terms of *cultural cosmopolitanism* has been made in respect of the nineteenth century imperial Russian cultural domain. As with the Ottoman case, in the sense of being both multi-ethnic and multi-religious, the Russian Empire during this period could have projected a cosmopolitan discourse as its own state of being. Illustrative of that possibility is the official title that Russian tsars as rulers of the empire held, namely "the emperor of all Russian (*rossiiskoie*) lands,"[20] where, as scholar Austin Jersild has pointed out, the adjective *rossiiskii* implied recognition of multiethnicity. This seems, in particular, to have been the way educated elites of Caucasus identified themselves within the empire from the 1830s as

---

18 Eldem, *Istanbul*, p. 205.

19 Deringil, Selim, *The Well-Protected Domains*, London, I.B. Tauris, 1998, p. 48.

20 Jersild, Austin, *Orientalism and Empire*, Montreal/Kingston, McGill-Queen's University Press, 2002, p. 7.

rossiiskii as opposed to *russkii*,[21] which referred to being ethnic Russian. Also, Richard Sakwa noted that this potential was and remains always there – in fact, Russia had "an innate cosmopolitanism". "In geographical and cultural terms," he noted, "Russia appears to have an innate cosmopolitanism in that its very existence refutes narrow definitions of East and West, Europe or Asia, nation-state, and empire, modernity and backwardness."[22] This innate cosmopolitanism, accordingly, was rooted in the Russian mind-set as illustrated by a Russian saying, "Russia is not a country; it is a world".[23] However, he specified that it was only in geographical and cultural rather than in political terms that Russia appeared so.

Following Tsar Alexander I's (reign 1801-1825) declaration of the Holy Alliance in 1815 – a vision for conducting European politics informed by Christian morality of brotherhood and solidarity – the imperial state intervened for the first time in the religious domain with the Decree of the Constitution of the Churches of 1817 in promoting a multi-religious empire. It recognised the freedom, plurality and equality of Christian religions, including also the Russian Masonry and Christian mystic groups, elevating the status of diverse Protestant churches to state church – a position held only by the Russian Orthodox Church.[24] Tsar Alexander I's openness in the religious sphere would be short-lived, however, as by 1822 he had caved in to pressure exerted by the Orthodox clergy to curb the proliferating activities of religious mystic groups and secret societies.[25] In 1833, in order to forge the loyalty of imperial subjects towards the tsar, the imperial state, through the doctrine of "Autocracy, Orthodoxy and Nationality",[26] began to promote a homogenising cultural politics around one religion and a vaguely defined notion of nationality. This was largely in response to a post-Napoleonic European order concerned with restraining the revolutionary impulse in the Continent and more importantly the perceived threat of that impulse at home following the Decembrist Uprising of 1825. In the ensuing decades, the state's attitude towards its multi-ethnic and multi-

21 *Ibid.*

22 Sakwa, Richard, "Russia as Eurasia. An Innate Cosmopolitanism," in Gerard Delanty (ed.), *Europe and Asia beyond East and West*, London, Routledge, 2006, pp. 215-227, p. 215.

23 *Ibid.*

24 Ley, Francis, *Alexandre 1er et sa sainte-alliance*, Paris, Librairie Fischbacher, 1975, p. 176.

25 *Ibid.*, p. 272.

26 Seton-Watson, Hugh, *The Russian Empire 1801-1917*, Oxford, Oxford University Press, 1967, p. 220.

religious populace became one of homogenisation around one dominant religious and increasingly ethnic marker.

Meanwhile, whereas Ottoman cultural and intellectual contacts and exchanges with Western European intellectual and cultural currents were rather insignificant until the first decades of the nineteenth century, Russian intellectual milieus had been permeated by these currents throughout the eighteenth and early nineteenth centuries. Some of these milieus responded to the "Spirit of Enlightenment" – perceived as an outwardly movement towards freedom, faith in man, progress and conducting life based on reason. Others tuned into an inward aspect of the West – a spiritual search for union between the earthly and the heavenly – which resulted in with the spread of secret societies of Western Masonry in Russia.[27] By the late 1830s, the "Spirit of Enlightenment" and, more particularly, German Idealism evolved into two intellectual currents; the so-called Westernisers and the Slavophiles – a division that continued throughout the century. While Westernisers sought to incorporate these ideas in the Russian context, Slavophiles came to reject Western thought and Westernisers' subscription to universalising European ideas as foreign and anti-national.[28] For Slavophiles, these were cosmopolitan views and attitudes, in which "cosmopolitan" had negative connotations. Instead, they took on the task of giving meaning to the notion of Russian nationality, emphasising the Russian ethnic element and the important role of Christian Orthodoxy.

Indeed, Slavophiles propagated a strong nationalistic rhetoric inside the empire. And beyond its confines, they embraced the doctrine of Pan-Slavism that called for the unity of all Slavic peoples. Such rhetoric permeated not only in the imperial state's attitude vis-à-vis nationalities inside the empire, but also with regards to the conduct of its international relations as in supporting Slavic nations within the Ottoman Empire at the outset of Russo-Turkish Wars of 1877-1878. For an ardent Slavophile such as publicist M.N. Katkov, who had actively embraced the cause of Pan-Slavism,[29] this doctrine was applicable solely outside the empire as inside it undermined the organic unity of the Russian nation. In light of the crushing of the 1863 Polish Rebellion by the imperial state, Katkov asserted that Russian nation was an organic entity and no separate nationalities could be tolerated within the empire. "Russia," he wrote, "thank God, is neither a heterogeneous state, like Austria, nor a

---

27 Zenkovskii, Vasilii Vasil'evick, *Russian Thinkers and Europe*, Ann Arbor, J.W. Edwards Publisher, 1953, pp. 6-7.

28 Malia, Martin, *Alexander Herzen and the Birth of Russian Socialism 1812-1855*, Cambridge, Harvard University Press, 1961, p. 279.

29 Morison, J.D., "Katkov and Panslavism," 46 *The Slavonic and East European Review* 107 (1968), pp. 422-441, p. 422.

disintegrating one, like Turkey [...] We consider that throughout the whole expanse of the Russian power no other political nationality can be recognised but the Russian one."[30] But his position was completely the opposite when it came to the Slavs of Habsburg and Ottoman empires, sympathising with their national grievances.[31] Meanwhile, for the prominent novelist Fyodor Dostoyevsky, Pan-Slavism was not only about the recognition of an exclusiveness based on ethnicity as a political and spiritual alliance for all Slavs, but also as an initial step to the ultimate aim of Russia, which was to render a universal service to mankind – meaning Western Europe. "We Russians have two fatherlands: Russia and Western Europe",[32] he had declared, and it was Russia's duty through its Pan-Slavism to save Western Europe from a moral decline. Writing in the context of the Russo-Turkish Wars of 1877-1878, when the rhetoric of Pan-Slavism was elevated, Dostoyevsky argued that Pan-Slavism was a universal message of the brotherly union of Europe, based on strong Christian values. This was because, in his view, the Russian nation, of all nations, was capable of containing the idea of pan-humanity.[33]

3. *Economic Cosmopolitanism* as Economic Imperialism

While in the domain of culture the imperial states attempted but ultimately did not succeed in upholding cosmopolitan cultural politics *vis-à-vis* their respective populaces, in the field of economy, which increasingly came to occupy a central role in their activities during the nineteenth century, they appeared more keenly engaged, through promoting a kind of *economic cosmopolitanism*. Openness and promotion of free trade among nations[34] was not a view strongly supported by economically active Ottomans and Russians, however. It became imperative to them only in the light of major crises, defeats in war, or economic depression at home. These imperatives, especially in the second half of the nineteenth century, gave rise, also, to positions that increasingly considered openness in trade and economic space as economic imperialism, calling instead for the erection of barriers and tariffs against free exchange between their respective economic spaces and other nations.

30 *Ibid.*, p. 423.

31 Quoted in *ibid.*, p. 431.

32 Quoted in Zenkovskii, *Russian Thinkers and Europe*, p. 5.

33 Florovsky, Anton, "Dostoyevsky and the Slavonic Question," 26 *Slavonic and East European Review* (1930), pp. 411-423, p. 414.

34 Kleingeld, "Six Varieties of Cosmopolitanism in Late Eighteenth-Century Germany", p. 518.

At the beginning of the nineteenth century the Ottoman state supported a closed internal economic space, and at the same time mediated contentious positions between rich merchants favouring open internal and external economic space and the highly regulated "guild system" of medium and small producers opposing it. Thus, nominally, until the reform period, which was set in motion in 1839, the state maintained the policy of supporting the guild system while rejecting any initiatives that would open up the economy and trade in relation to Western European industrial capitalism.[35] However, at the same time, it also had signed a series of international treaties that became tangible steps through which it opened up its economic space. The Peace Treaty of Adrianople with the Russian Empire in 1829, besides settling new borders, following the Russo-Turkish Wars of 1828-1829, had a strong economic component. It coerced the Ottoman state into granting Russian merchants freedom of commerce and navigation in relation to Ottoman lands and seas. The Balta Limani Treaty with the British Empire in 1838, following the Ottoman Empire's political crisis with Mohammed Ali of Egypt and growing political pressure exerted by Russia since the Treaty of Adrianople, forced the imperial state to open up its economy to free trade with Britain as a way of getting long term political and military support from it to ensure territorial integrity.[36]

But the discourse of *economic cosmopolitanism* was not entirely an ideology forced upon the Ottoman state by Russian and British interests. Sultan Mahmud II, a reformer under whose reign (1808-1839) the above treaties were signed, subscribed to the language of openness and *laissez-faire* in the economic domain of the empire. In 1831, he commissioned a French journalist, Alexander Blacque, to promote the *laissez-faire* ideology in a newly established official newspaper called *Le Moniteur Ottoman*.[37] Also, David Urquhart, who had been instrumental in the preparation stages of the Balta Limani Treaty of 1838, extended his thesis of non-intervention into the Ottoman economic realm as the best policy for free trade in the empire. He put forward these ideas in the same newspaper and sought to persuade Ottoman statesmen and intellectuals of their benefits.[38] And such an ideology – it is noteworthy that

---

35 Inalcik, Halil, "Capital Formation in the Ottoman Empire," 29 *The Journal of Economic History* (1969), pp. 97-140, pp. 135-36.

36 Pamuk, Şevket, *The Ottoman Empire and European Capitalism, 1820-1913*, Cambridge, Cambridge University Press, 2010 [1987], p. 20.

37 Kasaba, Reşat, "Treaties and Friendships. British Imperialism, the Ottoman Empire, and China in the 19th Century," 4 *Journal of World History* (1993), pp. 215-241, p. 220.

38 Bulbul, Yasar, "Transfer of Political Economy by a Traditional Society. Ilm-I tebdir-I menzil in the Ottoman Empire," <www.econ.uba.ar/www/institutos/epistemologia/marco_archivos/ponencias/Actas%20XIII/Trabajos%20Episte/BULBUL_paper.pdf>

Smith's ideas of free trade did not enter the discourse under his name – was sanctioned, to some extent, by the reform decrees of Hatt-ı Sherif of Gülhane 1839[39] and Hatt-ı Hümâyun 1856.[40] Still, statesmen like Sadik Rifat Paşa, who was closely involved during the early stages of reform, was not convinced of this doctrine and wrote in favour of economic protectionist measures to support the Ottoman economy.[41]

It was not until the second half of the century, however, that *economic protectionism* would start to gain currency among Ottomans as a countervailing doctrine to that of *economic cosmopolitanism.* As much as the reforms had been effective in opening up its economic space, it had become clear to some that this openness had only benefited a small number of merchants, rather than all trade and traders as provided, for instance, in the Balta Liman Treaty. This was especially the case for British traders, who maintained a privileged position in the Ottoman economy backed by the British government,[42] hurting local traders and producers and manufactures (the guild system).[43] Economic openness produced uneven outcomes – internal winners and losers were becoming obvious and this new division was imbued with ethno-religious differences. It had benefited some parts of the empire, such as areas around Thessaloniki – where Christians and Jewish merchants had principally benefitted – but deprived others, such as in Western Anatolia,[44] the heartland of Muslim Turks.

The two doctrines came into conflict in Ottoman intellectual and political circles, especially following the Ottoman economic crisis of 1870, its indebtedness to foreign lenders, the collapse of the First Constitutional Government in 1876 and the Russo-Turkish Wars of 1877-1878. The principles of *economic cosmopolitanism* had become entrenched in the teaching of economics in Ottoman schools; however, as mentioned above, Adam Smith was not a name associated with this doctrine in the Ottoman context. Indeed, the Ottoman Council of Science, established

---

(visited 8 November 2012); see also Urquhart, David, *Turkey and Its Resources. Its Municipal Organisation and Free Trade*, London, Sounders and Otley, 1833.

39 Palmer, Alan, *The Decline and Fall of the Ottoman Empire*, New York, Barnes & Noble Books, 1994, p. 106.

40 Davison, Roderic H., *Reform in the Ottoman Empire, 1856-1876*, Princeton, Princeton University Press, 1963, p. 6.

41 Mardin, *The Genesis of Young Ottoman Thought*, p. 188.

42 Kasaba, "Treaties and Friendships", p. 230.

43 *Ibid.*, p. 232.

44 Doğan, Necmettin, "The Origins of Liberalism and Islamism in the Ottoman Empire, 1908-1914," Dissertation zur Erlangung des Doktorgrades der Philosophie am Institut für Soziologie, Fachbereich Politik – und Sozialwissenschaften der Freien Universität, Berlin, 2006, p. 165.

in 1851, tasked to select books for translation into Turkish, also on political economy, decided on French classical economist Jean-Baptise Say's *Catéchisme d'Économie Politique*. Seen as a key text for liberal economics, it was translated in 1852 under the title *Ilm-I Tebdir-I Menzil* and was followed by a series of textbooks on economics designed to educate Ottoman bureaucrats. Not long after, however, these principles came under criticism, especially from an Ottoman scholar of economics Ahmet Midhat Effendi who, in his book *Ekonomi Politik* (Political Economy), published in 1881, argued that the doctrine of free trade had been good for Britain, which was the first country to industrialise, but not for the Ottoman state. He suggested along the lines of List's principal contention that the state needed to protect the economy, restrict imports, and support native merchants and bourgeoisie as opposed to foreign and Levantine traders who had controlled the empire's domestic and foreign trade.[45]

In the Russian Empire, meanwhile, free trade as an economic doctrine had permeated intellectual and political circles since late eighteenth century. Smith's ideas on free trade had been taught in Russian universities during his lifetime. Russian economics Professor Ivan Andreyevich Tret'yakov attended Smith's lectures at the University of Glasgow in 1761 and, being impressed by his ideas, lectured on them for nearly seven years later at the Imperial Moscow University.[46] In 1772, in one of his university lectures, Tret'yakov spoke in favour of free trade among nations. "The poverty of a nation," he emphasised, "cannot originate from trade with foreign countries provided this trade be conducted with prudence and wisdom."[47] Smith's magnum opus, *An Inquiry into the Nature and Causes of the Wealth of Nations* (1776) was translated in Russian twice, in 1802 and 1806, and was even popularised into the wider intellectual circles by the prominent poet Alexander Pushkin during the first three decades of the century. Pushkin highlighted the prominence of *the Wealth of Nations* among Onegin's circles in a short passage of his verse novel *Eugene Onegin* ("Yevgeny Onegin"):

If true delight you would afford him
You'd give him Adam Smith to read
A deep economist, indeed
He talked about the wealth of nations
The state relied, his friends were told

---

[45] *Ibid.*, pp. 167-168.

[46] Taylor, Norman W., "Adam Smith's First Russian Disciple," 45 *The Slavonic and East European Review* (1967), pp. 425-438, p. 434.

[47] *Ibid.*

Upon its staples, not on gold –
This subject filled with conversation.[48]

In the light of the Continental Blockade imposed by Napoleonic France in November 1806 against Britain, which Russia politically supported, negatively resulting in the prohibition of the grain trade from Odessa through the Black Sea, Russian Chancellor Michael Speransky used Smith's ideas on the advantages of free trade to convince Tsar Alexander I to approve the Tariff of 1810. As a result, permission was granted to open all Russian ports to free trade in grain. The export of Russian goods and import of manufactured products from Britain was also permitted. This led to an increase in trade between the two empires while complicating relations with France, leading to the two countries finding themselves at war in 1812.[49] Yet, in terms of economic policy, while with the Adrianople Treaty Russia had forced the Ottoman Empire to open its economic space to commerce with Russian subjects; it enacted a Free Trade Tariff Act only in 1868.[50]

As in the Ottoman case, this doctrine came to be challenged by that of *economic protectionism* in the light of a growing social question, a global economic crisis and demands for domestic industrial growth. For the Russian social commentator and founder of Russian revolutionary populism Nicholas Chernyshevsky, who was concerned with Russia's rapidly proliferating social questions, Smith's ideas were not suitable to solve contemporary Russian problems. He believed that the Smithian school reflected the psychology of the middle classes rather than that of the poor.[51] By 1867, a newly established Russian economic forum, the Russian Industrial Society – which included not only leading merchants and industrialists as its members, but also bureaucrats, journalists and scientists such as the prominent chemist Dmitrii I. Mendeleev – became a powerful voice against the discourse of free trade.[52] They saw it as being supported by Western European economists, commercial and major city ports and in turn espoused List's ideas of national economic protectionism, calling for moderate tariffs protection as a way of sup-

48 Quoted in Taylor, "Adam Smith's First Russian Disciple", p. 425.

49 Raeff, Marc, *Michael Speransky. Statesman of Imperial Russia 1772-1839*, The Hague, Martinus Nijhoff, 1957, pp. 78-160.

50 Gerschenkron, Alexander, "The Rate of Growth in Russia. The Rate of Industrial Growth in Russia, Since 1885," 7 *The Journal of Economic History* (1947), pp. 144-174, p. 147.

51 Turin, S.P., "Nicholas Chernyshevsky and John Stuart Mill," 9 *The Slavonic and East European Review* (1930), pp. 29-33, pp. 29-30.

52 Owen, Thomas C., "The Russian Industrial Society and the Tsarist Economic Policy, 1867-1905," 45 *The Journal of Economic History* (1985), pp. 587-606, p. 587.

porting emerging domestic industries.[53] In their view, free trade had placed the Russian economy in a "terrible struggle" with European exporters in world markets.

However, while stressing the dangers of European "economic imperialism", they favoured a Russian economic space dominated by ethnic Russians. Keen to pursue their economic interests inside an expanding empire, the Moscow-based members, in particular, strongly pushed a campaign of political and economic imperialism in support of the conquest of Central Asia by the Russian Empire.[54] Within this society, there were, however, as scholar Tomas C. Owen has argued, other leading members, intellectuals and bureaucrats who "tended to frame their policy statements in a somewhat more cosmopolitan economic language, so as to mute the blatant and self-serving xenophobia of the merchants".[55] With all these pressures, however, it took nearly 25 years from the enactment Free Trade Tariff Act before a strong protectionist tariff was enacted. The Tariff Act of 1 July 1891 was put in place under the guidance of Russian Minister of Finance I.A. Vyshnegradsky – a strong advocate of domestic industrialisation and high protectionist barriers, described as a convinced adherent of List's ideas.[56]

4. Conclusion

As noted above, the idea of cosmopolitanism is problematic in itself, and is even more so when seeking to apply it comparatively to two diverse settings. So, is it still possible to locate it in the Russian and Ottoman empires of the nineteenth century when contemporaries did not use it directly to describe their cultural interactions and economic relations? And then, can one view these empires as cosmopolitan during this long century? The first question can be answered affirmatively, in that there were slight attempts in both empires to adopt positions favouring certain overtures towards openness in their cultural and economic realms. But the second question cannot be answered in the same manner, precisely because of the contingency of these attempts and resurfacing or emergence of countervailing discourses and positions during this century as highlighted above.

Still, as outlined here, there are at least three aspects that made it difficult, if not impossible, to draw straightforward conclusions on whether the concept of cosmopolitanism can be effectively used in relation to the two imperial settings. Firstly, the discourses of contemporaries were

---

53 *Ibid.*, p. 595.

54 *Ibid.*, p. 594.

55 *Ibid.*

56 *Ibid.*, pp. 147-148.

almost bereft of direct usage of the notion – and yet articulated views of openness and plurality in the realms of culture and economy. Secondly, both Ottoman and Russian scholars made limited use of the concept to describe cultural plurality. Thirdly, there are a number of open questions related to whether the terms *cultural cosmopolitanism* and *economic cosmopolitanism* can be used when trying to locate cosmopolitan moments of the two imperial histories. Notwithstanding the virtual impossibility of reaching a definite conclusion, at least it becomes clear that questions and debates related to the concept of cosmopolitanism – homogenisation versus plurality, identity versus identities, and closure versus openness – were greatly relevant to the cultural and economic lives of both the Ottoman and Russian empires.

"Napoleonic Constitutionalism"

Legal Universalism or Political Particularism?

Markus J. PRUTSCH

1. Introduction

Analysing Napoleonic constitutionalism and politics in an anthology on *Cosmopolitanisms in Enlightenment Europe and Beyond* might sound unusual if not hazardous and misplaced, especially when focusing on a philosophical understanding of cosmopolitanism as a form of moral and ethical universalism. It sounds less unusual, however, when the reading of cosmopolitanism is broadened to include forms of "political cosmopolitanism" trying to overcome the nation-state model and aiming at universalisation of rule and government – particularly, though not exclusively, by means of (constitutional) law. With such a wider meaning in mind, "cosmopolitanism" in this essay essentially refers to a hegemonic form of "anti-nationalism", an early version of "Europeanism" by the means of "legal universalism".

It can reasonably be argued that the era of the Napoleonic wars brought about not only far-reaching political, economic and social, but also legal and constitutional changes. Under French – and particularly Napoleon's personal – influence, the codification of constitutional law made rapid progress, as did the formal guarantee of individual rights and representative government. These developments went hand in hand with questioning the validity of traditional concepts of political and above all monarchical legitimacy. Considering this, much of the existing research literature tends to interpret the Napoleonic Age as a breakthrough in legal developments and universalism essentially inspired by the ideals of the French Revolution, thus laying the foundations for modern European constitutionalism.

However, one might ask whether the historical interpretation of Napoleonic constitutionalism as a transnational and integrating phenomenon of the period is perhaps one-sided. More specifically, one could also ask whether such an interpretation does not in fact underestimate the importance of political and constitutional particularism and nationalism even in parts of Europe under direct French influence. One might certainly argue that constitutionalisation processes throughout Europe were initiated by Napoleon's military successes and that there were a number of common elements in the constitutional documents of the time, originating from French (revolutionary) constitutional law. Conversely, however, constitutional ventures carried out in the Napoleonic sphere of influence may be viewed less as an expression of legal universalism, and more as a distinctive and direct response to French hegemonic aspirations and constitutional imperialism. Seen thus, constitutionalism would be perceived differently: both as a means to safeguard sovereignty and as a focal point for nation-building.

Against this background, this essay has two aims: firstly, to shed light on the driving force of "Napoleonic constitutionalism" as a means of restructuring Europe politically; secondly, to evaluate the extent to which Napoleonic constitutionalism can actually be claimed to have paved the way for legal universalism, and to assess its political repercussions in the long term. It will hopefully provide food for thought rather than put forward anything like a comprehensive account of the subject. With this in mind, focus is put on the German Confederation of the Rhine and the Bavarian Constitution of 1808 in particular, which is reputed to have been one of Napoleon's "satellite constitutions". First, however, some observations on Napoleon's own personal vision of the political future of Europe may be appropriate at this point.

2. Napoleon's Concept of a "United Europe": Myth or Policy?

Napoleon's exile on Elba and later Saint Helena after his military defeat at Waterloo in 1815 gave him plenty of time to assess political (non-)achievements, appraise his global and historical role and reflect upon the "bright future" he had once envisaged. Despite his political downfall, he was in no doubt that the more time passed, the brighter his legacy would shine: "It is a fact that my destiny is the inverse of other men's. Ordinarily, a man is lowered by his downfall; my downfall raises me to infinite heights. Every day strips me of my tyrant's skin, of my murderousness and ferocity."[1] Modesty had never been a particular strength of the Corsican, and it was in this vein that Napoleon continued to depict himself as a "man of destiny" and the "prophet of a new world" – even after his fall. The most pervasive picture he sought to convey through his memoirs and writings in exile was that of his being the spearhead of global progress and liberal ideas:

1 2 November 1816. In Bonaparte, Napoléon, *The Mind of Napoleon. A Selection from his Written and Spoken Words*, ed. and transl. by H.J. Christopher, New York NY, Columbia University Press, 1955, pp. 273-274.

Liberal opinions will rule the universe. They will become the faith, the religion, the morality of all nations; and in spite of all that may be advanced to the contrary, this memorable aim will be inseparably connected with my name; for after all it cannot be denied that I kindled the torch and consecrated the principle, and now persecution renders me the Messiah. Friends and enemies, all must acknowledge me to be the first soldier, the grand representative of the age. Thus I shall forever remain the leading star.[2]

Whilst portraying himself as a leader who had only taken up and defended the cause of the people, popular sovereignty and democracy, at the same time Napoleon tried to downplay the authoritarian elements of his regime and present them as a necessary evil on the road to establishing durable peace in Europe. He declared at one stage that after peace had been attained: "I would have proclaimed the immutability of boundaries, all future wars [would have been] purely defensive; all new aggrandisement, anti-national; […] my dictatorship would have terminated, and […] constitutional reign commenced".[3]

An integral part of the image as the "liberal prophet" he wished to portray was the vision of a peacefully united Europe entrusted with progressive institutions, intended to overcome national(istic) peculiarities and idiosyncrasies:

One of my great plans was the rejoining, the concentration of those same geographical nations which have been disunited and parcelled out by revolution and policy. There are dispersed in Europe, upwards of 30,000,000 of French, 15,000,000 of Spaniards, 15,000,000 of Italians, and 30,000,000 of Germans; and it was my intention to incorporate these people each into one nation. It would have been a noble thing to have advanced in prosperity with such a train, and attended by the blessings of future ages. […] it would have been possible to indulge the chimera of the *beau ideal* of civilization. In this

2 Memoirs dictated to Count Las Cases, 9/10 April 1816, in de Las Cases, Emmanuel-Augustin-Dieudonné-Joseph, *Mémorial de Sainte Hélène. Journal of the Private Life and Conversations of the Emperor Napoleon at Saint Helena*, Vol. 2, 29, 8 [4] Vols., London, H. Colburn and Co, 1823. On Napoleon's (self-)depiction as "Prince of Liberal Ideas" see Hazareesingh, Sudhir, *The Legend of Napoleon*, London, Granta Books, 2005 [2004], pp. 151-183.

3 24 August 1816. In Las Cases, *Mémorialde Sainte Hélène*, Vol. 3, p. 267. For never having reached this durable peace he openly blamed Britain: "At Amiens [1802], I sincerely thought the fate of France and Europe and my own destiny were permanently fixed; I hoped that war was at an end. However, the English Cabinet again kindled the flame. England is alone responsible for all the miseries by which Europe has since been assailed. For my part, I intended to have devoted myself wholly to the internal interests of France; and I am confident I should have wrought miracles. I should have lost nothing in the scale of glory; and I should have gained much in the scale of happiness. I should then have achieved the moral conquest of Europe, which I was afterwards on the point of accomplishing by force of arms. Of how much glory was I thus deprived." 11 November 1816. *Ibid.*, Vol. 4, pp. 132-133.

> state of things, there would have been some chance of establishing, in every country, a unity of codes, principles, opinions, sentiments, views, and interests. Then, perhaps, by the help of the universal diffusion of knowledge, one might have thought of attempting, in the great European family, the application of the American Congress, or the Amphictyons of Greece. What a perspective of power, grandeur, happiness, and prosperity, would thus have appeared![4]

What he was actually indicating was that he had hoped to establish a European confederacy in the not too distant future:

> The same principles, the same system everywhere. An [*sic*] European code; a court of European appeal, with full powers to redress all wrong decisions [...] Money of the same value but with different coins the same weight, the same measures, the same laws, etc. etc. Europe would soon in that manner [...] have really been but the same people, and every one, who travelled, would have everywhere found himself in one common country.[5]

Obviously, hearing a seasoned political and military leader such as Napoleon declaring his vision of a "common Europe" united in peace and governed by universal values and institutions *ex post* sounds too noble to be true. Therefore, it could be all too easy to dismiss Napoleon's utterances as pure rhetoric or calculated attempts to save his name in the history books. Yet one might reasonably ask whether such a rebuff is in fact justified, and whether it is legitimate to deny Napoleon any personal fervour in wanting to liberalise and modernise "old" Europe in order to push it towards a more uniform, perhaps even "cosmopolitan" form. Be that as it may, if Napoleon's "universalising" reform agenda during his reign was subordinated to his striving for personal power, and guided primarily by Machiavellian reasoning, this would only be proof of the profane nature of his personal motivation. The agenda as such can nevertheless hardly be overlooked: the almost missionary zeal with which the Corsican promoted change and reform in economy, society and above all law throughout Europe under French hegemony is all too obvious.

To ask whether Napoleon was interested in some degree of political and especially legal universalism in his sphere of influence – and indeed to respond in the affirmative to that question – is, however, just one side of the coin. The other side would be to ask to what extent his ambition

---

4 11 November 1816. In *ibid.*, Vol. 4, p. 134. Nevertheless, he expressed confidence that: "this concentration will be brought about, sooner or later, by the very force of events. The impulse is given; and I think that since my fall, and the destruction of my system, no grand equilibrium can possibly be established in Europe, except by the concentration and confederation of the principal nations." *Ibid.*, p. 139.

5 4 August 1816. In *ibid.*, Vol. 3, p. 266.

could be put into real political practice. This would be particularly true for those parts of Europe under French hegemony yet at the same time enjoying a degree of political independence (i.e. not incorporated into the Empire) and for the policy area most directly linked with state sovereignty, namely constitutional policy. In this respect, the analysis of the impact and implications of Napoleonic constitutionalism within the context of the Confederation of the Rhine can serve as an instructive example.

3. "Napoleonic Constitutionalism" in Germany

In the course of the revolutionary wars and the expansion of Napoleonic France, the creation of several German *Mittelstaaten* ("middle states") was propelled by French foreign policy.[6] Under the aegis of Bonaparte, these states were finally bound together in the Confederation of the Rhine (established 1806)[7] to form a political counterweight to the dominant German powers Austria and Prussia. As an instrument of

---

6 The most important step towards defragmenting the Holy Roman Empire, traditionally composed of a multitude of independent territories and free cities, in favour of a smaller number of *Mittelstaaten* was the *Reichsdeputationshauptschluss* (formally the *Hauptschluss der außerordentlichen Reichsdeputation*, or "Final Recess of the Imperial Deputation"). Huber, Ernst Rudolf (ed.), *Dokumente Zur Deutschen Verfassungsgeschichte. 1, Deutsche Verfassungsdokumente 1803-1850*, 3rd ed., W. Kohlhammer, Stuttgart [u.a.], 1978 [1961]), pp. 1-28. Passed on 25 February 1803 by the *Reichstag* ("Imperial Diet") and ratified in March 1803, this resolution proved to be the last significant law enacted by the Empire before its dissolution. Based on a plan agreed in June 1802 between France and Russia, and broad principles outlined in the Treaty of Lunéville of 1801, the law established a major redistribution of territorial sovereignty within the Empire, achieved by the secularisation of ecclesiastical principalities and mediatisation of numerous small secular principalities. See Knecht, Ingo, *Der Reichsdeputationshauptschluß vom 25. Februar 1803. Rechtmäßigkeit, Rechtswirksamkeit und verfassungsgeschichtliche Bedeutung*, Berlin, Duncker & Humblot, 2007. For the history of the Holy Roman Empire as such, see e.g., Schmidt, Georg, *Geschichte des Alten Reiches. Staat und Nation in der Frühen Neuzeit 1495-1806*, Munich, C.H. Beck, 1999.

7 The "Confederation of the Rhine" or "Rhine Confederation" (German: *Rheinbund*; French: *États confédérés du Rhin* [officially] or *Confédération du Rhin* [in practice]) was initiated by Napoleon after his victory in the Battle of Austerlitz (2 December 1805) and the Peace of Pressburg (26 December 1805) and established on 12 July 1806 by the "Treaty of the Confederation of the Rhine" (*Rheinbundakte*; in Huber, *Dokumente*, pp. 28-34). In this treaty, 16 German states – among them Bavaria, Baden and Württemberg – formally left the Holy Roman Empire and joined together in a confederation under the "protection" (Art. 12) of Napoleon. On 6 August, following a French ultimatum, Francis II finally gave up his title of Emperor and declared the Holy Roman Empire dissolved. *Ibid.*, pp. 37-38. In the years that followed, 23 more German states joined the Confederation, which collapsed in 1813 in the course of Napoleon's defeat in Russia and the lost Battle of Leipzig. Interesting enough is there as yet no detailed study on the history of the Confederation of the Rhine.

French hegemonic politics, its main task was to form a military glacis against potential enemies, to contribute to the Continental System and to mobilise financial, material and military resources for the French Empire.

However, the creation of the Confederation of the Rhine did not only aim at creating a power-political buffer zone. Napoleonic policy also strove for ideological and social reform in Germany and beyond. In this context, the newly created "Napoleonides", namely the Grand Duchy of Berg (1806), the Kingdom of Westphalia (1807) and later the Grand Duchy of Frankfurt (1810), fulfilled a special role: by means of a "revolution from above", these satellite states were to be transformed into paragons of political progress and demonstrate the achievements of the Revolution and the Napoleonic Age in an exemplary fashion. This included replacing the old feudal order with a modern civic society based on French administrative and constitutional principles. Power, reform and modernisation converged in Napoleon's foreign policies in order to stabilise the Empire as a political entity with uniform social, administrative and constitutional frameworks. Moreover, by increasing the disparity with the absolutist powers Prussia and Austria, Napoleon's political and social modernisation agenda might serve as a tool to win over and tie the political powers and society in Germany.[8]

The key cornerstones of the modernisation agenda were civil equality and the implementation of a liberal legal system based on property rights and economic freedom. Further hallmarks were the adoption of the *Code Napoléon*, establishing an independent judiciary system and an efficient administrative structure. The core element of Napoleon's "reform programme", however, was the enactment of constitutions. They signalled most effectively the "on-the-ground" remodelling of state and society and the setting up of an innovative order promising to be egalitarian and abolish any remaining feudal structures.

Given that Napoleon authorised and screened the granting of constitutions personally, it will come as no surprise that it was under his direct personal involvement that in 1807 a written constitution was drafted and proclaimed in the most important of the Napoleonides, namely the Kingdom of Westphalia. This document followed earlier Napoleonic constitutions in Italy (1801/02 and 1805) and Holland (1805/06) and

8 See Hecker, Michael, *Napoleonischer Konstitutionalismus in Deutschland*, Berlin, Duncker & Humblot, 2005, pp. 28-30. Hecker's study is a most valuable contribution to the understanding of constitutional politics during the Napoleonic Age: by focusing on the constitutions of Berg, Westphalia and Frankfurt, Hecker not only analyses the presence of revolutionary and Napoleonic constitutional elements in those states, but also ascertains the connections between Napoleonic power politics and social-political reform processes in the Confederation of the Rhine.

was designed as a role model for the rest of Germany. In a letter to his brother Jérôme, King of Westphalia, accompanying the new Westphalian Constitution, Napoleon elaborated on the importance of constitutional government as follows:

> I am concerned for the happiness of your subjects, not only as it affects your reputation, and my own, but also for its influence on the whole European situation. [...] The benefits of the *Code Napoléon*, public trial, and the introduction of juries, will be the leading features of your government. And to tell you the truth, I count more upon their effects, for the extension and consolidation of your rule, than upon the most resounding victories. I want your subjects to enjoy a degree of liberty, equality and prosperity hitherto unknown to the German people. I want this liberal regime to produce, one way or another, changes which will be of the utmost benefit to the system of the Confederation, and to the strength of your monarchy. Such a method of government will be a stronger barrier between you and Prussia than the Elbe, the fortresses, and the protection of France. What people will want to return under the arbitrary Prussian rule, once it has tasted the benefits of a wise and liberal administration? In Germany, as in France, Italy, and Spain, people long for equality and liberal ideas. I have been managing the affairs of Europe long enough to know that the burden of the privileged classes was resented everywhere. Rule constitutionally. Even if reason, and the enlightenment of the age, were not sufficient cause, it would be good policy for one in your position; and you will find that the backing of public opinion gives you a great natural advantage over the absolute Kings who are your neighbours.[9]

Considering Napoleon's personal commitment and involvement, and the actual dictates of its enactment, constitutionalism in the French sphere of influence during the Napoleonic Age has frequently been interpreted as a tool in the service of power politics, but nevertheless a common phenomenon of the era with a certain amount of consolidating capacity.[10] Whether this is regarded as something good or bad depends very much on the point of view taken, particularly within the German context. While national scholars of the nineteenth and twentieth century – such as Heinrich von Treitschke and Ernst Rudolf Huber – branded Napoleonic constitutionalism unequivocally as *octroi*, imperialism or

9 Napoleon to Jérôme Bonaparte, King of Westphalia, Fontainebleau, 15 November 1807. In Bonaparte, Napoléon, *Correspondance de Napoléon Ier. Publiée par ordre de l'empereur Napoléon III*, 32 Vols., Paris, Imprimerie impériale, 1858-1869, Vol. 16, Doc. 13361, pp. 166-167.

10 See, e.g., Kirsch, Martin, *Monarch und Parlament im 19. Jahrhundert. Der Monarchische Konstitutionalismus als europäischer Verfassungstyp – Frankreich im Vergleich*, Göttingen, Vandenhoeck & Ruprecht, 1999, p. 231.

Scheinkonstitutionalismus ("pseudo-constitutionalism") of vassal states,[11] more recent assessment tends to be less critical and emphasise the impetus of legal transfer and the role of constitutionalisation processes for modernisation in general.[12] At all events, there is common agreement on the French origins of these new constitutions.

In line with this interpretation, the Bavarian Constitution of 1808 would seem to be nothing more than a mere copy of former Napoleonic constitutions, particularly the Constitution of Westphalia, and hence as another component of French integration and/or domination politics. Indeed, at first sight, this line of argument does make sense, especially against the backdrop of Bavaria's role as one of France's closest allies during the Napoleonic wars and the timing of the Bavarian constitutionalisation process.

4. Napoleon and the Bavarian Constitution of 1808

In the wake of Napoleon's military success between 1802 and 1805, Bavaria was able to extend its borders and population considerably.[13] Moreover, in the course of the Peace of Pressburg (26 December 1805), Bavaria finally achieved the status of a sovereign state and became a kingdom (1 January 1806). Nonetheless, due to the fact that these achievements were essentially based on French military success, the country's formal sovereignty was rather of a limited nature, manifest in the growing pressure from Napoleon for Bavaria to abolish its traditional *landständische* order[14] and establish a new administrative and constitutional system.[15] This pressure increased further after the formation of

---

11 On the term Scheinkonstitutionalismus see Huber, Ernst Rudolf, *Deutsche Verfassungsgeschichte seit 1789. Band 1: Reform und Restauration 1789 bis 1830*, 2nd ed., Stuttgart, W. Kohlhammer, 1967 [1957].

12 See, e.g., Fehrenbach, Elisabeth, "Verfassungs- und sozialpolitische Reformen und Reformprojekte in Deutschland unter dem Einfluss des Napoleonischen Frankreich," in Helmut Berding and Hans-Peter Ullmann (eds.), *Deutschland zwischen Revolution und Restauration*, Düsseldorf, Königstein/Ts, Athenäum, Droste, 1981.

13 The main stages in reshuffling the territorial borders of Bavaria were the *Reichsdeputationshauptschluss* (1803), the Peace of Pressburg (1805) and later the Treaty of Schönbrunn (1809).

14 The German *Landstände* traditionally signifies the assembly of the (feudal) representatives of the estates of the realm, called together for legislative purposes or deliberation. They are also known as *Landtag*, or, as in the case of Bavaria, *Landschaftsverordnung*.

15 On the history of the Bavarian Constitution of 1808 see among others: Zimmermann, Fritz, *Bayerische Verfassungsgeschichte vom Ausgang der Landschaft bis zur Verfassungsurkunde von 1818. Ein Beitrag zur Auseinandersetzung Deutschlands mit den Ideen der Französischen Revolution und Restauration. Erster Teil. Vorgeschichte und Entstehung der Konstitution von 1808*, Munich, C.H. Beck, 1940; Wegelin, Peter, "Die Bayerische Konstitution von 1808," *Schweizer Beiträge zur*

the Confederation of the Rhine. The need for the Bavarian government to react and act grew even stronger because of increasing demands from within its own ranks for fundamental political rights: personal and civic liberty on the one hand, active participation in the political process on the other. Both, it was felt, should ideally be laid down in a written constitution.

In 1807 the preparations for a Bavarian Constitution were finally launched. On 8 June of the same year, together with a decree that abolished the fiscal rights of the estates and thus did away with the traditional *landständische* system, King Maximilian I Joseph (1756-1825) assigned to his Prime Minister Maximilian von Montgelas (1759-1838) the task of drawing up a constitutional document.[16] However, it took more French intervention before work on the constitution could begin in earnest in late 1807. At the end of November 1807, King Maximilian I and Montgelas were invited to Milan by Napoleon. Here, the French Emperor urged Bavaria to take the initiative by emphasising – according to Montgelas – that: "in Teutschland nun etwas geschehen müsse – um den unruhigen Zustand, der noch immer da herrsche, zu entfernen und Ruhe und Ordnung zurückzuführen."[17] As a result, concrete discussions on a new Constitution were initiated immediately after their return to Bavaria. This document was to be based on the Westphalian model, which had been prepared by Napoleon himself.[18] Within a short time, the draft was completed, and on 25 May 1808 the first written Bavarian constitution was published in the country's law gazette.[19] The Constitution, encompassing 45 articles, was divided into six parts, namely

---

Allgemeinen Geschichte 16, 1958, pp. 142-206; Tiainen, Jorma, "Die Bayerische Konstitution von 1808 und die öffentliche Diskussion darüber," *Acta Societatis Historicae Ouluensis* 1, 1967, pp. 166-184; Möckl, Karl, "Die Bayerische Konstitution von 1808," in Eberhard Weis (ed.), *Reformen im rheinbündischen Deutschland*, Munich, Oldenbourg, 1984, pp. 151-166. Most recently – on occasion of its 200th anniversary – Schmid, Alois (ed.), *Die bayerische Konstitution von 1808. Entstehung – Zielsetzung – Europäisches Umfeld*, Munich, C.H. Beck, 2008.

16 On the drafting of the Constitution: Rumschöttel, Hermann, "Die Entstehung der bayerischen Konstitution," in Schmid, *Die bayerische Konstitution*, pp. 211-228.

17 *Protocoll über jene Gegenstände, die in der heute gehaltenen königlichen Geheimen Staats-Conferenz vorgetragen und entschieden worden* (20 January 1808), in Michael Doeberl, *Rheinbundverfassung und bayerische Konstitution*, Munich, G. Franz, 1924, pp. 73-74.

18 See *ibid.*, pp. 73-74 and 78-79: "Seine Königliche Majestät [haben] die Anträge des Freyherrn von Montgelas wegen Entwerffung [*sic*] einer Constitution für das gesamte Königreich nach den Grundlinien der vorliegenden Constitution des Königreiches Westphalen und wegen Annahme des Code Napoleon in dem gesamten Königreiche allergnädigst genehmiget […]." *Ibid.*, p. 79.

19 *Konstitution für das Königreich Baiern* (25 May 1808), in *Königlich-Baierisches Regierungsblatt* 1806, Columns 985-1000.

1) *Hauptbestimmungen* ("Main Regulations"); 2) *Von dem königlichen Hause* ("On the Royal Dynasty"); 3) *Von der Verwaltung des Reiches* ("On the Administration of the Realm"); 4) *Von der National-Repräsentation* ("On National Representation"); 5) *Von der Justiz* ("On the Judiciary"); and 6) *Von dem Militär-Stande* ("On the Armed Forces"). It replicated French (revolutionary) ideas and notions in general and the Westphalian Constitution of 1807 in particular, not only with regard to the terminology, using the term *C(K)constitution*[20] instead of the traditional German *Verfassung*, but also concerning actual structure and content.[21]

Consequently, it can be surmised that the outlining of the Bavarian Constitution was started at Napoleon's personal behest and signified yet another step in his "constitutional project" for Germany. Many observers of the time and a number of later authors adopted this interpretation and view, among them the Bavarian official and writer Joseph von Hazzi (1768-1845), who in his work on the Bavarian Constitution of 1818 observed: "Here [in Milan; MJP], Bavaria's constitution was now decided. The founder of the Bavarian kingdom and of its territorial expansion [Napoleon; MJP] pressed for it, and the King [...] had no objection to accepting it. If one asked, what kind of constitution? the answer was, that of Westphalia."[22] For such observers there was no doubt that the constitutional document had been imposed upon Bavaria from outside. However, this understanding does prove to be somewhat biased and slightly misleading.

---

20 The Westphalian Constitution, designed as a formal decree by Napoleon and published by his brother Jérôme, King of Westphalia (in the German text he appears as "Hieronymus Napoleon"), was entitled *Königliches Dekret vom 7. Dezember 1807, wodurch die Publikation der Constitution des Königreichs Westfalen verordnet wird* (7 December 1807). In *Bulletin des lois du Royaume de Westphalie/Gesetz-Bulletin des Königreichs Westphalen* 1808 (1), pp. 1-31.

21 For a detailed comparison between the Bavarian Constitution of 1808 and its Westphalian predecessor of 1807 see Oeschey, Rudolf, *Die bayerische Verfassungsurkunde vom 26. Mai 1818 und die Charte Ludwigs XVIII. vom 4. Juni 1814. Ein Beitrag zur Lehre vom monarchischen Prinzip. Unter Berücksichtigung der bayerischen Konstitution vom 1. Mai 1808 und deren Vorbildes, der westfälischen Verfassung vom 15. November 1807*, Munich, C.H. Beck, 1914, pp. 29-45.

22 "Hier [in Milan; MJP] entschied sich nun Baierns Constitution. Der Gründer des baierischen Königthums und der Ländermehrung [Napoleon; MJP] drang nämlich darauf, und der König [...] nahm keinen Anstand [*sic*] sie zuzusagen. Was für eine Constitution frug man, die von Westfalen war die Antwort." von Hazzi, Joseph, *Ueber die Standpuncte der baierischen Verfassungs-Urkunde von 1818 in Beziehung anderer Constitutionen*, Munich, J. Lindauer, 1819, p. 6. Similar interpretations can be found in the works of the leading Bavarian jurists Joseph von Mussinan (1766-1837) and Max von Seydel (1846-1901).

5. The National Drive of the Bavarian Constitution

In sharp contrast to the idea of the Bavarian Constitution having been imposed by Napoleon, the French envoy in Munich, Count Otto, had an entirely different reading in a report dated 14 May 1808, just a few days after the Constitution had been proclaimed. Otto argued that the Bavarian Constitution was the first of its kind to have been drawn up under the free will of the Bavarian king and people, with no influence whatsoever from the French.[23]

Although the idea that there was no influence at all is certainly an overstatement, Otto's remark does draw our attention to the problematic nature of an interpretation that focuses solely on the dependent character of the Bavarian Constitution of 1808. What is true is that the French government and especially Napoleon *in persona* speeded up the constitutionalisation process in Bavaria. It also goes without saying that references to the Constitution of Westphalia were based on political necessity and were in line with Napoleon's personal wishes. However, the particularist, national(ist) and even anti-Napoleonic elements peculiar to this constitution must also be borne in mind.

There was in fact a range of domestic challenges which necessitated the proclamation of a constitution, of which satisfying public opinion and meeting the growing demands for political reform were just two. Even more important was the need for "political amalgamation". On account of the immense number of territorial (ex) changes in the course of the expansion of Napoleonic France, the main challenge faced by Bavaria was that of integration. Formerly a medley of independent territories and towns with their own traditions, the task in hand was to create a single administrative and political unit: to create a "Bavarian consciousness" from this hotchpotch of regional and social groups, and to deal with the problem of the former *Standesherren* ("mediatised nobles"). The need for political integration was therefore pressing, since the future existence of Bavaria as a political entity was at stake.

In order to complete the task of integration, in the first stage priority had been given to enlightened absolutist reforms on an administrative level, by which the whole country was made subject to centralised "state absolutism".[24] Nevertheless, there was also growing awareness in Bavar-

---

[23] See Doeberl, Michael, *Ein Jahrhundert bayerischen Verfassungslebens*, Munich, Lindauer, 1918, p. 7.

[24] See the works of Walter Demel: *Der Bayerische Staatsabsolutismus 1806/08-1817. Staats- und gesellschaftspolitische Motivationen und Hintergründe der Reformära in der ersten Phase des Königreichs Bayern*, Munich, C.H. Beck, 1983, and *Vom aufgeklärten Reformstaat zum bürokratischen Staatsabsolutismus*, Munich, Oldenbourg, 1993.

ia that having a written constitution and guaranteeing political rights would act as a bonding agent and were vital components of a comprehensive modernisation agenda. The proclamation of a constitution thus became the key ingredient in Montgelas' reform agenda, and it therefore comes as no surprise that the idea of "integration" is the central motivating factor in the preamble to the 1808 Constitution. The preamble frankly states that any administrative regulatory system had to be accompanied by an overall binding legal framework, namely a constitutional document:

> Led by the conviction that the State, so long as it remains a mere aggregate of differing constituent parts, will not achieve the full collective strength located in its resources, nor can it offer to the individual members thereof all the advantages of civil union to the extent according to which that union is intended, We have already sought by means of several decrees to improve as much as was possible the variety of forms of administration in our realm, to establish a more uniform system for direct as well as indirect obligations, and to make the most important public institutions more commensurate with the mutuality of their purpose through arrangements that simultaneously protect their particularity. In addition, in order to obtain the advantage of appropriately equivalent civil and criminal laws in our entire State, We have also ordered the preparations necessary for this purpose, which are already partially completed. But as these particular instructions for specific parts of State organisation lead only imperfectly to the goal, and leave behind gaps whose closing is an essential requirement of the necessary unity of the whole; so We have resolved to give all constituent parts of legislation and government in Our Kingdom, with consideration for their external and internal relations, complete continuity through organic laws, and to lay the ground for this through the present constitutional document, which is intended by means of its respective arrangements and stipulations to provide guarantee of the fulfilment of the rightful demands of the State upon its individual members just as those of the individual members upon the State as based in the State's general purpose, to afford a fixed bearing and connection to the whole, and to provide each part of State authority its proportionate efficacy according to the requirements of the common good […].[25]

[25] "Von der Überzeugung geleitet, daß der Staat, so lange er ein bloßes Aggregat verschiedenartiger Bestandtheile bleibt, weder zur Erreichung der vollen Gesamtkraft, die in seinen Mitteln liegt, gelangen, noch den einzelnen Gliedern desselben alle Vortheile der bürgerlichen Vereinigung, in dem Maaße, wie es diese bezwecket, gewähren kann, haben Wir bereits durch mehrere Verordnungen die Verschiedenheit der Verwaltungsformen in Unserm Reiche, so weit es vor der Hand möglich war, zu heben, für die direkten Auflagen sowohl, als für die indirekten ein gleichförmigeres Sistem [*sic*] zu gründen, und die wichtigsten öffentlichen Anstalten dem Gemeinsamen ihrer Bestimmung durch Einrichtungen, die zugleich ihre besondern sichern, entsprechender zu machen gesucht. Ferner haben Wir, um Unsern gesamten Staaten den Vortheil angemessener gleicher bürgerlicher und peinlicher Geseze zu verschaf-

The need for a written constitution became all the more urgent as serious problems gained increasing momentum, above all public debt. Public debt was a knock-on effect of the expensive reform agenda as well as the debts and state pensions inherited from the annexed territories. Most importantly, the excessive military expenses which the country incurred as a member of the Confederation of the Rhine, weighed heavily on state finances, and Bavaria ran the risk of losing its creditworthiness.[26] Under these circumstances, the guarantees provided by a constitution offered an obvious means of strengthening faith in the security of public debt and preventing the financial collapse of the country. Moreover, by granting constitutional rights, new taxes could be reasonably justified.[27]

Apart from these practical requirements, an inherent national-political reasoning advanced the 1808 Constitution: on the one hand, it provided an opportunity to demonstrate progressiveness, not only to the Bavarian people, but also to other states. For this reason, constitutionali-

---

fen, auch die hiezu nöthigen Vorarbeiten angeordnet, die zum Theil schon wirklich vollendet sind. Da aber diese einzelnen Ausbildungen besonderer Theile der Staats-Einrichtung nur unvollkommen zum Zwecke führen, und Lücken zurück lassen, deren Ausfüllung ein wesentliches Bedürfniß der nothwendigen Einheit des Ganzen ist; so haben Wir beschlossen, sämtlichen Bestandtheilen der Gesezgebung und Verwaltung Unsers Reichs, mit Rücksicht auf die äußern und Innern Verhältnisse desselben, durch organische Geseze einen vollständigen Zusammenhang zu geben, und hiezu den Grund durch gegenwärtige Konstitutions-Urkunde zu legen, die zur Absicht hat, durch entsprechende Anordnungen und Bestimmungen den gerechten, im allgemeinen Staatszwecke gegründeten Foderungen [*sic*] des Staats an seine einzelnen Glieder, so wie der einzelnen Glieder an den Staat, die Gewährleistung ihrer Erfüllung, dem Ganzen feste Haltung und Verbindung, und jedem Theile der Staatsgewalt die ihm angemessene Wirkungskraft nach den Bedürfnissen des Gesamt-Wohls zu verschaffen […]." *Konstitution für das Königreich Baiern, Königlich-Baierisches Regierungsblatt* 1806, Columns 985-1000.

26 In the fiscal year 1806/1807, public revenue amounted to 26.92 million guilders, government spending, however, 32.51 million guilders. The deficit was thus 5.59 million guilders or about one quarter of the ongoing revenue. On the relation between public debt and reforms in Southern Germany see Ullmann, Hans-Peter, *Staatsschulden und Reformpolitik. Die Entstehung moderner öffentlicher Schulden in Bayern und Baden 1780-1820*, 2 Vols., Göttingen, Vandenhoeck & Ruprecht, 1986, and Ullmann, Hans-Peter, "Die öffentlichen Schulden in Bayern und Baden 1780-1820," 242 *Historische Zeitschrift* (1986), pp. 31-67. For a comparative analysis of contemporary political reforms in the Southern German states see Paul Nolte, *Staatsbildung und Gesellschaftsreform. Politische Reformen in Preußen und den süddeutschen Staaten 1800-1820*, Frankfurt am Main/New York, Campus, 1990, especially pp. 109-189.

27 Not only in Bavaria, but also in other (southern) German states the first concrete constitutional plans were triggered by the rise in debt. In 1808, for example, when national bankruptcy was a distinct possibility, the Badenese government also considered setting up a representative constitution based on the Westphalian model.

sation could be perceived as an act – indeed the seal – of "superior legitimation" for the state authorities. On the other hand, the government hoped that the Constitution would not only contribute towards integration at the domestic level, but also consolidate Bavaria's foreign policy, since the actual text of the Constitution would cement Bavaria's state borders and territorial status, both of which were anything but undisputed. This aspect refers to the perhaps most important purpose of the Bavarian Constitution of 1808: safeguarding, or rather reclaiming, national sovereignty. By taking the initiative and forcing through its own constitution, the Bavarian government pre-empted the impending creation of a framework constitution for the Confederation of the Rhine,[28] which would have had a far-reaching restrictive impact on Bavaria's future political development. At the same time enacting a home-grown constitution prevented any direct French interference, such as Napoleon drafting a constitution himself – as happened in the case of Westphalia. By circumventing this scenario, the royal cabinet maintained space to manoeuvre and even regained a degree of independence from France.

All in all, the Bavarian Constitution of 1808 was thus a political feat, by which – metaphorically speaking – two birds were to be killed with one stone. Outwardly, the Bavarian government left no doubt that it was a loyal ally of France and wanted to comply with Napoleon's wishes. Accordingly, the authorities were willing to follow French constitutional principles together with the model of the Westphalian Constitution, and promised to introduce the *Code Napoléon*.[29] Essentially, however, the "national card" was played, promising not only domestic stability and offering a possible solution to financial misery, but underlining and strengthening Bavarian claims to sovereignty and independence. The constitutionalisation of Bavaria in 1808 can thus be interpreted as an act both of statesmanlike pragmatism and political craftiness, which is revealing in understanding the practice of Napoleonic constitutionalism in general.

6. From Universal Constitutionalism to Constitutional Nationalism

In the wake of the Napoleonic Age, fundamental legal and constitutional changes took place. It was in this era that the codification of

[28] The plan to draw up a framework constitution for the Confederation of the Rhine was prominent in political debates of the time, but was never fulfilled. On the connections between this plan and the enactment of the Bavarian Constitution of 1808, see Doeberl, *Rheinbundverfassung*.

[29] The *Code Napoléon* was rewritten by Anselm von Feuerbach (*Allgemeines bürgerliches Gesetzbuch für das Königreich Baiern*), but never actually came into force in Bavaria: evidence of the ambivalent nature of French legal takeovers.

constitutional law made rapid progress, and universalised French "constitutionalism" became an important element of Napoleonic hegemonic politics. However, although French revolutionary constitutionalism was certainly a tangible phenomenon of the time and despite the fact that certain types of constitution could be termed as genuinely "Napoleonic" (e.g. the Constitution of Westphalia), "Napoleonic constitutionalism" was distinctly Janus-like.

What has become clear, as the case of the 1808 Bavarian Constitution proves, is that the constitutionalisation processes of the time cannot be assessed exclusively in terms of top-down politics, in which constitutions were created by Napoleon, then exported to and foisted upon other countries: these processes were on the contrary of a more complex and ambivalent nature. In Bavaria, the promulgation of a constitution was in fact as much a result of domestic constraints and national-political reasoning as French intervention. This reasoning can be interpreted as quasi "foreign politics" via "domestic polity": it was directed against the impetus of Napoleonic constitutional politics, which aimed at imposing political conformity on dependent states. In contrast to French ambitions, the Bavarian Constitution of 1808, though not fundamentally questioning the special relationship with its French patron, sought to achieve national sovereignty guaranteeing political autonomy. Or to put it in another way: in the case of Bavaria, Napoleon's hegemonic ambitions essentially provoked a "constitutional reflex" and the Constitution of 1808 thus became a means to safeguard sovereignty and a main driving force behind own nation-building processes.

Taking this into account, the actual "presence" of Napoleonic constitutionalism proved to be of a limited nature, even within the French sphere of influence. Moreover, most European countries did not undergo a constitutionalisation process during the Napoleonic Age at all, and those without a written constitution included not only the great European powers Russia, Austria and Prussia, but also a number of smaller states under French supremacy (e.g. the Kingdoms of Württemberg and Saxony).[30] In other countries, the framing of constitutions occurred without French influence (e.g. the Swedish Constitution of 1809)[31] or in declared opposition to Napoleon (e.g. the Spanish Cádiz-Constitution of

30 Both countries had gained the status of kingdoms by Napoleon in 1806 and were members of the Confederation of the Rhine.

31 The Swedish Constitution of 1809, which replaced the Constitution of 1772 in the course of the lost Swedish-Russian War 1808/1809, can be characterised as parliamentarian-corporatist and incorporated both traditional and modern elements. On its history see Lagerroth, Fredrik, *1809 års regeringsform: dess ursprung och tolkning*, Stockholm, Norstedt & Söner, 1942.

1812).[32] Even in those countries in which Napoleon himself was the (co-)author of the constitutional texts, such as the Kingdom of Westphalia, the Grand Duchy of Frankfurt or the Duchy of Warsaw, the concrete significance of these documents in constitutional practice was minor, if not negligible. In all these states, including Bavaria, doubt was cast on these constitutions shortly after their enactment and/or they never came into full effect, and actually nowhere was the promised democratisation of the political system achieved.[33] In France itself the Imperial Constitution of 1804 was essentially suspended from 1810 onwards by an autocratic regime that granted Napoleon absolute power.

It can thus be clearly seen that Napoleonic constitutionalism at the time was far from being a universal phenomenon with strong integrative capacities since it lacked both width and depth. Despite this fact, however, its legacy is considerable. The history of modern constitutionalism cannot be comprehended without the experience of the Napoleonic Age, in which the notions of "constitution" and "constitutionalism" gained enormously in prestige and became a crucial element of public discourse, whether in the context of pro- or anti-Napoleonic rhetoric. At the end of French hegemony in Europe, it was no longer possible to refute the relevance of "constitution". The call for constitutional government was now more distinct than ever before, especially because such constitutional government had been withheld in the previous years or had been ineffectively implemented. Consequently the main challenge for Europe's political class after 1814/1815 was to fulfil post-revolutionary society's expectations of the political innovations generated by the Revolution and the Napoleonic Regime being safeguarded – innovations, which had been voiced rather than implemented in Napoleonic Europe.

Even among the conservatively minded, popular opinion realised that rigid neo-absolutism as practised by the Spanish King after his return to

32 The Spanish Constitution of 1812 was promulgated on 12 March 1812 by the Cádiz Cortes, the national legislative assembly of Spain acting while in refuge. The document was based on the principle of popular sovereignty, but acknowledged the legitimacy of Ferdinand VII as King of Spain. The Constitution was later to become a considerable point of reference in post-Napoleonic European constitutional discourse, particularly among liberals. See Badia, Juan Ferrando, "Die Spanische Verfassung von 1812 und Europa," *Der Staat: Zeitschrift für Staatslehre, öffentliches Recht und Verfassungsgeschichte* 2 (1963), pp. 153-180, Dippel, Horst, "Die Bedeutung der spanischen Verfassung von 1812 für den deutschen Frühliberalismus und Frühkonstitutionalismus," in Martin Kirsch and Pierangelo Schiera (eds.), *Denken und Umsetzung des Konstitutionalismus in Deutschland und anderen europäischen Ländern in der ersten Hälfte des 19. Jahrhunderts*, Berlin, Duncker & Humblot, 1999, pp. 219-237.

33 The parliamentary assembly which was foreseen in the Bavarian Constitution, for example, was never convened.

power was not a suitable solution in the longer-term.[34] Rather, the example of the French Restoration under Louis XVIII in his aspirations to achieve a lasting settlement by offering constitutional guarantees incorporating many of the legal achievements of the Revolutionary and Napoleonic Age seemed a much more appropriate and reasonable solution. Hence it was again the "French model" that became important for European constitutionalism, namely the *Charte constitutionnelle*,[35] which formed the foundation of the new "monarchical constitutional"[36] regime in France and generated ideas as to how the diverging aspirations of rulers and post-revolutionary society might be reconciled. Accordingly, rather than a decline, the post-Napoleonic Age saw a new wave of constitutionalism throughout Europe, with constitutions following the example of the French *Charte* being enacted in several states, such as the newly created Kingdom of the United Netherlands, the Kingdom of Poland (Congress Poland) and – in 1818, ten years after its first experience with a written constitution – Bavaria.

All these constitutional projects were spin-offs of what can be called "Napoleonic constitutionalism" and perpetuated the tradition of *octroi* as the principal means of enacting constitutions. At the same time, however, such projects launched a new phase in European constitutionalism, in which the key principle of the previous decades, namely popular sovereignty, was replaced by a consistent anti-revolutionary counter concept based on the principle of dynastic legitimacy and monarchical sovereignty.

---

34 See Talleyrand's *Rapport fait au Roi pendant son voyage de Gand à Paris* (June 1815), in Georges Pallain (ed.), *Correspondance inédite du Prince De Talleyrand et du Roi Louis XVIII pendant le Congrès de Vienne. Publiée sur les manuscrits conservés au dépôt des Affaires étrangères, avec préface, éclaircissements et notes*, 3rd ed., Paris, Londres, Leipzig, E. Plon et Cie, 1881, pp. 436-484, citation at p. 474. And indeed, this critical opinion was soon to be confirmed: only six years after the advocates of the 1812 Cádiz-constitution had been forced into exile, in 1820 the Revolution started in Spain.

35 On the *Charte* and its role as a European model see Sellin, Volker, *Die geraubte Revolution. Der Sturz Napoleons und die Restauration in Europa*, Göttingen, Vandenhoeck & Ruprecht, 2001, especially pp. 275-325, Prutsch, Markus J., *Die Charte constitutionnelle Ludwigs XVIII. in der Krise von 1830. Verfassungsentwicklung und Verfassungsrevision in Frankreich 1814 bis 1830*, Marburg, Tectum, 2006, especially pp. 153-170.

36 "Monarchical constitutionalism", also referred to as "constitutional monarchism" – see Anderson, Eugene N. and Anderson, Pauline R., *Political Institutions and Social Change in Continental Europe in the Nineteenth Century*, Berkeley, University of California Press, 1967, pp. 39-40 and 78-79, can be defined as a constitutional system in which the monarch is the central political power and holder of the *pouvoir constituant*, in which, however, a written (representative) constitution restricts the sovereign by providing civil liberties and allowing citizens to take part in the political, and, most important, legislative process.

While Napoleon had failed to make French-type "(revolutionary) constitutionalism" a common European standard, the language of constitution(alism) had obtained quasi-universal validity by 1814/1815. The bell had tolled for the "age of constitutions".[37] But paradoxically, however universal the wish for constitutional government had become, the actual outcome of the constitutional wave was clearly "anti-cosmopolitan". Quite in contrast to Napoleon's vision of a common Europe united by universal laws and institutions, so eloquently elaborated in the writings he produced in exile, constitutionalism became *the* focal point of burgeoning nationalism. The ultimate result was a Europe united in believing in constitutionalism, but in political terms separated more than ever before through the sheer plurality of ideologically charged national constitutions. Far from having promoted "anti-Nationalism", the final result of the Napoleonic Age was hence "Europeanism" of a somewhat heterodox nature.

---

37 See, e.g., Carl von Rotteck, who declared in 1830 "Es ist heute ganz eigens das Zeitalter der Constitutionen." Rotteck, Carl von, *Lehrbuch des Vernunftsrechts und der Staatswissenschaften*, Stuttgart, Hallberg, 1829-1835, Vol. 2 (1830), p. 172.

Haiti and the Cosmopolitan Imagination

Liliana OBREGÓN

> L'ironie du sort fit de nous le porte-étendard de la civilisation, la démonstration de vérités vainement et inutilment proclamées.
>
> Frederic Marcelin, *Haiti et l'indemnité francaise*, 1897

> It is true that in ... the 19th century France had to negotiate very hard conditions for diplomatic recognition of Haiti and imposed on its government a debt that would be ... inconceivable today... But that is a part of history, and we can't go back over the historical conditions today...It does not make sense, history turns...
>
> Thierry Burkhard, France's Ambassador to Haiti, 2004 Interview

1. Introduction

The Haitian Revolution (1791-1803), declaration of independence (1804), first constitutions (1801 and 1805) and the subsequent obstacles to state recognition are uncomfortably situated in the immediacy of Immanuel Kant's foundational texts proposing the utopia of a cosmopolitan law that would bring perpetual peace to the world.[1] Instead of hailing Haiti for complying with Kantian constitutional requirements in search of diplomatic recognition and participation in the first attempt at an amphictyonic project in the Americas, the new state was feared, ostracized, isolated and seen as a model of devolution.

This essay explores the underlying tension between the legacy of Kantian cosmopolitanism and the teleological understanding of international law. First, it will consider Kant's writings on race as central to his cosmopolitan view. Second, it will argue that the legality of the slave trade and slavery were broadly accepted institutions of eighteenth and nineteenth century legal consciousness despite the conventional view

1 The Kantian texts most referred to by international legal scholars are *Idea for a Universal History from a Cosmopolitan Point of View* (1784) and *Project for a Perpetual Peace. A Philosophical Essay* (1795).

that we have of the Enlightenment as leading to the "century of progress." Third, it will describe the process of searching for sovereign independence through constitutional forms as well as the process of recognition, or rather of "non-recognition" of Haiti, during the early nineteenth century.

2. Kant's Anthropological Thought and the Cosmopolitan Imagination

In the earlier half of the eighteenth century, a cosmopolitan was a polyglot traveller, a self-designated citizen of the world[2] who acted as an ambassador of enlightenment ideas. A learned man "stranger nowhere in the world,"[3] the cosmopolitan felt "at home in all companies and all countries."[4] Less generous observers viewed cosmopolitans as "selfish wanderers," men without a grounding or a *patrie* or as national traitors.[5]

But for Immanuel Kant the French Revolution radically transformed the voyaging dilettante. The unexpected event came as a hopeful "historical sign" that remembered the past, revealed a moral disposition both "pure and universal" in the present and showed a future of progressive improvement.[67] The human race viewed as a "complete association of men" indicated "the *right* of every people to give itself a constitution ...without interference from other powers...and the *aim*, which is also a

2 Boyer, Abel and Prieur, J.C., *Le Dictionnaire Royal Francois-Anglois Et Anglois-Francois (the Royal Dictionary, French and English, and English and French)*, 2, London, C. Bathurst, 1773.

3 Anonymous, *Dictionnaire Universel François Et Latin. Contenant La Signification Et La Definition Tant Des Mots De L'une & De L'autre Langue*, Paris, Trevoux & se vend chez F. Dalaulne, 1721, Vol. 5, p. 170.

4 Fenning, D., *The Royal English Dictionary or a Treasury of the English Language*, 2nd ed., London, Baldwin, Richardson, Crowder, Collins, 1763.

5 Archibugi, Daniel, "Immanuel Kant, Cosmopolitan Law and Peace," 1 *European Journal of International Relations* (1995), pp. 429-456, pp. 441-442. For dictionary definitions see Anonymous, *Dictionnaire Universel François Et Latin*. For a better understanding of the cosmopolitan in the early modern period see Jacob, Margaret C., *Strangers Nowhere in the World. The Rise of Cosmopolitanism in Early Modern Europe*, Philadelphia, Univ. of Pennsylvania Press, 2006.

6 Kant, Immanuel, "The Contest of the Faculties," in Hans S. Reiss (ed.), *Kant. Political Writings*, 2nd enl. ed., Cambridge Texts in the History of Political Thought, Cambridge, Cambridge University Press, 1991, pp. 176-190, p. 181. On this point I follow Michel Foucault's observation, Foucault, Michel, "The Art of Telling the Truth," in Lawrence D. Kritzman (ed.), *Politics, Philosophy, Culture. Interviews and Other Writings, 1977-1984*, New York, Routledge, 1988, pp. 91-92.

7 Kant, "The Contest of the Faculties", p. 181.

duty, of submitting to those conditions by which war, the source of all evils and moral corruption can be prevented."[8]

The famed philosopher, who never travelled far from his home or his habits, gave the cosmopolitan a serious makeover. Kant's cosmopolitan man abandoned his dandy life, to build institutions and secure stable international relations. Through "a universal cosmopolitan existence", the selfish wanderer of yesterday would construct "perfect political constitutions", "a civil union of mankind," "a federation of people" and a "universal justice."[9] Kant's "citizen of the world" no longer dwelled in his narcissistic education but rather used his *Weltkenntnis* (or "cosmopolitan knowledge") of human nature to contribute to the "moral development of the species" and the "common evolution of the cosmopolitan ideal."[10]

If the French revolution woke Kant from his political slumber[11] he fell back asleep for the Haitian one. Why was the uprising of half a million slaves[12] in "that place of the most refined and cruel slavery," as Kant called it in *Perpetual Peace*, not read as another historical sign, unexpected but more encouraging towards a cosmopolitan ideal than the first? Kant most likely knew about the revolt from German newspapers that informed about it more than any other American event of its time;[13]

8 *Ibid.*, pp. 182-183.

9 Kant, Immanuel, "Perpetual Peace," in Hans S. Reiss (ed.), *Kant's Political Writings*, Cambridge, Cambridge University Press, 1996.

10 Wilson, Holly L., *Kant's Pragmatic Anthropology. It's Origin, Eaning, and Critical Significance*, Albany, State Univ Of New York Press, 2007, p. 28.

11 Arendt, Hannah and Beiner, Ronald (eds.), *Lectures on Kant's Political Philosophy*, Chicago, University of Chicago Press, 1992, p. 16.

12 The population for Haiti in 1791 consisted of 40,000 white (stratified and divided in *grands blancs* – plantation owners and government officials, and *petits blancs* – overseers, artisans), 28,000 mulattoes and free blacks (who possessed one third of the real estate but were denied legal equality with the *blancs*) and nearly half a million slaves (many of whom were recent arrivals from Africa) These numbers were first calculated by the landmark work Philip D. Curtin, *The Atlantic Slave Trade; a Census* (Madison, University of Wisconsin Press, 1969), who carefully evaluated the historiography on the subjects and the actual data available at the time. Though Curtin explained his numbers as "a range of possibility" and not a set figure, his estimate continues to be accepted as the most probable. Commenting on Curtin's numbers see more recently Eltis, David and Richardson, David, "The 'Numbers Game' and Routes to Slavery," *Routes to Slavery. Direction, Ethnicity, and Mortality in the Transatlantic Slave Trade*, Studies in Slave and Post-Slave Societies and Cultures, London, Portland OR, Frank Cass, 1997, pp. 1-15, p. 1; and Klein, Herbert S., *The Atlantic Slave Trade*, 2nd new ed., New Approaches to the Americas, Cambridge/New York, Cambridge University Press, 2010, p. xviii.

13 Schuller, Karen, "From Liberalism to Racism. German Historians, Journalists, and the Haitian Revolution from the Late Eighteenth to the Early Twentieth Century," in

through his personal inquiries of foreign events or through the *Amis des Noirs* who wrote about the uprising in Saint Domingue from its beginning in 1791.[14]

My purpose, however, is not to prove that Kant knew what happened in the French colony, to accuse him of disregarding the events or to excuse him for forgetting them.[15] In fact, we can suppose that Kant would not or could not recognize an event he deemed improbable: "if ever revolutions occurred, they were always realized by whites. [...] Negroes have never had a part in them [...]."[16]

Haiti's invisibility is not unique to Kant or to the history of international law: the topic of silencing or forgetting Haiti has become somewhat of a redundancy in the historical literature elsewhere.[17] But the background to Kant's cosmopolitan imagination represents two ignored aspects of the legal consciousness of early nineteenth century scholars and practitioners which did not permit Haiti's recognition as part of the community of civilized nations until the second half of the nineteenth century: the normalcy of slavery, the legality of the slave trade and the construction of a scientific concept of race.

David P. Geggus (ed.), *The Impact of the Haitian Revolution in the Atlantic World*, Columbia, University of South Carolina, 2001, pp. 23-43.

14 Buck-Morss, Susan, "Hegel and Haiti," 26 *Critical Inquiry* (2000), pp. 821-865, p. 837.

15 It is sufficient to know, as Susan Buck-Morss has demonstrated, that "the Haitian Revolution was the crucible, the trial by fire for the ideals of the French Enlightenment. And every European who was part of the bourgeois reading public knew it" including Hegel, whose master-slave dialectic was inspired by it. See *ibid.*, p. 845; and Buck-Morss, Susan, *Hegel, Haiti, and Universal History*, Illuminations, Pittsburgh PA, University of Pittsburgh Press, 2009.

16 From Immanuel Kant's private writings in the *Menschenkunde* as cited in Carter, J. Kameron, *Race. A Theological Account*, Oxford, Oxford University Press, 2008, p. 91.

17 The trope of forgetting and silencing Haiti was initiated with Michel-Rolph Trouillot's "An Unthinkable History. The Haitian Revolution as a Non-Event," in *Silencing the Past, Power and the Production of History*, Boston, Beacon Press, 1995. Other recent texts are Dwyer, Philip, "Remembering and Forgetting in Contemporary France. Napoleon, Slavery and the French History Wars," 26 *French Politics, Culture & Society* (2008), pp. 110-122; Reinhardt, Thomas, "200 Years of Forgetting. Hushing up the Haitian Revolution," 35 *Journal of Black Studies* (2005), pp. 246-261; Miller, Christopher L., "Forget Haiti. Baron Roger and the New Africa," 107 *Yale French Studies*, The Haiti Issue: 1804 and Nineteenth-Century French Studies (2005); Dorigny, Marcel, "Aux origines. L'indépendance d'Haïti et son occultation," in *La fracture coloniale. La société française au prisme de l'héritage colonial*, Nicolas Bancel Pascal Blanchard and Sandrine Lemaire (eds.), Paris, La Découverte, 2005; Nettleford, Rex, "The Haitian Revolution and the Struggle against Slavery. Challenges to Knowledge, Ignorance, and Silence," 58 *International Social Science Journal* (2006), pp. 195-202.

Indeed, Kant believed that "Negroes" were born slaves and did not have the capacity for self-government or to make revolutions.[18] By his time, slavery had been practiced on European territory for centuries[19] and the more recent commerce in Africans had become a multinational enterprise. Expanding past the Spanish and Portuguese who made it a lucrative business in the sixteenth and seventeenth centuries, merchants from Copenhagen to Geneva joined the trade in the eighteenth century.[20] Of the estimated 11.8 million Africans enslaved between 1500 and 1867, 1.6 million were brought to the Americas in the seventeenth century with a peak of 6.4 million by the end of the eighteenth century. The remaining 3.8 million were brought in the nineteenth century.[21]

The French colony of Saint Domingue was the major exporter of wealth and the main importer of slaves in the Americas. Towards the end of the eighteenth century, French planters imported a yearly average of 30,000 slaves to the island, a sum which represented a third to a half of the entire transatlantic trade for that period.[22] One year after France's National Assembly approved the famed Declaration of the Rights of the Man and the Citizen, 55,000 slaves were unloaded in the Caribbean, a record number shipped under any national flag.[23] On the eve of the Haitian Revolution, France imported more slaves into her colonies than any other imperial power.

Thus Kant lived in a world in which slavery and the slave trade was legal, part of normal commercial relations, and justified by the law of nations. It was in this world that he developed his idea[24] of a cosmopoli-

---

18 Carter, *Race*, p. 91.

19 Herbert Klein, points out that despite a quarter century of studies, there still continues to be much ignorance on the nature of the Atlantic slave trade and its impact on the world. He attributes this gap of knowledge to the connection with European imperialism, the political and emotional connotations of the slave trade and the complexity of its study.

20 Curtin, *The Atlantic Slave Trade*, p. 117; Drescher, Seymour, *Abolition. A History of Slavery and Antislavery*, Cambridge, Cambridge University Press, 2009, p. 147.

21 These numbers were first calculated by the landmark work Curtin, *The Atlantic Slave Trade*. Commenting on Curtin's numbers see more recently Eltis and Richardson, "The 'Numbers Game' and Routes to Slavery", p. 1; and Klein, *The Atlantic Slave Trade*, p. xviii.

22 Curtin, *The Atlantic Slave Trade*, p. 75.

23 Drescher, *Abolition*, p. 147.

24 Eigen Figal, Sara and Larrimore, Mark J. (eds.), *The German Invention of Race*, Suny Series, Philosophy and Race, Albany, State University of New York Press, 2006, p. 7.

tan law but more significantly he also constructed the first "scientific" account of race.[25]

Kant's ideas of race and human difference were central to answer the most important question for his critical project: "what is man?" His thinking about the nature and destiny of "man" was central to his philosophical project and to his normative one, as expressed in his own words. In 1764 Kant described how Europeans' were naturally predetermined – through their superior moral and intellectual capacities – in accessing the "beautiful" and the "sublime." Among these, the Germans faired above all while the Spaniards were the least appreciated but all Europeans had the possibility of understanding the "sublime" and the "beautiful" as well as religion.[26] Kant described the "rest of the world" (Arabs, Persians, Japanese, Indians, Chinese, Orientals, Negroes and Savages) through national, religious, geographical and racial distinctions.[27]

In later essays, Kant characterized a unitary nature of humanity as descending from the same "stem genus" and the universal capacity to generate fertile children.[28] Only one race was close to the original stem genus: "white brunettes" from the Old World "where the best mixtures of climate and earthly creatures coexist."[29] After the "white brunettes" Kant provided a hierarchy of four "genuine" races identified by colour, climate and geography: 1) Whites, or "first race of very blonds (Northern Europe) who live in damp cold; 2) second race, who are copper red (America) and live in dry cold; 3) the third race, Negro or blacks (Senegambia) of dry heat, and 4) the fourth race, olive-yellow (Indians) of dry heat."[30]

25 Kant's notions of race were well known and discussed since his first publications on race in the eighteenth century and his role in inventing the scientific notion of race was recognized throughout the twentieth century. See Bernasconi, Robert, "Who Invented the Concept of Race. Kant's Role in the Enlightenment Construction of Race," in Robert Bernasconi (ed.), *Race*, Blackwell Readings in Continental Philosophy, Malden Mass., Blackwell, 2001, pp. 11-36.

26 Kant, Immanuel, "On the Different Races of Man (1775)," in Emmanuel Chukwudi Eze (ed.), *Race and the Enlightenment. A Reader*, Cambridge Mass., Blackwell, 1997, pp. 38-48.

27 *Ibid.*

28 *Ibid.*, p. 39. For a more recent translation see Kant, Immanuel, "Of the Different Races of Human Beings (1775)," *Anthropology, History, and Education*, The Cambridge Edition of the Works of Immanuel Kant, Robert B. Louden and Günter Zöller (eds.), Cambridge UK/New York, Cambridge University Press, 2007, pp. 82-97, pp. 84-85.

29 Kant, "On the Different Races of Man (1775)", p. 48.

30 *Ibid.*

In addition to differences in physical appearance, Kant distinguished non-physical characteristics such as capacity for reason, education, revolution and access to moral and aesthetic sensibilities. These differences determined their potential, as a racial group, to be sovereign. Kant's scientific notions belonged to a natural taxonomy, a system of natural laws in which each race had an inherent predisposition for reaching certain developments.[31] Man was disposed for all climates and geographies, but individual races were "born to a place and made for it."[32] However, only "Negroes" and "Whites" classified as fundamental races[33] because Kant believed their differences were as great with the "capacities of the mind as... with colour."[34] Kant's granted "Africans", "blacks" or "Negroes" immutable natural characteristics: they "have by nature no feelings that rises above the ridiculous...not a single one has ever been found who has accomplished something great in art or science or shown any other praiseworthy quality,"[35] they profess a "religion of fetishes...which sinks so deeply into the ridiculous as ever seems possible for the human race;"[36] they are "very vain ...and so talkative that they must be driven apart from each other by blows;"[37] "all Negroes stink...and are strong, fleshy, supple...but...lazy, soft and trifling;"[38] they are "born slaves" that do not have the capacity to rule themselves; they cannot make revolutions.[39]

Kant's understanding of race was a part of a tense discussion in eighteenth century Germany that spread across Europe and by the beginning of the nineteenth century had made race a stable and historically evolved scientific concept, constituted by the disciplines of the human sciences, history and philosophy.[40] Nonetheless, Kant's view of blacks is not important as an isolated interpretation of the works of one

31 *Ibid.*

32 *Ibid.*, pp. 43-45.

33 *Ibid.*, p. 42.

34 Kant, Immanuel, "On the Feeling of the Beautiful and the Sublime (1764)," *Anthropology, History, and Education*, The Cambridge Edition of the Works of Immanuel Kant, Robert B. Louden and Günter Zöller (eds.), Cambridge UK/New York, Cambridge University Press, 2007, pp. 18-62, p. 59.

35 *Ibid.*

36 *Ibid.*

37 *Ibid.*, p. 60.

38 Kant, "Of the Different Races of Human Beings (1775)", p. 93.

39 Carter, *Race*, p. 91.

40 Eigen Figal, Sara and Larrimore, Mark J., "Introduction. The German Invention of Race," in Sara Eigen Figal and Mark J. Larrimore (eds.), *The German Invention of Race*, Suny Series, Philosophy and Race, Albany, State University of New York Press, 2006, pp. 1-22, p. 1.

philosopher (or rather, *the* philosopher), but rather as an exemplary view that circulated during his time and was underlying the European legal consciousness of the early nineteenth century.

3. Haiti and the Cosmopolitan Constitutional Requirement

3.1. Toussaint's Colonial Constitution of Saint Domingue, 1801

On December 15, 1799, one month after the *coup d'État* of 18 Brumaire, Napoleon Bonaparte proclaimed the Constitution of the Year VIII and the end of the French Revolution.[41] Article 91 stated that the colonies would be ruled by "special laws," modifying the French Republic's fundamental principle of indivisibility proclaimed in the Constitution of the Year III (1795). The colonies were no longer "integral parts of the Republic…subjected to the same constitutional law."[42]

Article 91 also challenged a law of 1798 which reviewed the colonial organisation and declared that

> [b]lacks or coloured individuals, removed from their Fatherland and transported to the colonies, are not reputed to be foreigners; they enjoy the same rights as an individual born on the French territory, if they are attached to the culture, if they are useful in the armies, if they exert a profession or trade.[43]

The law also declared that any individual "born in Africa or in foreign colonies, and transferred to the French islands, would be free as soon as he laid feet upon French territory" but "to acquire citizenship for the future, he would have to comply with article 10 of the Constitution." To comply meant three unlikely conditions for a former slave: marriage to a French women, seven-year residence in France and proof of property ownership. Though the 1798 law granted colonial free blacks and

41 Bonaparte, Napoleon, Gourgaud, Gaspard, and Montholon, Charles-Tristan, *Memoirs of the History of France During the Reign of Napoleon*, London, H. Colburn and Co., 1823, p. 403.

42 However, Boissy d'Anglas, the drafter of the 1795 Constitution clarified that this did not mean an equality status for the colonies since "absolute equality is a chimera" and in similar ideas to Kant's racial thinking, he argued for climatic differences that would support the colonial domination over those territories. D'Anglas, Boissy, *Plan of the New Constitution of the French Republic; To Which Is Prefixed, the Report Presented to the Convention, from the Commission of Eleven*, Edinburgh J. Robertson, No. 4, 1795.

43 Duvergier, J.B., "12 Nivose an 6 (1er Janvier 1798) 'Loi Concernant L'Organisation Constitutionnelle Des Colonies'," in France (ed.), *Collection Complète Des Lois, Décrets, Ordonnances, Réglemens Et Avis Du Conseil D'état, Publiée Sur Les Éditions Officielles Du Louvre, De L'imprimerie Nationale Par Baudouin Et Du Bulletin Des Lois, De 1788 À 1824 Inclusivement*, 10, Paris, A. Guyot et Scribe, 1825, p. 193.

former male slaves almost impossible conditions for citizenship, it at least recognized them as "not foreign" and guaranteed freedom from slavery on French territory.[44]

The new constitution marked a definitive moment in which the rights of citizens in the metropole were differentiated from those of the colonies, but did not apply to Saint Domingue or other colonies where slavery had been abolished since 1793.[45] Anticipating a reaction from the island, Napoleon addressed the "citizens of Saint-Domingue" to explain that the laws of the French colonies would be tailored according to the "nature of things" as well as their different "habits, morals, interests, climate, cultures, and products." The proclamation also informed that one of the first acts of the new government would be to provide Saint Domingue with new laws and the promise that it would continue to recognize the liberty and equality of the island's "brave blacks."[46] Napoleon's strategic move looked to regain presence in the colonies while using Saint Domingue as a stronghold against the British and as a provider of sugar and soldiers.[47]

Though the rebels had been fighting for their freedom since 1791, Saint Domingue was still considered a colony despite France's effective loss of control over the island and the French Assembly's official recognition of their freedom in 1794. After the abolition of slavery, Toussaint Louverture, the famous former slave turned general and ruler of the island, accepted French support in order to defeat both British and Spanish armies that attacked them. By 1800, Toussaint's authority was well established and recognized both in Saint Domingue and abroad. However, he was conscious that their revolutionary gains were in danger as they were internally divided and externally threatened. The general's priority was to secure French support while retaining authority within.

---

44 *Ibid.*

45 Décret qui abolit l'Esclavage des Nègres dans les Colonies. Du 4 Février, 1794 (No. 2262) "La Convention Nationale déclare que l'esclavage des négres dans toutes les colonies est aboli; en conséquence, elle décrète que tous les hommes; sans distinction de couleur, domiciliés dans les colonies, sont, citoyens français, et jouiront-de tous les droits assurés par la constitution." Convention Nationale De France, "Décret Qui Abolit L'Esclavage Des Nègres Dans Les Colonies. Du 4 Février, 1794," in L. Rondonneau (ed.), *Collection Générale Des Lois, Décrets, Arrêtés, Sénatus-Consultes (1789-1814)*, IV, Paris, Imprimerie Royale, 1818, p. 918.

46 Bonaparte, Napoléon, "'Aux Citoyens De Saint-Domingue' Paris, 4 Nivose an VIII (25 Decembre, 1799)," *Correspondance De Napoléon I; Publiée Par Ordre De L'empereur Napoléon III*, Paris, H. Plon, J. Dumaine, 1858, p. 42.

47 Fink, Carolyn E., "The Saint Domingue Slave Revolution and the Unfolding of Independence 1791-1804," in David Patrick Geggus and Norman Fiering (eds.), *The World of the Haitian Revolution* (Blacks in the Diaspora), Bloomington, Indiana University Press, 2009, pp. 179-196, p. 182.

Napoleon's constitution warned Toussaint of future impositions so he pre-empted the special laws by drafting the first constitution for Saint Domingue. By arguing that laws imposed on them in the past were incoherent and chaotic and that only the people of Saint Domingue could truly represent their "spirit and pain," Toussaint invoked the constitution as a "rock" that would ground his people together.[48] On March 22, 1801 a constitutional assembly of ten deputies began to work. Three months later, the colonial constitution of 1801, also known as "Toussaint's Constitution," was read by the leader and promoted by the assembly with a grandiose celebration in Port-Au-Prince.

The 1801 document established the constitutional basis for the "French colony of Saint Domingue," as a "single colony…ruled under particular laws" but part of the "French empire."[49] The constitution gave Toussaint the authority of Governor General "for life" in recognition of the services rendered to the colony "in its most dire moments of revolution" and the right to pick his successor who would rule for periods of five years. Despite its recognition of a colonial status, the constitution called it a "new colony" as if designating a different status of autonomous government *vis-à-vis* the metropole. Indeed, Toussaint's constitution organized the colony's government and determined a broad scope of sovereign decision-making for himself: from the definition of territorial boundaries and the abolition of slavery, to the regulation of commerce, finances and military activities.

Toussaint's constitution appropriated French functions and looked for foreign recognition while searching for ways of unifying the disparate groups of former African slaves.[50] First, it was written in French, the language of the metropole and of "civilisation" which the majority did not speak. Second, the citizens of Saint Domingue were proclaimed to "live and die free and French" – the nationality of their former masters – but the only one which could grant security in face of menacing foreign powers. Third, the Catholic religion was recognized as official despite the majority practice of Voudon, a syncretic religion of African roots. The colonial constitution also gave incentives for former plantation owners to return and re-invest in Saint Domingue in contrast with the majority population which preferred small- self-subsistence farming.

Contrary to its purpose, the constitution's underlying contradictions resulted in both internal and external opposition and a direct affront to

---

48 Janvier, Louis Joseph, *Les Constitutions D'haiti (1801-1885)*, Paris, C. Marpon & E. Flammarion, 1886, p. 7.

49 Article 1, *ibid.*, p. 8.

50 See Gaffield, Julia, "Complexities of Imagining Haiti. A Study of National Constitutions 1801-1807," 41 *Journal of Social History* (Fall 2007), pp. 81-103.

the Napoleonic regime.[51] The colonial constitution not only assigned equal rights to employment, punishment and protection "regardless of colour," it also put Toussaint Louverture practically at the same level as Bonaparte. From his designation as Governor General "for life" Toussaint was invested with the authority to represent the colony directly with the metropole, legislate and propose laws as well as changes to the constitution, nominate civilian and military employees, command and organize the armed force, determine territorial divisions, organize the colony's internal and external security, determine the measures necessary to ensure the subsistence and the supply of goods of all sorts, direct and supervise the colony's payments and finances, inform receipts and disbursements and censor printing on the island or from abroad.[52] The only role left for the French government was to sanction it, but even that power was pre-empted in the document by granting the Chief General (Toussaint) power to immediately implement the constitution due to its urgent and necessary character.[53]

Toussaint sent the constitution for Napoleon's sanction one week after it was read in Port-Au-Prince. Not surprisingly, Napoleon was outraged with the affront and answered directly to Toussaint that the constitution "contains some [provisions] that are contrary to the dignity and sovereignty of the French people, of which Saint Domingue forms only a portion" and considered him a traitor.[54] Soon thereafter, Napoleon sent the French empire's largest military expedition consisting of more than fifty thousand men, to recover Saint Domingue and reimpose slavery. Most of the men died in combat or from yellow fever, including Napoleon's brother in law, General Leclerc, who headed the infamous expedition, detained Toussaint and sent him to exile in France where he died of pneumonia while in prison. The news of Toussaint's betrayal by Napoleon, the information that slavery had been reinstated in Martinique in 1802 and Toussaint's death in 1803 forced the definitive combat and final declaration of independence by the surviving leaders of Saint Domingue on January 1, 1804.

---

[51] This observation is made by Victor Schoelcher an early biographer of Toussaint whose research is based on extensive primary sources. However, Schoelcher also argued that the constitution aided Toussaint in organising the colony successfully, at least for the short period before Napoleon's intervention. Schœlcher, Victor, *Vie De Toussaint-Louverture*, 2nd ed., Paris, P. Ollendorff, 1889, p. 309.

[52] Janvier, *Les Constitutions D'haiti (1801-1885)*, p. 8.

[53] *Ibid.*

[54] As cited in Schœlcher, *Vie De Toussaint-Louverture*, pp. 304-305, 17.

3.2. The Declaration of Independence and the Birth of Haiti, 1804

The Haitian declaration of independence, authored by Jean Jacques Dessalines, a former slave and vociferous revolutionary leader, was clear: a radical break with France and any European power that might not take their sovereignty seriously.[55] The declaration begins with the heading "Liberté ou la Mort" directed to an "Armée Indigène." Instead of establishing a forward-looking set of principles on which to base the state, the declaration documents the violent fourteen years of fighting against the French and makes several radical breaks from its enslaved and colonized past.

Though written in the language of the French revolution, the declaration ends its history with France: 1804 is declared year I of independence and the name of Hayti was given to the new State, as a way of paying tribute to the original indigenous peoples that were annihilated by the first colonizers.[56] The document claimed Haiti's leaders as sworn "before eternity" and "before the entire universe" to "forever renounce France" and to die rather than live under its domination. The constitution refers to Haitians as *indigenes*, as natives, and declared to have "expelled the barbarians who have bloodied our land for two centuries." In a passionate account of its continued independence, the declaration recognized Haitians as inevitably tied to their European past despite the insurmountable differences between them and the "barbarous French":

> The French name still haunts our land. Everything revives the memories of the cruelties of this barbarous people: our law, our habits, our towns, everything still carries the stamp of the French. But what do we have in common with this nation of executioners? The difference between its cruelty and our patient moderation, its colour and ours the great seas that separate us, our avenging climate, all tell us plainly that they are not our brothers, that they never will be, and that if they find refuge among us, they will plot again to trouble and divide us.

---

55 Dessalines was illiterate and because of this, the declaration was frequently attributed to one of his mulatto Paris educated secretaries: Louis Boisrond-Tonnerre. However, more recently, historian Deborah Jenson has argued for recognition of Dessaline's authorship due to the similar structure, symbolism, and rhetorical style that is recurrent in Dessaline's other attributed documents. Dessaline's authorship is important for attributing agency to a former slave in the making of a text that speaks, for the first time, of a postcolonial State in the Americas denouncing slavery and colonialism. Jenson, Deborah, "Dessaline's American Proclamations of the Haitian Independence," 15 *The Journal of Haitian Studies* (2009), pp. 72-102.

56 For more on the possible origins of the name Haiti see Geggus, D., "The Naming of Haiti," 71 *New West Indian Guide/ Nieuwe West-Indische Gids* (1997), pp. 43-68.

The declaration threatened to terrify and put to death anyone who tried to take their liberty and declared Haiti an empire without imperialism. Dessalines recognized the role model Haiti would play for the region and stated in the document that they did not want to fall into a "missionary spirit" or to declare themselves lawgivers of the Caribbean, nor let their new independence trouble the peace of the neighbouring islands. He summarized in a telling phrase: "Peace to our neighbours but eternal hatred of France!"

3.3. Haiti's First Constitution, 1805

Haiti's first independent constitution promulgated on May 20, 1805 complied with fundamental Kantian requirements: "freedom of the members of a society (as men)," "a single common legislation (as subjects)," and, the "law of their equality (as citizens)."[57] But it defied France and other colonial powers by declaring itself an empire while it acknowledged all Haitians as "black," prohibited "all whites" from owning property and confiscated all property from any "white Frenchman," declared no predominant religion, tolerated freedom of worship, made marriage a purely civil act and authorised divorce.

Dessalines, was designated as "emperor," "avenger" and "deliverer" of the new state. In the preamble, the constitution declared Haiti as an equal sovereign whose source was a "Supreme Being" and nature, despite being so "unjustly and for so long a time considered as outcast children."

The first article departed from the colonial name of Saint Domingue to "the empire of Hayti" and declared the island "a free state sovereign and independent of any other power in the universe." The following articles upheld equality as their main purpose: slavery was "forever abolished" (art. 2); "the Citizens of Hayti are brothers at home; equality in the eyes of the law is incontestably acknowledged, and there cannot exist any titles, advantages, or privileges, other than those necessarily resulting from the consideration and reward of services rendered to liberty and independence" (art. 3); and "the law is the same to all, whether it punishes, or whether it protects" (art. 4).

Citizenship, however, was limited to black males who possessed a mechanic skill and could be lost by emigration, naturalisation in another country, criminal condemnation, bankruptcy or by not being "a good father, good son, a good husband, and especially a good soldier" (art. 9). The constitution made an important racial distinction: "Haytians shall

[57] First definitive article of Perpetual Peace as found in Kant, Immanuel, *Project for a Perpetual Peace. A Philosphical Essay*, London, printed by S. Couchman for Vernor and Hood, 1796.

hence be known by only by the generic appellation of Blacks" and "no white man of whatever nation he may be, shall put his foot on this territory with the title of master or proprietor, neither shall he in future acquire any property therein" (art. 12). Exceptions to this article included naturalized white women and their children, as well as the Germans and Poles who had defected from Napoleon's army and remained in Haiti.

The constitution designated Dessalines as emperor and commander in chief of the army with the authority to name his successor. In continuity with the declaration of independence, it also stated that Haiti was a non-imperial empire as "the Emperor shall never form any enterprise with the views of making conquests, nor to disturb the peace and interior administration of foreign colonies." The desire for recognition was made clear in the constitution's final words: "we present it to the friends of liberty, to philanthropists of all countries as a signal pledge of the Divine Bounty, who in the course of his immortal decrees, has given us an opportunity of breaking our fetters, and of constituting ourselves a people, free civilized and independent."

4. The Quest for Recognition

After declaring independence, Haitians lived in a constant state of flux both internally and externally. Haitian territory was still disputed among different factions of revolutionary leaders despite a functioning constitutional process. In 1807 Alexandre Pétion, signer of the declaration of independence and the constitution of 1805, was chosen president by a constituent assembly and re-elected three more times. In 1816, the constitution was modified for him to be "president for life," with the right of naming a successor. His purpose to unite the Haitian territory made for continual strife with Christophe with much internal dissension among his followers.[58] Externally, Haiti's declaration of independence and new constitution did not bring a cosmopolitan embrace but the contrary: an active rejection of recognition of the new state. The nervousness that ran through the slave states of Europe and the United States since the revolution began in 1791 was augmented to an intense fear. The terrifying possibility of another Haiti and the power exerted by France through the Napoleonic wars made diplomatic recognition of Haiti virtually impossible. In 1805 and 1806, the United States, for example, imposed a trade embargo on Haiti under pressure from the French government.[59]

58 Mackenzie, Charles, *Notes on Haiti, Made During a Residence in That Republic*, 1st ed., London, H. Colburn and R. Bentley, 1830, 2 Vols., pp. 80-81.

59 Matthewson, Tim, "Jefferson and the Nonrecognition of Haiti," 140 *Proceedings of the American Philosophical Society* (1996) pp. 22-48, p. 31.

4.1. Haiti's Paid Recognition and the "Double Debt"

Former plantation owners exercised constant pressure on France's policy towards Haiti. The *anciens colons* carried out incessant political, legal and publicity strategies aimed at recovering the colony and at obtaining compensation. Exhausted with the constant threat of recolonisation and re-enslavement, President Pétion proposed the first indemnity solution in 1814. He anticipated indemnifying France in exchange for Haiti's recognition as a small price to pay.[60] The French government accepted the proposal but the following negotiation sessions failed due to their disparate claims and France's offensive threats.[61] On July 4, 1825, fourteen army ships docked in Port-au-Prince with a final offer that then president Boyer could not refuse. The royal ordinance signed by King Charles X on April 17, 1825 would concede "full and entire independence" under two unilaterally imposed conditions: French ships would pay half of docking rights for future commerce and the citizens of Haiti would compensate former plantation owners with 150 million Francs.[62] The indemnity amount was five times France's total annual budget and almost twice as much of the 80 million that the United States paid Napoleon for Louisiana, the sum which Pétion had argued would be the maximum they were willing to pay.

Unable to pay the first instalment, the Haitian government was forced to take a 30 million loan from a French bank, with another 30 million for principal at a 6% annual interest rate and an additional 6 million for handling fees. Thus the indemnity payment turned into Haiti's "double debt." Another loan was taken to finance the second instalment, but this time under yearly payments of 6.5 million for 35 years.[63] The Haitian government once again defaulted.[64]

By 1829, the planters were enraged at not having been paid their legitimate indemnity claims. They hired the law firm of Dalloz & Cie to evaluate the French government's responsibility in their delayed payment. The firm's report recognised that Haiti had accepted to pay an amount that was beyond its resources but it also insisted that the

60 Brière, Jean-François, *Haïti Et La France, 1804-1848. Le Rêve Brisé*, Paris, Éd. Karthala, 2008, p. 65.

61 For a brief history of the negotiations see Beauvois, Frédérique, "L'indemnité De Saint-Domingue. 'Dette D'indépendance' Ou 'Rançon De L'esclavage'?," 10 *French Colonial History* (2009), pp. 109-124.

62 MM. Delagrange Dalloz, Hennequin, Dupin, *Consultation de MM. Dalloz, Delagrange, Hennequin, Dupin Jeune et autres jurisconsultes, pour les anciens colons de St-Domingue (15 avril 1829)*, Paris, Impr. de Vve Agasse, 1829, p. 15.

63 Brière, *Haïti Et La France, 1804-1848.*

64 *Ibid.*

150 million was only a fraction (12%) of the losses suffered by the planters. Dalloz argued that the French government was directly responsible for the indemnity, even if Haiti defaulted because it had abandoned its sovereignty, had disposed of their private property and had legitimated a dismemberment of their country that had been violently effectuated.[65]

As Haiti defaulted, it entered into debt renegotiations between 1834 and 1838, opposed by the planters who argued their full indemnity right had been violated. It was only in 1838 that France fully recognized Haiti, but with a new balance of 60 million to be paid in thirty years with loans from French banks. Haiti continued to borrow over 166 million francs to pay the 60 million francs with more than half used to pay bank commissions, fees and interest. If the 26,000 planters or their descendants had received a proportional payment they would receive only 116 francs per year for thirty years. If they had received the full amount of the initial indemnity in one payment, they would have received a total of 58,000 francs.[66] These sums indicate that France's recognition of Haiti was not more than a symbolic gesture to save face after having lost their most profitable colony. France's final payment was made in 1910 after almost a century of crippling debt.

4.2. Opposition to Haiti's Recognition and the Panama Congress

Towards the end of 1815, Simón Bolívar landed in Aux Cayes looking for support from the Haitian government for his independence actions in Venezuela. President Pétion received Bolívar and re-equipped him with men, money, muskets, gunpowder and a printing press. Before sailing back to Venezuela, Bolívar thanked Pétion and asked to publicly acknowledge him as the "author of our liberty" in the independence proclamation. Pétion responded by requesting that Bolívar grant freedom to all those under the yoke of slavery but requested to be anonymous so as not to acquire the Spanish crown as a new enemy of Haiti.[67]

Bolívar's oath became an opportunity to recruit men for his army. Soon after he landed in Venezuela in 1816, he decreed a conditional state of "absolute freedom for slaves who have been under the Spanish domination for three centuries." Women, children, invalids and the elderly were exempted but men 14 to 60 years of age could become citizens if they joined the Venezuelan rebel forces. If males decided not

65 Mm. Dalloz, *Consultation De Mm. Dalloz, Delagrange, Hennequin, Dupin Jeune Et Autres Jurisconsultes, Pour Les Anciens Colons De St-Domingue (15 Avril 1829).*

66 Beauvois, "L'indemnité De Saint-Domingue", p. 199.

67 Bolívar, Simón, "Latin-American Correspondence author(S). Simon Bolivar and Alexandre Sabès Pétion," 7 *Phylon (1940-1956)* (1946), p. 196.

to "defend their own liberty" they would continue to be slaves as would their children, wife and elderly parents.[68] One month later, Bolívar proclaimed citizenship for emancipated slaves though the conditional status of the previous decree still held but Spanish troops defeated Bolívar's. Therefore, Bolívar returned to Haiti in search for more support where he obtained supplies and volunteers for the second time. On 28 December 1816, Bolívar sailed from Haiti and soon thereafter won the final independence battle in Caracas, and claimed Pétion as the "author of our independence."

A few years later, on December 2, 1823 United States President James Monroe issued a policy statement declaring that "the American continents, by the free and independent condition which they have assumed and maintained, are henceforth not to be considered as subjects for future colonisation by any European powers." The Monroe Doctrine was taken seriously by Bolívar and other Latin American leaders as signalling a continental effort to oppose re-colonisation of their territories by the Holly Alliance and to deter United States imperialist interventions.

Bolívar planned to hold an amphictyonic congress in Panamá of the newly independent states in order to form a permanent union that would serve as council and mediator on regional conflicts and promote and interpret regional treaties.[69] He expressed ideas of regional integration as early as 1815, but it was only after Spanish recognition of several states that he decided to go forth with the congress. Invitations to participate in an "American Confederation" were issued on December 7, 1824 to Colombia, Mexico, Peru, Chile and Buenos Aires.[70] Though the heading of the invitation mentioned all of the American republics, the text clarified that it was a matter of urgency to unite the former Spanish colonies in an effort to consolidate their governments eternally, celebrate the "power of Columbus' world" and carry out diplomatic alliances and international treaties.[71]

---

68 Bolívar, Simón, "Decreto Sobre Libertad De Los Esclavos – Carúpano, 2 De Junio De 1816," in Vicente Lecuna (ed.), *Bolívar, Simón. Proclamas Y Discursos Del Libertador, 1811-1830*, Biblioteca De Autores Y Temas Mirandinos, 1983, pp. 148-149.

69 Vieira Posada, Edgar, *La Integración De América Latina. Del Congreso Anfictiónico De Panamá En 1826 a Una Comunidad Latinoamericana O Sudamericana De Naciones En El Año 2010*, Colección Biblioteca Del Profesional, Bogotá, Editorial Pontificia Universidad Javeriana, 2004, p. 43.

70 Bushnell, David, *Simón Bolívar. Hombre De Caracas, Proyecto De América. Una Biografía*, 1ra. ed., Colección Historias Americanas, Buenos Aires, Editorial Biblos, 2002, p. 130.

71 Bolívar, Simón, *Coleccion De Documentos Relativos Á La Vida Pública Del Libertador De Columbia Y Del Perú Para Servir a La Historia De La Independencia*

Bolívar chose the Isthmus of Panama as the congress location because it was geographically equidistant between Mexico and Buenos Aires, its symbolic value as centre of the globe and its idealisation the origins of American integration surpassing the Isthmus of Corinth, where the Greeks had held their amphyctionic congresses.[72]

The Haitian government expected an invitation in hope that it would lead to her recognition by the United States. Bolívar did not originally invite the United States because he wanted an alliance of the Spanish American nations that would counteract its growing hegemony and recognition by Britain. Despite Bolívar's initial hesitation General Santander, president of Colombia, took it upon himself to invite the United States. Only the government of Guatemala proposed that Haiti be invited but it received a heated rejection from the United States, Colombia and Peru.

President Adams announced that he had accepted an invitation for the United States to send a representative to Panama and would like the opinion of the Congress on how to proceed and who to represent them. The US delegates' priority was to preserve US neutrality in relation to Haiti and the Spanish American states. Adams was concerned "whether Hayti ought to be recognized by them as an independent State; and whether any decision taken, in that respect, should be joint, or each Power behest to pursue the dictates of its own policy."[73] Adams considered Haiti's "nature and the manner of the establishment of the governing power in that island", "the little respect which is there shown to other races than the African" as well as its re-colonisation through the French indemnity payment as limiting the possibilities of US recognition:

> If the colonial relation may be correctly described to be the monopoly of the commerce of the colony, enjoyed by the parent State, it cannot be affirmed that Hayti has not voluntarily, by that arrangement, consented to its revival [...]. Prior to the conclusion of that arrangement, Hayti enjoyed, no matter how established, a sort of independence [...]. By that arrangement, she has voluntarily [...] changed her character, and has become, to say the least, not an independent State. Under the actual circumstances of Hayti, the President does not think that it would be proper, at this time, to recognize it as a new State.[74]

Del Suramérica. Tomo Tercero, 3, Carácas, Impr. de Devisme Hermanos, 1826, p. 175.

72 *Ibid.*, p. 178.

73 March 15, 1826.

74 Register of the Debates in Congress of the second Session of the twentieth Congress, volume V, Appendix to Gales & Seaton's Register, *Documents relative to the Panama Mission*, Washington, 1830, p. 47.

A more heated debate in the US Congress focused on the issue of slavery and the recognition of Haiti. With respect to the first issue, Senator Hayne, representing the Southern States, regarded that slavery "must be considered and treated entirely as a domestic question":

> Let me solemnly declare, once for all, that the Southern States never will permit, and never can permit, any interference whatever in their domestic concerns; and that the very day on which the unhallowed attempt shall be made by the authorities of the federal government, we will consider ourselves as driven from the Union. It is a subject of too delicate a nature – too vitally interesting to us – to be discussed abroad. On this subject, we committed an error when we entered into treaties with Great Britain and Colombia for the suppression of the slave trade. That error has been happily corrected.[75]

With respect to the recognition of Haiti, Haynes was also very emphatic:

> It is altogether hopeless that we could, if we would, prevent the acknowledgment of Haytien independence by the Spanish American states. Our policy with regard to Hayti is plain. We never can acknowledge her independence [...] Let our government direct all our ministers in South America and Mexico to protest against the independence of Hayti. But let us not go into council on the slave trade and Hayti. These are subjects not to be discussed anywhere. There is not a nation on the globe with whom I would consult on that subject; and least of all, the new republics.[76]

Several other Congressmen opposed US participation in Panama because of the Spanish Americans' "different manner of regarding Africans," the possibility of severing relations with Spanish American states,[77] and because the black skin of South Americans impeded their capacity for administering a republican form of government.[78]

Spanish American opposition was equally harsh. Colombia's Minister of Foreign Affairs Gual showed "great repugnance against maintain-

---

75 United States Congress (1826), Executive Proceedings on the Panama Mission: March 14, 1826. Register of Debates in Congress: Comprising the Leading Debates and Incidents of The First Session of The Nineteenth Congress, Washington, Gales & Seaton, Vol. II, p. 165.

76 The debates in the several State conventions, on the adoption of the Federal Constitution as recommended by the General convention at Philadelphia, in 1787 together with the Journal of the Federal Convention, Luther Martin's Letter, Yate's Minute, Congressional Opinions, and others, Vol. IV, Washington, 1836, pp. 483-485.

77 Congressional Debates, Vol. II William Jay, View of the action of the Federal Government in Behalf of Slavery, published by the American-Anti-slavery society, 1839, pp. 176, 177, 178.

78 The American Whig Review, new series Vol. VIII, New York, Published at 120 Nassau Street, 1851, pp. 156-157.

ing with Haiti [...] relations [...] generally observed among civilized nations." He instructed the Colombian delegates not recognize Haiti. Despite Bolívar's earlier debt to Haiti, President Santander was adamant that by recognising "a republic of colour, it would bring negative consequences to the cause of the Spanish American states before the European powers." The Peruvian minister Hipólito Unanue argued that the presence of Haitian delegates would spread the idea of freedom throughout the continent and cause a disastrous racial revolution.

Several states did not send delegates or could not participate. One of the US representatives died on the way (Ricardo C. Anderson), the other arrived late (John Sargeant), and a third waited for the congress to be moved to Mexico (Joel R. Poinsett). On June 22, 1826, eight delegates from Central America, Colombia, México and Peru met and held ten sessions in which they approved several treaties, discussed the issues of slavery, Cuban and Puerto Rican independence, and decided to create a continental army.

Bolívar acknowledged that the American states must have Spanish and other European support to be accepted in their sphere of the world. He promoted the idea of unification of principles, forms of government and institutions as proof of internal stability and civilisation because:

> She [Europe] expects us, as republicans, to be virtuous and wise; she demands firmness, stability, and permanence in our institutions. She will not forgive the errors of youth, for she holds that a people which aspires to be free must be expert, strong, and well informed regarding its best interests [...] If they find our governments firm and stable and possessed of sufficient willingness to forget the past [...] it is almost certain that recognition will be granted with the inestimable benefits of peace and acknowledgement of the freedom and independence of our republics.[79]

The US Congress continued to reject Haiti's recognition despite receiving many petitions favouring recognition between 1825 and 1860 because of Haiti's growing importance as a trade partner and progress of the abolition movement. The United States finally recognized Haitian independence in 1863 under Abraham Lincoln.

5. Conclusion: Haiti's Challenge to the Cosmopolitan Imagination

Kant's cosmopolitan ideal imagined states participating in a federation of peoples in which every state, even the smallest, could expect to derive its security and rights "from a united power and the law governed

[79] Bolívar, Simón, *Selected Writings of Bolívar*, New York, Colonial Press, 1951, p. 253.

decisions of a united will."[80] However, his utopian vision was grounded in his theory of race that answered the philosophical inquiry of "what is man" in the cosmopolitical sense.[81] Seen from this duality, the contemporary event of the revolution on the island of Saint Domingue and Haitian independence could only be read in two ways: 1) either that the "black race" could not achieve or contribute to the cosmopolitan ideal because they were inherently incapable of progress and sovereignty, or 2) that they contributed to achieving the cosmopolitan ideal by acting out their predetermined condition of servitude. Though Haiti complied with the constitutional requirements and interest in being part of a federation of states as Kant proposed, in reality recognition by her most important neighbours and trading partners was delayed or burdened by the weight of racism, the legitimacy of slavery and the continued profitability of the slave trade during the early half of the nineteenth century.

80 Kant, "Perpetual Peace", p. 47.

81 Crampton, Jeremy W. and Elden, Stuart, *Space, Knowledge and Power. Foucault and Geography*, Aldershot, England/Burlington VT, Ashgate, 2007, p. 43.

How British Colonialism Underdeveloped Nigeria

Adedokun Olatokunbo OGUNFOLU*

1. Introduction

Portugal was the first European state to make contact with the territory of present-day Nigeria in the fifteenth century. The Kingdom of Benin traded with Portugal in pepper and subsequently slaves. The intrusion of more than European states accelerated the slave trade. It was dominated by Britain and Portugal, and led to the export of between 30 million to 40 million young Africans – mainly Nigerians – to sugar plantations in the Americas. Africa has still not recovered from this most monumental loss of human resources in human history.[1] The European-controlled slave trade led to wars which decimated agriculture and economic progress in Africa. The industrialisation of Britain changed the demand from slaves to palm oil,[2] to fuel its industries and provide raw material for its industrial products and the ambitious project to make West Africa the market for the surplus produce of British industrialisation. This set the stage for the scramble for Africa and its physical conquest by European powers that used the 1884-1885 Berlin

* I greatly appreciate the kind support of Mónica García-Salmones and Professor Omoniyi Adewoye, the foremost Nigerian legal historian and a former Deputy Vice-Chancellor of the University of Ibadan, Ibadan, Nigeria.

1 Rodney, Walter, *West Africa and the Atlantic Slave Trade*, Nairobi, East African Publishing House, 1967; Lord Lugard, "Slavery in All Its Forms," 6 *The Journal of the International African Institute* (1933), pp. 1-14; Baron Lugard, "Native Policy in East Africa," 9 *Foreign Affairs* (1930), pp. 65-78.

2 "Great Britain abolished the slave trade in 1807 [...] Once abolition was legislated, Great Britain had to effectively suppress the slave trade if palm oil was to emerge as West Africa's chief export... an anti-slavery patrol force of the British Navy, the West African Squadron was inaugurated in 1810 [...] In these places, British efforts were relatively successful. Palm oil began to supplant slaves when the export of the latter was forcibly prevented. In 1806, Liverpool received 150 tons of palm oil from West Africa. By 1819, the quantity jumped to 3,000 tons; to 13,000 tons by 1839." Ehrensaft, Philip, "The Political Economy of Informal Empire in Pre-Colonial Nigeria, 1807-1884," 6 *Canadian Journal of African Studies/Revue Canadienne des Études Africaines* (1972), pp. 451-490, p. 456.

Conference to formalise the balkanisation of Africa into their colonial projects of state-building,[3] and exploitation of African resources.[4]

British colonial policies formulated to exploit the resources of its Nigerian colony, resulted in the creation of some indigenous political elites programed to protect British colonial interests and the trend continued after independence.[5] This was not surprising as England has had a predatory pedigree for centuries in Africa as Adam Smith noted in 1776, of the English Royal African Company:

> In 1732, after having been for many years losers by the trade of carrying negroes to the West Indies, they at last resolved to give it up altogether; to sell to the private traders to America the negroes which they had purchased upon the coast; and to employ their servants in a trade to the inland parts of Africa for gold dust, elephant teeth, dying drugs, &c.[6]

Even though Japanese colonialism was brutal and its colonial templates in Taiwan and Korea stood apart from the colonized peoples; Japan in contrast with predatory Britain, created in the two colonies: "complex financial systems, as well as heavy industry, including steel, chemicals, hydroelectric facilities, metallurgy, and transportation."[7] The visionary developmental state was crucial in the industrialisation of nineteenth century Japan and Germany (then known as Prussia) through the adaptation to autochthonous conditions, of imported institutions and factories from other countries.[8] A responsible state provides basic

---

3 Uzoigwe, G.N., "European Partition and Conquest of Africa. An Overview," in A. Adu Boahen (ed.), *General History of Africa. Volume VII Africa under Colonial Domination 1880-1935*, Abridged Edition, Ibadan, Heinemann Educational Books LTD, 1990, pp. 10-24.

4 Ayandele, E.A., *The Missionary Impact on Modern Nigeria, 1842-1914*, London, Longmans, 1966; Ajayi, J.F.A., *Christian Missions in Nigeria 1841-1891*, London, Longmans, 1966; Ajayi, J.F.A., *A Thousand Years in West African History*, Ibadan, Ibadan University Press, 1967; Tamuno, T.N., *The Evolution of the Nigerian State. The Southern Phase, 1898-1914* London, Longmans, 1972; Ikime, O., *Niger Delta Rivalry and the European Presence 1884-1936*, London, Longmans, 1969.

5 Laitin, D.D., "Hegemony and Religious Conflict. British Imperial Control and Political Cleavages in Yorubaland," in P.B. Evans, D. Rueschemeyer and T. Skocpol (eds.), *Bringing the State Back In*, Cambridge, Cambridge University Press, 1985, pp. 285-316.

6 Smith, Adam, *An Inquiry into the Nature and Causes of the Wealth of Nations*, New York, Modern Library Edition, 1937, p. 701.

7 Pempel, T.J., "The Developmental Regime in a Changing World," in Meredith WooCumings (ed.), *The Developmental State*, New York, Cornell University Press, 1998, pp. 137-181, p. 163.

8 Chang, Ha-Joon, "The Economic Theory of the Developmental State," in Woo-Cumings (ed.), *The Developmental State*, pp. 182-199, p. 195.

services like education and healthcare for its citizens as well as access to affordable housing for a minimum standard of living.[9]

The British invasion of Africa was supposedly "not colonization but the prevention of the slave trade, organized on the basis of a Declaration from Vienna in 1815 and through bilateral treaties that granted Britain the privilege of patrolling the African coasts in search of vessels suspected of slaving".[10] From 1945 to 1951, humanitarian Britain looted £140 million in its colonies and put "in only about £40 million under the Colonial Development and Welfare Acts".[11] The focus of this essay will be Nigeria's destructive experience of British colonialism. The conquest of the Ijebu nation in 1892 is used to demonstrate the devastating colonial effects wreaked by Britain on a proud and prosperous people.

2. The Introduction of English Law into Nigeria

1863 was the year English law was introduced into Nigeria though Ordinance No. 3 of Lagos colony.[12] This provided that:

> all laws and statutes which were enforced within the realm of England on the 1st day of January, 1863, not being inconsistent with any Ordinance in force in the colony, or with any rule made in pursuance of any such Ordinance should be deemed and taken to be in force in the colony and should be applied in the administration of justice, so far as local circumstances would permit.[13]

The entity now known as Nigeria had for centuries before Britain's imperialist conquest evolved complex and sophisticated strands of customary law amongst its hundreds of nationalities, which Professors Elias[14] and Allot[15] have researched extensively in the past. These strands

---

9 Marshall, T.H., *Citizenship and Social Class, and other essays*, Cambridge, Cambridge University Press, 1950, p. 54.

10 Koskenniemi, Martti, *The Gentle Civilizer of Nations. The Rise and Fall of International Law 1870-1960*, Cambridge, Cambridge University Press, 2002, p. 111.

11 Davidson, Basil, *The Black Man's Burden. Africa and the Curse of the Nation-State*, New York, Three Rivers Press, 1992, p. 219.

12 Park, A.E.W., *The Sources of Nigerian Law*, Lagos, African Universities Press, 1963, p. 16.

13 Reproduced in Asei, John O., *Introduction to Nigerian Legal system*, Ibadan, Sam Bookman Publishers, 1998, p. 95.

14 Elias, T.O., "Colonial Courts and the Doctrine of Judicial Precedent," 18 *The Modern Law Review* (1955), pp. 356-370; Elias, T.O., *The Nigerian Legal System*, London, Routledge & Kegan Paul Ltd, 1963; Elias, T.O., *British Colonial Law A comparative study of the Interaction between English and Local Laws in British Dependencies*, London, Stevens & Sons Limited, 1961.

15 See for example proceedings of the conference on "Integration of Customary and Modern Legal Systems in Africa" directed by Dr Antony Allot at the Institute of

of customary law had a common character which – with the exception of the written Sharia Islamic law used in most of Northern Nigeria – lay in its unwritten nature.[16] Britain's imperialist conquest of Lagos in 1861 marked the beginning of a forced grafting of the common law upon the existing legal traditions of what is now known as Nigeria. The Romans and Normans knew the efficacy of law as an instrument for lubricating the stranglehold of empire in Rome and England respectively.[17] "The story of British advent in Nigeria since about the middle of the nineteenth century has been told by many writers. What has not been emphasised sufficiently is the role of the law in Britain's conquest."[18] The law was employed in the form of treaties to pacify the indigenous populace. This was the period when the Industrial Revolution had made the use of slaves unprofitable for Britain's economy and in order to maximise the benefits of industrialisation the slave trade sustaining other imperial competitors had to be stopped. "By this time, the overseas slave had become anachronistic and irrelevant to Britain's economy and it had been abolished as far back as 1807. As a result of the Industrial Revolution, products like palm oil, ivory, cotton and indigo were more useful to Britain's economy than slaves."[19] It was ostensibly under the guise of suppressing the slave trade which destroyed African economy, in which "Britain had previously taken as great a hand as any other nation"[20] that Lagos was colonised by Britain. The treaty signed with the hapless King Dosunmu of Lagos read as follows:

> In order that the Queen of England may be the better enabled to assist, defend, and protect the inhabitants of Lagos, and to put an end to the slave trade in this and the neighbouring countries, and to prevent the destructive wars so frequently undertaken by Dahomey and others for the capture of slaves, I, Docemo, do, with the consent and advice of my council, give, transfer, and by these presents, grant and confirm unto the Queen of Great

---

African studies at University of Ife from 24 August to 29 August 1964 reported in the 8 *Journal of African Law* (1964), pp. 55-56; Allot, A.N., "Towards a definition of 'Absolute ownership'," 5 *Journal of African Law* (1961), pp. 99-102; Allot, A.N., "The Authority of English Decisions in Colonial Courts," 1 *Journal of African Law* (1957), pp. 23-39.

16 Obilade, A.O., *The Nigerian Legal System*, Ibadan, Spectrum Law Publishing, 2000, p. 83.

17 See the work of the foremost Nigerian legal historian, Adewoye, Omoniyi, *The Judicial System in Southern Nigeria, 1854-1954 Law and Justice in a Dependency*, New Jersey, Humanities Press, 1977, p. 12.

18 *Ibid.*, p. 11.

19 Atanda, J.A., *An Introduction to Yoruba History*, Ibadan, Ibadan University Press, 1980, p. 41.

20 Roberts-Wray, Sir Kenneth, *Commonwealth and Colonial Law*, London, Stevens & Sons, 1966, p. 792.

> Britain, her heirs and successors for ever, the port and Island of Lagos, with all the rights, profits and revenue as the direct, full, and absolute dominion and sovereignty of the said port, island and premises, with all the royalties thereof, freely, fully, entirely and absolutely. I do also covenant and grant that the quiet and peaceable possession thereof shall, with all possible speed, be freely and effectively delivered to the Queen of Great Britain, or such person as Her Majesty shall thereunto appoint for her use in the performance of this grant; the inhabitants of the said island and territories, as the Queen's subjects, and under her sovereignty, Crown, jurisdiction and government being still suffered to live there.[21]

The British interest consisted purely of looting Nigeria's natural resources through the Royal Niger Company in the form of 360 treaties with coerced indigenous communities:[22]

> They purported in recognition of the 'benefit accorded to our country and people by the intercourse with the company' to cede 'the whole of our territory to the company, their heirs and assigns forever'. Power was also ceded to the company to settle all native disputes arising from any cause whatever. The ceding chiefs undertook not to enter into any war with other tribes without the sanction of the company and further not to have any intercourse with any stranger or foreigners except through the company which was to have power at its discretion to exclude any such stranger or foreigners.[23]

The colonial authorities appropriated the land and mineral resources of Nigeria through the States Land Law of 1 April 1918. In 1878, Sir James Fitzstephen drafted a criminal code to codify the criminal law elements of English common law, but the British parliament did not enact it. The rejected British criminal code became the major component of the 1899 criminal code of the state of Queensland in Australia. In 1904, Lugard, the British Governor of the northern part of present-day Nigeria, foisted the Queensland code on Northern Nigeria, and in 1914 the Northern criminal code was foisted on Southern Nigeria after the amalgamation of Northern and Southern Nigeria in 1914 by Lugard.[24] On 24 November 1915, the Governor of Nigeria, Lugard, promulgated the Collective Punishment Law, which provided for the imposition of fines on villages and communities that sheltered or colluded with a person declared a criminal by the colonial administration.

---

21 Reproduced in Nwabueze, B.O., *Constitutional Law of the Nigerian Republic*, London, Butterworths, 1964, p. 9.

22 *Ibid.*, p. 10.

23 *Ibid.*

24 Okonkwo, C.O., *Okonkwo and Naish on Criminal Law in Nigeria*, Ibadan, Spectrum Law Publishing, 1990, pp. 4-5.

3. The Berlin Conference of 1884-1885

French lobbying, King Leopold's "philanthropic" campaigns and the German quest for African colonies led Prince Bismarck of Germany to invite Austria-Hungary, Belgium, Denmark, Spain, the United States, France, Great Britain, Italy, the Netherlands, Portugal, Russia, Sweden and Norway, and Turkey as a concert of powers to a conference in Berlin which he declared open at 2 p.m. on Saturday 15 November 1884 and closed on 26 February 1885.[25] The aim of this conference was to lay down ground rules for the almost completed conquest of African territories by European military powers. Bismarck's opening address stated that the main goals of the conference were free trade in the Congo, modalities for valid territorial annexation in the years to come and free navigation through the Congo and Niger rivers. Bismarck declared that issues of sovereignty were not to be discussed, while service to humanity and peace were the *raison d'être* of the conference. Articles 26 to 33 of Chapter V of the Act of Berlin provided for the free navigation of merchant ships through the river Niger.[26] Chapter VI was the kernel of the Berlin Conference and was captioned: "Declaration relative to the essential Conditions to be observed in order that new Occupations on the Coasts of the African Continent may be held to be effective."[27] It stipulated in Article 34 that:

> Any power which henceforth takes possession of a tract of land on the coasts of the African Continent outside of its present possessions, or which being hitherto without such possessions, shall acquire them, as well as the Power which assumes a protectorate there, shall accompany the respective act with a notification thereof, addressed to the other Signatory Powers of the present Act, in order to enable them, if need be, to make good any claims of their own.[28]

The most prescient observation about the ramifications of the Berlin Conference for empire, peace and war was made on 15 November 1884 by the *Economist*, which stated that:

> The English public is not interested in the Congo. The majority of electors know little about the area and are completely unaware of any bearing it may have on British trade. Among the more informed, there is a certain disgust with the colonies and particularly with the African enterprises from the Egyptian expedition to the operations in Bechuanaland. They watch the

[25] Gavin, R.J. and Betley, J.A., *The Scramble for Africa. Documents on the Berlin West African Conference and Related Subjects 1884/1885*, Ibadan, Ibadan University Press, 1973, pp. 128-301.

[26] *Ibid.*, p. 297-299.

[27] *Ibid.*, p. 300.

[28] *Ibid.*, p. 300-301.

Congo affair with more curiosity as to the machinations of Germany than anything else. Nonetheless, to those with an historical eye, the Conference is an important incident. It represents the first time that Europe as an informal group has assumed any jurisdiction over a large uncivilized area [...] This distribution of land is perhaps the last to be made, the remainder of the globe being already parcelled out. Any further changes [...] will probably be the result of war.[29]

4. Humanitarian Britain

Following King Henry VIII's break with the Roman Catholic Church, the English became free of any restraint over trade formerly exercised by the pope. This led to their attempting to break the Portuguese monopoly of trade in West Africa, including the slave trade. Slavery, the greatest tragedy of imperial Britain, commenced in full swing and eventually led to a backlash by humanitarian elements within its society against this horrendous trade.[30] "Britain sent manufactured goods to West Africa to exchange for slaves who were shipped to the West Indies in return for sugar and similar tropical products."[31] Slave labour was pivotal to the development of the cotton industry in Britain and the United States.[32] It was the binary technology of cotton production that laid the basis for the Industrial Revolution and the digital age. The first English expedition to West Africa was captained by Windham in 1533, but it returned to Plymouth with only 40 men after 100 had died at sea. It was not until 1562 that John Hawkins led a successful trip to Sierra Leone. He came back with 300 slaves and was knighted by Queen Elizabeth.

The English slave trade was officially stopped on 31 March 1808 when a British Act of Parliament to this effect came into force. British slave owners were compensated in the sum of £20 million by Britain. She also paid Portugal £300,000 and Spain £400,000 to acquire the right to search their ships for slaves. Slavery continued in certain areas in present-day Nigeria until 1850.[33] From 1787 to 1807, William Wilber-

---

29 Louis, William Roger, "The Berlin Congo Conference," in Prosser Gifford and William Roger Louis (eds.), *France and Britain in Africa. Imperial Rivalry and Colonial Rule*, New Haven/London, Yale University Press, 1971, pp. 167-220 and pp. 214-215.

30 Perham, Margery, *The Colonial Reckoning. The End of Imperial Rule in Africa In the Light of British Experience*, New York, Alfred A. Knopf, 1962, pp. 128-133.

31 Chamberlain, M.E., *The Scramble for Africa*, Harlow, Longman, 1974, p. 18.

32 Luxemburg, Rosa, *The Accumulation of Capital* (1913), Agnes Schwarzschild (ed.), London, Routledge and Kegan Paul Ltd, 1951, p. 362.

33 Awolowo, Obafemi, *The People's Republic*, Ibadan, Oxford University Press, 1968, pp. 6-8.

force and his fellow British compatriots championed the abolition of the slave trade in England. Granville Sharp was also a prominent abolitionist who fought for the rights of Somerset, a slave who escaped from his captors.[34] The defeat of Britain by its settlers in North America in 1776 birthed a new policy of commercial pursuit as opposed to the expensive policy of colonisation. Lord Shelburne, Britain's Secretary of State declared in 1783 that "we prefer commerce to dominion".[35] British commercial interests dovetailed into the slave trade abolition movement. Unlike the Catholic Church and the French middle classes, which were preoccupied with domestic turmoil, the English Anglican Church and middle class were interested in the abolition of the slave trade. "Liberal and soon Free Trading Britain linked its anti-slave-trade passion to its need for commercial expansion."[36]

> Nothing is more revealing in this matter than the numerous treaties concluded between 1830 and 1880 with the Negro chiefs of the coast. Almost all British texts insist on four points: the abolition of the slave trade, freedom to trade for all white men, help for ships in peril and a share in wrecks, and the protection of missionaries. Cession of sovereignty is rare, and when it occurs it is dictated by local conditions: the need to repress smuggling in the slave trade, or the need to augment revenue by the control customs. This was so in the case of the annexation of Lagos in 1861 and its extension to Badagri, Palma, and Lekki in 1863. [...] Franco-African agreements on the contrary always start by the granting of political sovereignty to France, and generally do not deal with slavery. They often seek a trade monopoly, which they frequently do not dare to claim openly from the Negro chief, who prefers British goods. It is clear from this comparison that the aims of the two countries were not the same; for the British they were material advantage and the satisfaction of a humanitarian ideal; for the French a thirst for political prestige.[37]

British missionaries initially came to Nigeria in the fifteenth and sixteenth centuries. Forceful collaboration with indigenous political power by the British Empire was game theory at play, with the acquisition of control of vital trade routes along the tributaries of river Niger. This game was greatly facilitated by the missionaries who needed to use such tributaries to spread the Gospel.[38] "The work started with powder and

---

34 *Ibid.*, p. 54.

35 Brunschwig, Henri, "Anglophobia and French African Policy," in Gifford and Louis (eds.), *France and Britain in Africa*, pp. 3-34, p. 5.

36 *Ibid.*, p. 5.

37 *Ibid.*, p. 6.

38 Robinson, Ronald and Gallagher, John, "The Partition of Africa," in William Roger Louis (ed.), *Imperialism. The Robinson and Gallagher Controversy*, New York, New Viewpoints, 1976, pp. 73-128.

shot could be completed with the New Testament, and many who came to fight remained to pray."[39] Such collaborators were maintained until Britain manipulated electoral processes in its colonies and handed political power to autochthonous collaborators instructed to protect British economic interests at all costs. After a hiatus the missionaries returned in the 1840s and were very active in building health and educational facilities, unlike the nonchalant British colonial authorities, up until 1899.[40] The recidivist colonial pursuits of Britain cast aside Lord Shelburne's concerns (see above) and from 1815 to 1865 she enjoyed "virtually unchallenged maritime and imperial pre-eminence".[41] By 1860, Britain was responsible for 20% of global trade and 40% of global output in manufactured goods.[42] Between 1841 and 1851 Britain acquired the Gold Coast, Hong Kong, Labuan, Natal, New Zealand, Punjab and Sind. Between 1851 and 1870 it grabbed Basutoland, Berar, British Columbia, Burma, Kowloon, Griqualand, Lagos, Sierra Leone and the Transvaal.[43] Disraeli, a stalwart of the Conservative party, lamented in 1852 that: "The Colonies are millstones around our necks."[44] Disraeli's speech in 1872 at the Crystal Palace, London introduced the theme of the Tory party for the 1874 election year as "Imperial Federation".[45] Disraeli also became the Conservative party flag-bearer in 1874. So it came to be that imperial fervour permeated the latter part of nineteenth century Britain and infused the consciousness of its youth in the academic centres of Oxford and Cambridge with "Preservation of the Empire".[46] Between 1830 and 1880 British firms, supported by the British Royal Navy, monopolised trade in the Niger Delta region of present-day Nigeria. Unimaginable profits were realised from this endeavour under an informal British empire.[47]

---

39 *Ibid.*, p. 102.

40 Awolowo, *The People's Republic*, p. 59.

41 Kennedy, Paul, *The Rise and Fall of the Great Powers. Economic Change and Military Conflict from 1500 to 2000*, New York, Random House, 1987, p. 226.

42 *Ibid.*, p. 151.

43 Gallagher, John and Robinson, Ronald, "The Imperialism of Free Trade," in Louis (ed.), *Imperialism*, pp. 53-72.

44 Quoted in Lenin, V.I., *Imperialism. The Highest Stage of Capitalism*, New York, International Publishers, 1939, p. 78.

45 Schumpeter, Joseph A., "A Sociological Theory of Imperialism. An Atavism," in Robin W. Winks (ed.), *British Imperialism. Gold, God and Glory*, New York, Holt, Rinehart and Winston, 1963, pp. 82-91.

46 *Ibid.*, p. 85.

47 Dike, Onwuka K., *Trade and Politics in the Niger Delta 1830-1885. An Introduction to the Economic and Political History of Nigeria*, Oxford, Clarendon Press, 1956, pp. 47-203.

5. From British Humanitarianism to Empire-building and Globalisation

The years from 1815 to 1914 witnessed the expansion of the European colonies from 35% of the earth's surface to 85%, with Africa and Asia bearing the brunt of this assault.[48] The nineteenth century witnessed the interconnection of the economies of European colonial powers and their colonies, resulting in a "global economy".[49] Eric Hobsbawm has described the period from 1875 to 1914 as the "Age of Empire", stating that: "It was an era of unparalleled peace in the western world, which engendered an era of equally unparalleled world wars."[50] The conclusion of the Berlin Conference in 1885, rather than achieving its main goal of preventing European disputes over colonial territories,[51] instead gave rise to a mad rush by Britain and France to possess territories around the river Niger in the hinterland of present-day Nigeria. They only narrowly avoided war at Kishi, Bode, Okuta, Gbasora and Kiama on 30 May 1898, and it was the Niger Convention signed by France on 14 June 1898 that averted war.[52] Fashoda, situated in the upper Nile, was also another place where war was averted and France was humiliatingly forced to pull out, just as she did in the Niger (see above).[53] France was forced to eat humble pie by signing the Anglo-French Declaration of 21 March 1899, which bequeathed the territory from Darfur to Lake Chad to France and gave the Nile Basin to Britain.[54]

> The Egyptian affair had started off the 'scramble'. It had ended the standstill arrangement in Africa. It had run British policy into a noose held by Bismarck […] It would seem that the claiming of the Niger in 1884 was motivated neither by increased enthusiasm for enlarging the empire nor by pressing economic need to exploit the region. The incentive to advance here was no stronger than of old. It sprang from a passing concatenation of minor trade rivalries in West Africa with major changes of front by the Powers in Europe and the Mediterranean, mainly provoked by British blunders and difficulties in Egypt. The Liberals claimed the Lower Niger merely to prevent an existing field of British trade from disappearing behind French tariff

48 Said, Edward W., *Orientalism*, New York, Vintage Books, 2003, p. 41.

49 Hobsbawm, E.J., *The Age of Empire, 1875-1914*, New York, Pantheon Books, 1987, p. 62.

50 *Ibid.*, p. 9.

51 Anghie, Antony, *Imperialism, Sovereignty and the Making of International Law*, Cambridge, Cambridge University Press, 2005, p. 71.

52 Pakenham, Thomas, *The Scramble for Africa. White Man's Conquest of the Dark Continent from 1876 to 1912*, New York, Random House, 1991, pp. 504-523.

53 *Ibid.*, pp. 547-556.

54 Robinson, Ronald and Gallagher, John, with Denny, Alice, *Africa and the Victorians. The Climax of Imperialism*, New York, Anchor Books, 1968, pp. 339-378.

walls; and they limited their new commitment to this negative purpose. They had not decided to found an ambitious West African empire.[55]

Revenue from tariffs was a crucial factor in 1870 in the partition of West Africa between France and Britain, with Germany in control of Togo and Cameroon.[56] Britain and France together controlled 80% of European trade in West Africa and the need to agree on the sharing of profits led to the abortive Tariff Convention of 1882.[57] When the terms of the Convention became public knowledge in 1883, this had a large influence on Bismarck's decision to intervene in West Africa.[58] The steeplechase for colonial profits had begun. In spite of the Berlin Conference, France and Britain had to conclude tariff agreements in 1889 and 1890 up until the end of the nineteenth century in order to avert war.[59] At the Berlin Conference, "Africa's boundaries were determined and agreed not in the interests of the newly subjected peoples but so as to ensure peace and stability in the international relations of nineteenth century Europe".[60] According to British policy, physical control was not needed, but rather a protectorate wherein chartered companies would extract profits from the protectorate under the British flag. But the French and German territorial acquisition binges both before and after the Berlin Conference threatened British protectorates exemplified by the excessive greed and military weaknesses of British chartered companies which depended on British soldiers on leave or on mercenaries. Sir George Goldie, the founder of the Royal Niger Company in 1881 had recruited Lord Lugard in 1894,[61] to participate in what the French called the "Steeplechase for Nikki" during the scramble for Northern Nigeria between France and Britain".[62] The panacea for Britain was "indirect rule [...] of co-operative devolution"[63] of her African colonies and "the development of the material resources of the colonies for the

55 *Ibid.*, pp. 178-180.

56 Newbury, C.W., "The Tariff Factor in Anglo-French West Africa Partition," in Gifford and Louis (eds.), *France and Britain in Africa*, pp. 221-259.

57 *Ibid.*, pp. 226-234.

58 *Ibid.*, p. 234.

59 *Ibid.*, pp. 239-259.

60 Abraham, Garth, "Africa and its Boundaries, a Legal Overview from Colonialism to the African Union," in Jeffrey Herbst and Greg Mills (eds.), *Big African State*, Johannesburg, Wits University Press, 2006, pp. 273-290.

61 Lugard, Frederick D., "Northern Nigeria," 23 *The Geographical Journal* (1904), pp. 1-27.

62 Perham, Margery, "Lord Lugard. A Preliminary Evaluation," 20 *Africa Journal of the International African Institute* (1950), pp. 228-339, p. 233.

63 Lord Lugard, "Colonial Administration," 41 *Economica* (1933), pp. 248-263.

benefit of the world at large".[64] Lord Lugard, the foremost British colonial soldier, provided a masterstroke of indirect rule in his "methods of ruling native races",[65] using autochthonous political institutions reworked in the interests of the British Empire to extract the maximum profit at the least cost. The treaties signed with traditional rulers were not understood by them. The subsidy promised to the Sultan of Sokoto by the Royal Niger Company was perceived by him to be a tribute. Numerous treaties were churned out which could not be comprehended by near-illiterate interpreters who translated the "The Protectorate of N. Nigeria […] as 'The instruction of compassion of the Sudan".[66] Lugard confessed that:

> Let it be admitted at the outset that European brains, capital, and energy have not been, and never will be, expended in developing the resources of Africa from motives of pure philanthropy; that Europe is in Africa for the mutual benefit of her own industrial classes, and that of the native races in their progress to a higher plane; that the benefit can be made reciprocal, and that it is the aim and desire of civilised administration to fulfil this dual mandate […] As Roman imperialism laid the foundations of modern civilisation, and led the wild barbarians of these islands along the path to progress, so in Africa to-day we are repaying the debt, and bringing to the dark places of the earth, the abode of barbarism and cruelty, the torch of culture and progress while ministering to the material needs of our own civilization […] British methods have not perhaps in all cases produced ideal results, but I am profoundly convinced that there can be no question but that British rule has promoted the happiness and welfare of the primitive races.[67]

Lugard had a messianic conviction in British colonial rule conferring greater benefits upon Africans[68] than other forms of European colonial practice,[69] as if there was any difference between the devil and the deep blue sea.[70]

64 Lord Lugard, "The Basis of the Claim for Colonies," 15 *International Affairs* (1936), pp. 3-25, p. 10.

65 Lord Lugard, *The Dual Mandate in British Tropical Africa*, London, Frank Cass & Co., 1965, pp. 193-229.

66 *Ibid.*, p. 15.

67 *Ibid.*, pp. 617-618.

68 Lord Lugard, "Africa and the Powers," 35 *Journal of the Royal African Society* (1936), pp. 4-17, pp. 6-7.

69 Lord Lugard, "The Claim to Colonies," 35 *Journal of the Royal African Society* (1936), pp. 115-122.

70 Lord Lugard, "Education and Race Relations," 32 *Journal of the African Society* (1933), pp. 1-11.

6. The 1892 British Conquest of Ijebu Kingdom[71]

The Ijebu Kingdom is part of "the very intelligent and progressive Yorubas"[72] located in the Yoruba Kingdoms situated in the south-western part of present-day Nigeria. In the nineteenth century just like the experience of Europe, the Yoruba Kingdoms of Ife, Owu, Oyo, Ijesha, Ondo and Ekiti were consumed by wars which resulted from the vacuum created by the fall of the Old Oyo Empire at the beginning of the nineteenth century.[73] The Ijaye War of 1860 to 1865 is an example of one of the major wars over Yoruba land, which Britain felt threatened its economic interests – in particular, access to palm oil readily available in Yoruba land. The Ijebu Kingdom was already well established in the fifteenth century with its capital at Ijebu-ode which was surrounded by an enormous 80-mile-long wall. It was headed by a king called the Awujale, who shared power with Agemo priests and the Osugbos (who exercised legislative and judicial roles).

Up until the eighteenth century, the Ijebus traded with the Portuguese in palm oil, ivory, pepper, guns, ammunition, slaves and Ijebu cloth which was highly valued by Yoruba slaves in Brazil. The British offer of Christianity and trade ties were rejected by Awujale Ademiyewo who ruled from 1841 to 1855. He regarded Ijebu's indigenous religion as superior to British Christianity.[74] His view was reinforced by the chicanery of the British in 1852 when a fake treaty purportedly signed by the Awujale surrendered Ijebu sovereignty to Britain. He denounced the British imperial slogan of "Christianity, Commerce and Civilization",[75]

71 "The only state in Yorubaland that had effectively resisted the missionaries, the British traders and the Lagos administration until the 1880s was Ijebu. Bent on occupying Yorubaland from the early 1890s, the British decided to teach Ijebu a lesson and at the same time demonstrate to the remaining Yoruba states the futility of opposing them. Using an alleged insult to Governor Denton in 1892 as a pretext, the British launched a well-prepared expedition of about 1,000 men armed with rifles, machine guns and a maxim gun. The Ijebu courageously raised an army of between 7,000 and 10,000 men. However, in spite of this huge numerical superiority, the Ijebu were routed by the invaders. It would appear that all remaining Yoruba states learnt this lesson very well and it is not surprising that between 1893 and 1899 Abeokuta, Ibadan, Ekiti-Ijesa and Oyo readily agreed to negotiate treaties and accepted British residents." Gueye, M. "African Initiatives and Resistance in West Africa, 1880-1914," in Boahen (ed.), *General History of Africa*, pp. 55-71, p. 65.

72 Lord Lugard, "British Policy in Nigeria," 10 *Africa Journal of the International African Institute* (1937), pp. 377-400.

73 Ajayi, J.F.A. and Smith, Robert, *Yoruba Warfare in the Nineteenth Century*, Ibadan, Ibadan University Press, 1971.

74 Ayandele, E.A., *The Ijebu of Yorubaland 1850-1950. Politics, Economy and Society*, Ibadan, Heinemann Educational Books, 1992, pp. 1-11.

75 *Ibid.*, p. 12.

which was subsequently promoted by Trojan horses in the form of indigenous collaborators working with the British. One of them was Otunba Payne, whose grandfather, Awujale Gbelegbuwa, reigned from 1760 to 1790. Otunba Payne was employed in 1863 as a civil servant by the British and he became the only African Chief Registrar of the Supreme Court of Lagos during the colonial period.[76]

Ijebu Kingdom was an oasis of peace and prosperity in Yorubaland from 1800 to 1892 which the British invaders of adjoining Lagos greatly coveted.[77] The Ijebus were well acquainted with the cunning machinations of the British in the forcible conquest of Lagos in 1861 and were wary of suffering the fate of Lagos. In 1863 the British Governor of Lagos wrote to the Colonial Office in London and stated that: "The people of Ijebu-Ode are the most retrograde party around us and the greatest check to the spread of civilisation. They must be forced to allow white men into their territory."[78] British Protestant missionary societies, fearing a French Catholic harvest of Yoruba souls, encouraged imperial Britain to attack Ijebu land. This coincided with British fears over a French incursion into territories assigned to Britain at the Berlin Conference from 1884 to 1885 supervised by Bismarck.

The best description of the resulting battle between the British and the Ijebus in 1892 at Imagbon is that given by Professor A.B. Aderibigbe and according to him:

> With the fordable Yemoji stream in their front the Ijebus held their own against the lethal efficacy of the Maxim gun for the first time being used in a major West African expedition. In consecutive relays they resisted the whole column of their expedition two miles long in a single file, until their adversaries forded the Yemoji to carry the day. About 1,000 Ijebus were said to have fallen in this unsuccessful stand in the defense of the route to Ijebu-Ode.[79]

With the conquest of Ijebu-Ode, everything indigenous was desecrated by the British in Ijebu land and the British missionaries swarmed in like locusts denigrating Ijebu culture and its belief system. "This was now violently dismantled."[80] In the words of the present Awujale: "Having conquered the land, the white men smashed our leadership and their spiritual hold. They took over our government, along with the

---

76 *Ibid.*, pp. 13-29.

77 *Ibid.*, p. 5.

78 *Ibid.*, p. 14.

79 *Ibid.*, p. 34.

80 *Awùjale. The autobiography of Oba Sikiru Kayode Adetona Ogbagba II CFR*, Ibadan, Mosuro Publishers, 2010, p. 51.

control of the land and our religious establishment."[81] In addition the "conquest whittled down the institutional forces that had long reigned before the advent of the whites. In replacement came the colonial government, the cross and much later the crescent."[82] The British had earlier tried to open a trade route through the Ondo Kingdom in order to bypass the Ijebu Kingdom.[83] "In fact, this route was an old one which the Ondo and Ijebu had used in trading with one another for a long time, but which had been abandoned because of troubles in the Ondo country."[84] The numerous wars in Yoruba land made the Ondo road unsafe. "Throughout the war it would seem that most Lagos merchants preferred the Egba and Ijebu roads, as is evidenced by their continual demands that the Lagos government should do something to ensure the opening of the Egba and Ijebu roads."[85] The conquest of Ijebu Kingdom by the British led to the reluctant submission of other Yoruba Kingdoms to the superior firepower of the British and the opening up of their resources to British exploitation.[86]

> For the Yoruba people the abject lesson of the Ijebu expedition went beyond the Ijebu region. It created a psychological weapon, cutting down the moral fibre of resistance which the Yoruba would have woven against further inroad into their sovereignty by the British. It in part explains the relative ease with which Governor G.T. Carter achieved his mission of extending the influence of the British into the interior of Yorubaland in 1893 [...] by subjugating the warriors and other recalcitrant elements, the hitherto unannexed areas, namely, Ibadan, Ijesa, Ekiti and Oyo districts.[87]

The missionaries completed the subjugation of the proud and prosperous Ijebu people with the introduction of British paternalistic education to spread the gospel of the Bible in the British image. Their forerunner was the anti-slave trade crusader, T.A. Buxton who in his 1840 book, *The African Slave Trade and Its Remedy* visualised a time when British traders and missionaries would facilitate the planting of crops in

---

81 *Ibid.*

82 *Ibid.*

83 Akintoye, S.A., "The Ondo Road Eastwards of Lagos, c. 1870-1895," 10 *The Journal of African History* (1969), pp. 581-589.

84 *Ibid.*, p. 585.

85 *Ibid.*, p. 589.

86 "Consequently Governor G. Carter who had achieved the conquest of Ijebuland, faced little or no opposition when he made his famous journey through Yorubaland in 1893 to put a final end to the Yoruba civil wars." Atanda, *An Introduction to Yoruba History*, p. 46.

87 Atanda, J.A., "The Wars and Imperial Conquests of Yorubaland," in Adeagbo Akinjogbin (ed.), *War and Peace in Yorubaland 1793-1893*, Ibadan, Heinemann Educational Books, 1998, pp. 307-320, p. 315.

present-day Nigeria for export to Europe. These would be processed and shipped back to Nigeria as finished goods to be sold for profit.[88] This suggestion was adopted as British colonial policy which manifested in the 1841 mission of 144 Britons and one Yoruba up the River Niger to Lokoja. Of this mission, 48 Britons died of malaria and other diseases. The Yoruba on the trip was no other than the first black African Bishop, Samuel Ajayi Crowther, who translated the King James Version of the Bible into Yoruba.[89]

> The primary objective of the early Christian missionaries was to convert the 'heathen' or the benighted Africa to Christianity via education. Knowledge of the Bible, the ability to sing hymns and recite Catechisms, as well as the ability to communicate both orally and in writing, were considered essential for a good Christian. The early missionaries also realised the importance of training – preferably through the media of English and the local language – the local clergy, catechists, lay readers and pious or godly teachers who would minister to the needs of their own people. However, they erroneously assumed that the African culture and religion (animist) had, in the words of Lord Lugard, 'no system of ethics, and no principle of conduct'. It is with this attitudes of mind they established their schools.[90]

Despite their condemnation of indigenous Ijebu culture, the British looted artefacts and spiritual totems of the Ijebus and carted them away to adorn private collections in Britain. Recollections of elderly Ijebus always note the hypocrisy of the British in condemning indigenous Ijebu culture on one hand, while at the same the Janus British carted away all the Ijebu artwork they could lay their hands upon in 1892 and during colonial rule.

> The contrast with Japan after 1867 could not really be more acute. Japan was able to accept 'Westernization' on its own terms, at its own speed, and with its own reservations, ensuring as far as possible that new technology and organization were assimilated by Japanese thinkers and teachers without dishonor to ancestral shrines and gods. Japanese self-confidence could be salvaged. Such an outcome was impossible in dispossessed Africa. In retrospect, the whole great European project in Africa, stretching over more than a hundred years, can only seem a vast obstacle thrust across every reasonable avenue of African progress out of preliterate and pre-scientific societies into the 'modern world'. It achieved the reverse of what occurred in a Japan made aware of the need to 'catch up with the West. It taught that nothing useful could develop without denying Africa's past, without a ruthless sev-

88 Fafunwa, A. Babs, *History of Education in Nigeria*, Ibadan, NPS Educational Publishers, 1995, pp. 76-77.

89 *Ibid.*

90 *Ibid.*, p. 81.

ering from Africa's roots and a slavish acceptance of models drawn from entirely different histories.[91]

7. The Colonial Heritage of Nigeria

A careful perusal of the agreements entered into by the British with various nationalities in present-day Nigeria, presents a distorted notion of these nationalities being enamoured of their "saviour", the Queen of England, and willing to sign away their land and natural resources.[92] Europe's superiority in armaments in the nineteenth century was crucial in its ability to colonise independent African states, and the development of new technologies secured the rapacious exploitation of Africa's natural resources.[93]

> Especially from the mid-nineteenth century, scientists were central, if not always direct actors in imperial development. They helped to pioneer new technologies that facilitated vastly more effective exploitation of natural resources, for agriculture and industry. Technology underpinned growing superiority in European armaments and communications. Constraints imposed by environment and disease were gradually driven back. The scale of European imperialism and its transformative capacities were shaped and facilitated by science, technology and environmental transformation. Science was intrinsic to the process of imperialism and settler colonialism. Clearly there were branches of colonial interest, such as racial sciences where it is difficult to separate these connections.[94]

As demonstrated above by the brutal attack of 1892 meted out by British firepower on the Ijebu, colonial Britain ruled its colonies with an

---

91 Davidson, Basil, *The Black Man's Burden. Africa and the Curse of the Nation-State*, New York, Three Rivers Press, 1992, p. 42.

92 These agreements initially made with the Royal Niger Company always included two clauses. For example, the one with Sultan of Sokoto on 26th day of June 1894 read as follows: "3. With the view of bettering the condition of my people, and having considered and taken counsel with my chiefs, I give to the company, and their successors forever, full power and rights in perpetuity over foreigners in my country, whether travelling or resident, including right of just taxation as they may see fit. My chiefs are in no way to interfere, and are to recognise no one but the Company. 4. I give to the Company and their successors forever, all power in any part of my dominions as to mining rights [...]. 6. I recognize that the Company receives its power from the Queen of Great Britain, and that they are Her Majesty's representatives to me. I will not recognize any other white nation, because the Company are (*sic*) my help." See Vandeleur, Seymour, D.S.O. Lieutenant and Scots Guards, *Campaigning on the Upper Nile and Niger*, London, Methuen & Co., 1898, p. 248.

93 Beinart, William, Brown, Karen and Gilfoyle, Daniel, "Experts and Expertise in Colonial Africa Reconsidered. Science and the Interpenetration of Knowledge," *African Affairs*, Advance Access Publication, 28 May 2009, pp. 413-433.

94 *Ibid.*, p. 418.

iron fist, and the resources of its colonies were shipped to London.[95] Christianity was the velvet glove over the iron fist of empire and "Europeans gave the Africans the bible and took away their land".[96] The fortunes of the British Empire were built up through the exploitation of its colonies like Nigeria.[97] In 1943, a British newspaper, the *Daily Mail*, reported the confession of a British district officer who admitted that: "Truth is that we have no colonial policy. For years we have drained West Africa of her wealth without putting anything back."[98]

Nigeria is a vast territory and has the most diverse number of ethnic nationalities in the world, with over 400 sub-ethnic groups in Northern Nigeria apart from the dominant Kanuri and Hausa-Fulani nationalities.[99] In order to check French incursion into West Africa the British government declared a protectorate over Southern Nigeria which was extended to Northern Nigeria in 1900, but both territories were governed separately.[100] Indirect rule was introduced into Northern Nigeria due to a "shortage of European staff"[101] and the Southern and Northern parts of

95 Falola, Toyin, *Economic Reforms and Modernization in Nigeria, 1945-1965*, Kent OH, The Kent State University Press, 2004, p. 5.

96 Cole, J.P., *The development Gap*, New York, John Wiley & Sons, 1981, p. 425.

97 Falola, Toyin, *Development Planning and Decolonization in Nigeria*, Gainesville FL, University of Florida Press, 1996, p. 7.

98 Pearce, Robert, "The Colonial Economy. Nigeria and the Second World War," in Barbara Ingham and Colin Simmons (eds.), *Development Studies and Colonial Policy*, London, Frank Cass, 1987, pp. 263-292.

99 Temple, C.L., *Notes on the Tribes, Province, Emirates and States of the Northern Provinces of Nigeria*, New York, Barnes & Noble, 1922; see also Schultze, A., *The Sultanate of Bornu*, originally published in German in 1913, translated by P.A. Benton, London, Frank Cass & Co. Ltd, 1968.

100 Perkins, William A. and Stembridge, Jasper H., *Nigeria. A Descriptive Geography*, Ibadan/London, Oxford University Press, 1963, pp. 10-11.

101 See Temple, Charles Lindsay, *Native Races and their Rulers. Sketches and Studies of Official Life and Administrative Problems in Nigeria*, London, Frank Cass and Co., 1968. This was a book originally published in 1918 and to Temple we owe the gravamen of indirect rule in Nigeria. He stated: "I trust it may be evident that the policy of ruling native races 'indirectly', which is advocated in the following pages, is recommended for application in the case of those native communities which are living in conditions, climatic or other, which preclude the entry among them of any large proportion of Europeans, and not to those where natives and Europeans are intermingled in anything like equal proportions as in the West Indian Colonies or the Southern States of America, for instance […] The world is turning faster and faster. Not the least effect of the employment in this war of large numbers of natives, fighting shoulder to shoulder with white men, in the white men's countries and against other white men, will inevitably be a great stride in the development, or at all events alteration, of the conception which the native mind has formed of the white man." *Ibid.*, p. xii.

Nigeria were amalgamated into one unit in 1914.[102] Nigeria in essence was created by the British who:

> Brought into one political entity a large number of communities many of which were warring against each other, and were at varying stages of development, with differing political and social organizations. They had nothing in common except that they were administered as one country by the British. Therefore, when the time came for the British to hand over power to the Nigerians, power was handed over to authorities who had no claim to the loyalties of the various peoples that made up Nigeria, except that they were the legitimate successors of the former British rulers.[103]

8. Conclusion

British colonialism jettisoned various indigenous modes of customary arbitration and imposed English law on present-day Nigeria under the British version of global capitalism practised in the late nineteenth century. The extractive industry and raw materials provider template, together with the role of importing substandard British products, was foisted upon Nigeria by British colonial policy. Hitherto economically and politically independent entities had their autochthonous systems destroyed by Britain and forced into a subservient position in Britain's empire. The experience of the Ijebu nation typifies the violent way in which Britain in the nineteenth century subjugated the independent sovereign nationalities she encountered in the Nigeria of the day.

The extractive industry template foisted upon Nigeria by British colonial policy continues to stifle the development of institutions crucial for economic development and explains to a large extent why Nigeria has failed to realise its potential.[104] The legal architecture put in place by Britain continues to dominate commerce and investment in Nigeria. British contract law, commercial law and company law permeate recent Nigerian legislation, while the legal structure retains huge chunks of oppressive colonial law regulating the socio-economic sphere.

---

102 Niven, C. Rex, *A Short History of Nigeria*, London, Longmans, 1965, p. 240; Ademoyega, Wale, *The Federation of Nigeria*, London, George Harrap & Co. Ltd, 1962, p. 108.

103 Williams, F.R.A., "Fundamental Rights and the Prospects for Democracy in Nigeria," 115 *University of Pennsylvania Law Review* (1967), pp. 1073-1090.

104 Acemoglu, Daron, Johnson, Simon and Robinson, James A., "The Colonial Origins of Comparative Development. An Empirical Investigation," 91 *The American Economic Review* (2001), pp. 1369-1401, pp. 1370-1373; see also Mahoney, Paul G., "The Common Law and Economic Growth. Hayek Might Be Right," 30 *The Journal of Legal Studies* (2001), pp. 503-525.

Upon gaining independence on 1 October, 1960, Nigeria joined the Commonwealth,[105] a group of former British colonies aligned with the metropolis and periphery divisions of capitalism "appending and distorting third world societies in order to extract their raw materials and economic surplus for the benefit of metropolitan centres [...] The Third World is not a world apart but one intimately linked to the First World of industrial capitalism in Western Europe, the United States, and Japan through relationships of economic, political, and cultural domination."[106] It epitomises Andre Gundre Frank's canonical work *The Development of Underdevelopment.*[107] Only structural transformation of the Nigerian economy from a supplier of raw materials into a manufacturing economy[108] can reduce the level of poverty experienced daily by 70% of her 150 million citizens. A manufacturing economy, in essence, is the route to economic emancipation, which is the antidote to poverty not aid. This fact has been proven by South Korea, Taiwan and more recently China.

---

105 Commonwealth Secretariat‹www.thecommonwealth.org/YearbookHomeInternal/138917/› (visited 29 November 2012).

106 Ehrensaft, Philip, "The Political Economy of Informal Empire in Pre-Colonial Nigeria, 1807-1884," 6 *Canadian Journal of African Studies/Revue Canadienne des Études Africaines* (1972), pp. 451-452.

107 Gundre Frank, Andre, "The Development of Underdevelopment", XVIII *Monthly Review* (1966), pp. 17-30.

108 Lewis, Peter, *Growing Apart. Oil, Politics, and Economic Change in Indonesia and Nigeria*, Ann Arbor, MI, University of Michigan Press, 2007.

EPILOGUE

The Cosmopolitical and the National

An Uneasy Relationship

BO STRÅTH

1. The Ambiguities of the Concept and the Failure to Address the Social Question

Cosmopolitan is derived from the Greek words *cosmos* and *polis*. *Cosmos* refers to the whole world, yes, indeed, the whole universe, although in practice the reference is to the world as the globe. *Polis* is the label of a bounded political community, normally a small city state. From there comes the term politics. Since the nineteenth century, the locus of the political is in Europe in particular the nation state. The unification of the unbounded world and the bounded polity means an ambiguous relationship and a crucial question is how the ambiguity has been addressed historically.

The ambiguity has been present in the historical discourses on cosmopolitanism since the eighteenth century. The cosmopolite has been seen as a citizen of the world transcending political territorial borders such as nation states and living in a vaguely discerned world state. The cosmopolite was imagined as standing above or between all bounded polities.

At the same time the term had a local demarcation. The unbounded cosmopolity did only make sense in relation to the bounded (national or local) polity. Global went hand in hand with local.

In the nineteenth century German debate, for instance, the cosmopolitan imagination was based on the idea of the nation state. Immanuel Kant's point that world government was a world federation of states, rather than something that transcended them, was ever more transformed into the imagination of the nation as carrier of the universal. The discourse on *Weltbürgertum* became a point of reference in the nineteenth century *Völkerrecht* project of international law where the interrelationships between the states of the world were regulated. Global meant interstate. The emphasis on the world as *inter*state or *inter*national counteracted without interruption attempts to transcend political borders.

Like liberalism, cosmopolitanism claims some kind of universalism, for instance the globally acceptable notion of human dignity that must be protected and enshrined in international law. Under cosmopolitanism, all humans have rights; however, history shows that recognition of these rights is not guaranteed. Kant in his 1795 essay "Perpetual Peace" staged a *ius cosmopoliticum* (cosmopolitan law/right) as a guiding principle to protect people from war, and morally grounded this cosmopolitan right on the principle of universal hospitality. Kant claimed that the expansion of hospitality with regard to "use of the right to the earth's surface which belongs to the human race in common would finally bring the human race ever closer to a cosmopolitan constitution."

The tensions, the ambiguities, and the contradictions in the term cosmopolitanism developed in new directions in the mass migration societies from the second half of the twentieth century onwards with a focus on the practices rather than on the idea of the concept. Self-imaginations of being a cosmopolitan city, for instance, refer to world-openness and tolerance, the intermingling of many nationalities and races under cultural adjustment. Being a cosmopolite connotes better-off intellectuals or businessmen, moving independently all over the world without restrictive ties, exploring and explaining it.

In many big European cities today one third or more of the inhabitants are immigrants of non-European origin. The bustling and exotic way of life in these cities is not referred to as cosmopolitan, however, but rather as multicultural. The bearing of the term multicultural is on immigrant ghettos, marginalisation, exclusion and poverty. There is in the binary terms of cosmopolitan and multicultural an important social bias evident in the conceptualisation of the transnational. The term cosmopolitan has come to connote revolt by the elites against the low culture of the masses stuck in local experiences without perspective or horizons.

As a viable concept, cosmopolitan would have to respond to the question that the term multicultural provokes. Etymologically cosmopolitan and multicultural are in many respects overlapping concepts but in social practices over the last decades they have become counter-concepts. The problem is how to unify them. The solution to this problem deals with the social issue. What was set out at the end of the eighteenth century as a problem of how to unify the cosmopolitan and the national has become a problem of how to unify the cosmopolitan and the social.

The locus of the social question, when it emerged as an issue in the 1830s in the industrialising societies, became ever more the nation, culminating in the idea of "national socialism". In the transnational space there was little scope for the social issue. The concept of cosmopolitan suffers from this absence.

Cosmopolitanism is an identity and a project, as Martti Koskenniemi notes in his contribution to this volume. An identity and a project in the mind of an enlightened elite, one might add, which, as Koskenniemi also notes, might end up suicidal or tyrannical, as a moral trap or a preface to destruction, as an illustration of those contradictions of modernity, which in some versions are called the dialectics of enlightenment.

When political economy emerged as a special discipline in the enlightenment discourse, as a development of moral philosophy, a key question dealt with wealth and distribution of wealth. Nobody talked about world wealth. Adam Smith talked about the wealth of nations (*sic*), and the Commonwealth was the continuity of the British Empire. National wealth as a term did not say anything about the distribution of the yields from the economy. The struggle about the social question, or the class question, as it also was called, settled this issue. It was a lengthy and often violent struggle which at the end kneaded together the oppositions into national communities of destiny. Nothing similar has occurred at the global level. The social issue separated the idea of the nation from the idea of the cosmopolity.

The problem of the genealogy of the concept of cosmopolitan is not only its failure to address the social question, but also its European centrism. One could argue that this problem has been solved by the fact that the cosmopolites of today all follow a Western pattern of behaviour in their jet-setting across the world irrespectively of whether they come from rich countries or poor. However, this is an argument that locks out the social question. A sustainable reconstruction of the term must integrate global social protest and activist movements for the environment, health and a fair distribution of wealth, like *Attac*, *Social Forum*, *Doctors Without Borders*, etc., much more.

Étienne Balibar has in this vein remarked that what truly unified the planet was not just colonial expansion, but the revolts, the liberation struggles that put into question the notion of "different natures" that separate peoples of the "metropolis" from those of the colonies, producing a dialectic between these two demographic groups that results in a reversal of roles, a "particularising" of the old metropolis and a "universalisation" of the former colonies. By universalisation of the former colonies, Balibar refers to the large and visible presence in contemporary Europe of groups from the ex-colonies.[1] He contributes to give the

1 Balibar, Étienne, *L'Europe, l'Amérique, la guerre: réflexions sur la médiation européenne*, Paris, La découverte, 2003; Balibar, Étienne, *We, the People of Europe? Re-*

term cosmopolitan the social dimension that has been absent from the beginning and therefore made it fail as a viable alternative to nationalism. Twenty years of hegemonic globalisation rhetoric has made this task of integrating the social more difficult but not less urgent.

Cosmopolitanism is suspected by many of escaping or bypassing the bounded social problems in the wake of global capitalism. Cosmopolitanism is suspected of fleeing social responsibility. The argument that follows from this connotation, is that a sustainable reconstruction of the term cosmopolitan must much more integrate the social question, among others, by focusing on the role of global social protest and activist movements as potential carriers of a an important cosmopolitan dimension.

There is a historical irony here, since cosmopolitan used to be an insult used by the national establishments against the international working class, meaning more or less *vaterlandslose Gesellen* whereas it was a label to be proud of in the early working class language before the movement had been nationalised in 1914. In the Soviet cosmopolitan language, the cosmopolite was an honorary figure. The Soviet case is hardly a point of departure for a reconstruction of the term today, however, filled with hypocrisy as it is.

In the nineteenth century, the cosmopolitan and world historical problem was how to merge the universal and the national. Cosmopolitanism was in the eighteenth and early nineteenth century seen as a concept in a rather unproblematic way linked to nationalism. By the end of the nineteenth century it had become a counter concept to nationalism. The social question became the ever more urgent problem in the industrialising and urbanising European societies. The social question became the key issue of national integration when ideas of National Socialism competed with ideas of class struggle socialism and put the cosmopolitan approach aside.

2. Kant on Cosmopolitanism

In his *Idea for a Universal History with a Cosmopolitan Intent*, Immanuel Kant (1784) tried to reconcile the fact that human beings do not behave in a human way with hopes of human progress.[2] One cannot suppress a certain indignation, Kant stated, when one sees men's action

flections on Transnational Citizenship, Princeton NJ, Princeton University Press, 2004.

2 Kant, Immanuel, "Idea for a Universal History with a Cosmopolitan Intent," in Immanuel Kant, *Perpetual Peace and Other Essays on Politics, History, and Moral Practice*, transl. by Ted Humphrey, Indianapolis, Hackett Publishing Company, 1983, pp. 29-40.

on the great world stage and finds, besides the wisdom that appears here and there among individuals, everything in the large woven together from folly, childish vanity, malice and destructiveness. In the end, one does not know what to think of the human race, so conceited in its gifts. It was difficult to see any purpose in the chaos of individual human action. The task of the philosophers was to see if one could find a natural purpose in this idiotic course of things human.

It remains strange, Kant argued, that earlier generations appear to carry through their toilsome labour only for the sake of the later, to prepare for them a foundation on which the later generations could erect the higher edifice which was Nature's goal, and that only the latest of the generations should have the good fortune to inhabit the building on which a long line of ancestors had unintentionally laboured without being permitted to partake of the fortune they had prepared. However puzzling it might be, this human condition was necessary in order to fulfil the assumption of mankind as a whole as "a class of rational beings", not as individuals but taken together. Each human being is bound to die while the species is immortal. Like a bee-hive (the metaphor was not Kant's) they developed their individual capacities for the long-term perfection of society but died before they could enjoy the perfection.

The means employed by Nature to bring about the development of all the capacities of men exposed their antagonism in society (Fourth Thesis). Kant referred to the social antagonism as the unsocial sociability, by which he meant their propensity to enter into society, bound together with a mutual opposition which constantly threatened to break up the society. Human beings have an inclination to associate with others, because in society they feel themselves to be more than individuals. However, this sociability is not enough. Without the human unsociability based on individual selfishness all talents would remain hidden, "unborn in an Arcadian shepherd's life, with all its concord, contentment, and mutual affection". Men, "good-natured as the sheep they herd, would hardly reach a higher worth than their beasts". Thanks to Nature, Kant said, for the incompatibility, for heartless competitive vanity, for the insatiable desire to possess and to rule. Without these features all the excellent natural capacities of humanity would forever sleep, undeveloped. "Man wishes concord; but nature knows better what is good for the race; she wills discord." Kant's problem of the unsocial sociability was an echo of Hobbes' question about how to prevent civil war, but the solution went in another direction.

The highest purpose of Nature was attainable only in societies with the greatest freedom meaning that there was mutual opposition among the members. In order to make each individual's freedom consistent with the freedom of others a "perfectly just civil constitution" was required. However, this was not sufficient, and on this point Kant played off his cosmopolitan argument (Seventh Thesis). A perfect civic constitution was dependent upon the problem of a lawful external relation among states:

> Through war, through the taxing and never-ending accumulation of armament, through the want which any state, even in peacetime, must suffer internally, Nature forces them to make at first inadequate and tentative attempts; finally, after devastations, revolutions, and even complete exhaustion, she brings them to that which reason could have told them at the beginning and with far less sad experience, to wit, to step from the lawless condition of savages into a league of nations. In a league of nations even the smallest state could expect security and justice, not from its own power and by its own decrees, but only from this great league of nations.[3]

3. Hegel, Cosmos, and the Nation

Kant's teleology in his universal history with a cosmopolitan purpose translated experiences of human diversity and division into a vision of human unification through progress. Hegel developed the idea in his philosophy of history where Reason was inherent in the idea of the nation and the torch moved from nation to nation in a movement towards ever higher stages of development. The world spirit inhabited one nation at a time. The westbound movement from the ancient world made Hegel in his own time see the *Weltgeist* incarnated in Napoleon on his white horse after the occupation of Jena. Later in the nineteenth century the emerging social sciences took over this imagination when they assumed universal laws for the development of societies and where the position of each could be described in terms of forward or backward, mature and old or young, early or late.

Despite the belief in universal progression there was a tension between cosmopolitanism and nationalism, independence and interdependence, unbounded and bounded. The tension or the ambiguity, yes, even the contradiction between these dichotomies did not make them mutually exclusive. On the contrary, they constituted each other. They were entangled categories. The term national required an international framework in order to make any sense. The nation required an *Other*. The imagination of an international order departed from the existence of nations. Rather than being separated they belonged together. The historical alliance between cosmopolitanism and nationalism must be seen in this view.

3 Seventh Thesis, Kant, "Idea for a Universal History with a Cosmopolitan Intent", p. 34.

4. Cosmopolitanism and Democracy in the View of Tocqueville

Terms like democracy, liberalism, cosmopolitanism, universalism, human rights and natural rights constitute a semantic field, which since the enlightenment describes how modern democracies function and how they at the end will develop. This field built up self-assessments of European societies after the French revolution.

The thoughts that derive their nourishment from this field fail to tell why, after the argued break-through of liberal democracy, totalitarian regimes dominated the world during the first half of the twentieth century. These thoughts have furthermore ignored the fact that the nineteenth century, as the time of the assumed break-through of liberal democracy, must be described in national(ist) rather than universal terms. The nation building in Europe was a bloody affair. Empirical observations of the opposite from the theoretically assumed enlightenment standard have been played down as deviations. The violent experiences in the nineteenth century have as a matter of fact been circumvented in a political and philosophical bypass operation, where a straight progressive line has been drawn from the enlightening eighteenth century towards our own times under key words like rationalisation, modernisation and globalisation.

On this point Tocqueville should be retrieved and made to enter the stage, as a voice for another, more realistic view on the nineteenth century, as Demin Duan convincingly demonstrates in his contribution to this volume.

Tocqueville saw problems with the label of the nineteenth century as the age of liberal democracy. In particular, he had problems with individualism as a key dimension of democracy. When people were driven to their own private sphere the "public spirit" and the mores eroded and were replaced by "the abasement of the mind" and "the mediocrity of tastes." Here Tocqueville seems to have developed opinions formulated by Kant in his contempt of the spirit of commerce. Like Kant, who in contrast to his idea of perpetual peace at times saw the solution in the ennobling war, Tocqueville opted for imperial war and conquest as the remedy for the consequences of the democratic individualism. As Duan demonstrates, quoting Jennifer Pitt, the Algerian conquests could according to Tocqueville help France avoid the threat of future dictatorships by uniting the French people behind a national cause.

The example demonstrates how important it is to historicise and contextualise the use of concepts that are argued to be universal. The contextual focus breaks down the imagination of cohesive logics and sheds light on paradoxical languages. In the same vein the liberal Max Weber's (who as opposed to Tocqueville looked positively upon individual autonomy as the basis of modern politics) and Joseph Chamberlain's support of imperial politics, in the decades after 1900, becomes understandable. Universal concepts like liberalism, socialism and cosmopolitanism become problematic if their uses are measured in comparison to theoretical postulates.

Contextualisation and historicisation furthermore emphasise the ambiguities of universal concepts. This was, in particular, the point where Tocqueville was sceptical of the democracy in America. The development could in the name of democracy take various directions and in some of them the outcome might be the opposite of democracy. The term of democracy has historically always been close to the term populism. These two concepts are far from opposites. Another example in the same vein is the occupation of the term cosmopolitan by the Communist International. The concept became a weapon in the arsenal of the Cold War confrontation and before that in the value clash of the interwar years.

Cosmopolitanism does not fit well with the existence of wars: between states or as civil wars. In the communist version the opposition was solved through the class war and the revolution which would put an end to all wars and pave the way for true cosmopolitanism.

Another field where the opposition was accommodated was colonial wars as civilising missions. When the whole world was civilized there would be no wars and the preconditions for cosmopolitanism would emerge. The enlightenment philosophers tried to get rid of the medieval scholastic debate on just wars. Rousseau and Vattel were two of the prominent thinkers who struggled with the development of new views on the still existing phenomenon of war. In the wake of Grotius and Hobbes they discussed the possibility of an *international* order analogous to the imagination of a peaceful *internal* order, a peaceful interstate order as a mirror of the peaceful domestic social order. They played down the debate about just war, *ius ad bellum*, and focused on the issue of *ius in bello*, i.e. they moved the problem from the right to make war to the rights or rules for warfare, which, of course, was a kind of capitulation to the existence of war and a defeat for the idea of a peaceful international order between sovereign states. The states framed sovereignty and were the locus of it. There, in the states, the link between sovereignty and peace was possible. At the level between the states this link ceased. Gabriella Silvestrini investigates thoughtfully these crucial debates in her contribution.

5. Cosmopolitanism and Colonialism

Adedokun Olatokunbo Ogunfolu investigates in his contribution the liberal language about trade and civilisation. The industrial revolution made the use of slaves unprofitable, and in Britain, the first industrialising country, strong interests emerged to stop the slave trade from sustaining competitors on the world markets in order to maximise the profits. Industrialisation changed from demand for slaves to demand for palm oil to fuel the factories and for raw material. Civilisation and cosmopolitan human rights became compatible with the scramble for Africa and for the violent opening of world markets. The Berlin conference of 1884 regulated geopolitical and geoeconomic spheres of interest in Africa. Rules were decided for peace in Europe through conquest of African lands by the European states. The main object of the conference was free trade in Congo and free navigation on the rivers Congo and Niger. In his opening address to the delegates Otto von Bismarck declared that the reason for calling the conference was service to humanity and peace. In paragraph 34 of the Treaty that was signed in 1885 any power which took possession of a tract of land on the coasts of the African continent was authorised to acquire it. Treaties were, in the wake of the decisions in Berlin, signed with the traditional chieftains in the conquered territories; they did not understand what they underwrote. Subsidies for the conquest were taken for tributes and many treaties could not be comprehended by the natives translated by illiterate interpreters as they were.

Liliana Obregón investigates the Haitian slave revolution of 1791-1803 in connection with Kant's cosmopolitan imagination. Kant's utopia of cosmopolitan law in 1790 was clearly inspired by the French revolution where he discerned a moral disposition within the human race. Five years later when he had witnessed the excesses of the revolution he had obviously become more hesitant about the concept of democracy as is clear from his essay on perpetual peace, however. But the belief in moral disposition as the basis of a cosmopolitan world remained. The slaves in Haiti made the disposition global.

The case of the slave revolt in Haiti represents a kind of boomerang from the European civilisation language. Enslaved people in a colony employed what had been proclaimed to be universal human rights. They translated the universalist language into their own experiences and implemented it in a way that came as a surprise to the protagonists of the civilisation project. They provide a perfect illustration of Dipesh Chakrabarty's thesis about provincialising Europe, where he argues that, although the colonised peoples try to create a demarcation to the enlightenment heritage, and emphasise their native traditions, they cannot get rid of it. However, they can translate it into their own experiences.

Each such translation of enlightenment values contains potential surprises for the originators. This was the case when the slaves in Haiti took one of the enlightenment core values seriously, that about critique and social protest as a universal human right.

Francisco Ortega deals with the same complex problem when he asks whether cosmopolitanism was always manipulated in favour of an anti-democratic agenda, or whether it occasionally was able to carry out its critical dimension and democratic potential. His focus in the discussion of this question is on early nineteenth century Latin America and on one of the protagonists in the second rank of the liberation movement, Simón Rodríguez. His cosmopolitanism was much more than openness to other cultures and a critical attitude to local attachments. Rodríguez was, in particular, interested in the social interdependence among individuals. Cosmopolitanism was in his understanding commonwealth with the active involvement of all citizens in state life. Cosmopolitanism was not a virtue of the few but of all members of the polity. General education was an instrument towards a cosmopolitan society.

Several of the contributions to the volume thus demonstrate the crucial overall role of colonialism in the cosmopolitan language. Colonialism and cosmopolitanism are entangled categories which are tied together by paradoxical language, contradictions and, not least, hypocrisy.

The approach by Adrian Brisku is similar, although he has a somewhat different object of analysis in his essay on cultural and economic cosmopolitanism versus political practices in the Russian and Ottoman empires in comparison. The issue at stake in the cosmopolitan language that he analyses deals with power. Pan-Slavist ideas of cultural cosmopolitanism in the Russian empire ended up in Russian nationalism. Cosmopolitanism and nationalism constituted each other but the long-term development was that nationalism gained the upper hand. In the economic sphere the development was similar. Initial ideas of economic cosmopolitanism based on free trade doctrine and on Adam Smith's theory were in the second half of the nineteenth century transformed into protectionism. The development was on this point the same in the Ottoman Empire where the rulers were exposed to European imperialism with claims to open the borders for free trade with protectionism as the long-term response. Brisku sheds light on the languages and political practices behind arguments about cosmopolitanism as universality and openness, multi-ethnicity, nationalism, Pan-Islamism and Pan-Slavism. Cosmopolitanism was not about universalism but rather about diversity and tolerance of diversity. The preconditions of this tolerance changed during the nineteenth century. The politics went from local self-government and non-interference towards centralised government and homogenisation of populations, in declining tolerance of diversity. The cosmopolitan language became trapped in the nationalist rhetoric. The cosmopolitical and the national constituted and constitute an uneasy relationship.

Bibliography

Books

Abbé de Saint-Pierre, *Projet pour rendre perpétuelle la paix en Europe*, Paris, Fayard, 1986.

Ademoyega, Wale, *The Federation of Nigeria*, London, George Harrap & Co. Ltd, 1962.

Adewoye, Omoniyi, *The Judicial System in Southern Nigeria, 1854-1954 Law and Justice in a Dependency*, New Jersey, Humanities Press, 1977.

Ajayi, J.F.A., *Christian Missions in Nigeria 1841-1891*, London, Longmans, 1966.

Ajayi, J.F.A., *A Thousand Years in West African History*, Ibadan, Ibadan University Press, 1967.

Ajayi, J.F.A. and Smith, Robert, *Yoruba Warfare in the Nineteenth Century*, Ibadan, Ibadan University Press, 1971.

Amend-Traut, Anja, *Wechselverbindlichkeiten vor dem Reichskammergericht: praktiziertes Zivilrecht in der frühen Neuzeit*, Köln [u.a.], Böhlau, 2009.

Amunátegui, Miguel Luis, *Ensayos biográficos*, 4 Vols., Santiago de Chile, Imprenta Nacional, 1896.

Anghie, Antony, *Imperialism, Sovereignty and the Making of International Law*, Cambridge, Cambridge University Press, 2005.

Anonymous, *Dictionnaire Universel François Et Latin. Contenant La Signification Et La Définition Tant Des Mots De L'une & De L'autre Langue*, Paris, Trevoux & se vend chez F. Dalaulne, 1721, Vol. 5.

Anderson, Eugene N. and Anderson, Pauline R., *Political Institutions and Social Change in Continental Europe in the Nineteenth Century*, Berkeley, University of California Press, 1967.

Appiah, Kwame Anthony, *Cosmopolitanism. Ethics in a World of Strangers*, New York, W.W. Norton & Company, 2006.

Aquinas, Thomas, *Political Writings*, R.W. Dyson (ed.), Cambridge, Cambridge University Press, 2007.

Arendt, Hannah and Beiner, Ronald (eds.), *Lectures on Kant's Political Philosophy*, Chicago, University of Chicago Press, 1992.

Armitage, David, *The Ideological origins of the British Empire*, Cambridge, Cambridge University Press, 2000.

Arneil, Barbara, *John Locke and America. The Defence of English Colonialism*, Oxford, Clarendon Press, 1996.

Asbach, Olaf, *Die Zähmung der Leviathane. Die Idee einer Rechtsordnung zwischen Staaten bei Abbé de Saint-Pierre und Jean-Jacques Rousseau*, Berlin, Akademie Verlag, 2002.

Asei, John O., *Introduction to Nigerian Legal system*, Ibadan, Sam Bookman Publishers, 1998.

Atanda, J.A., *An Introduction to Yoruba History*, Ibadan, Ibadan University Press, 1980.

Awolowo, Obafemi, *The People's Republic*, Ibadan, Oxford University Press, 1968.

Awùjale, *The autobiography of Oba Sikiru Kayode Adetona Ogbagba II CFR*, Ibadan, Mosuro Publishers, 2010.

Ayandele, E.A., *The Ijebu of Yorubaland 1850-1950. Politics, Economy and Society*, Ibadan, Heinemann Educational Books, 1992.

Ayandele, E.A., *The Missionary Impact on Modern Nigeria, 1842-1914*, London, Longmans, 1966

Balibar, Étienne, *L'Europe, l'Amérique, la guerre: réflexions sur la médiation européenne*, Paris, La découverte, 2003.

Balibar, Étienne, *We, the People of Europe? Reflections on Transnational Citizenship*, Princeton NJ, Princeton University Press, 2004.

Bartelson, Jens, *The Critique of the State*, Cambridge, Cambridge University Press, 2001.

Beck, Ulrich, *Cosmopolitan Vision*, London, Polity Press, 2006.

Belissa, Marc, *Fraternité universelle et intérêt national (1713-1795) Les cosmopolitiques du droit des gens*, Paris, Kimé, 1998.

Bély, Lucien, *L'art de la paix en Europe. Naissance de la diplomatie moderne XVIe-XVIIe siècle*, Paris, PUF, 2007.

Bentham, Jeremy, *The Works of Jeremy Bentham, Now First Collected; Under the Superintendence of His Executor, John Bowring*, Vol. VIII, Edinburgh, 1839.

Berkes, Nyazy, *The Development of Secularism in Turkey*, Montreal, McGill University Press, 1964.

Bernardi, Bruno, *La fabrique des concepts. Recherches sur l'invention conceptuelle chez Rousseau*, Paris, Champion, 2006.

Bewes, Timothy, *Cynicism and Postmodernity*, London, Verso, 1997.

Bolívar, Simón, *Coleccion De Documentos Relativos Á La Vida Pública Del Libertador De Columbia Y Del Perú Para Servir a La Historia De La Independencia Del Suramérica*, Tomo Tercero, 3, Carácas, Impr. de Devisme Hermanos, 1826.

Bolívar, Simón, *Selected Writings of Bolívar*, New York, Colonial Press, 1951.

Bonaparte, Napoléon, *Correspondance de Napoléon Ier. Publiée par ordre de l'empereur Napoléon III*, 32 Vols., Paris, Imprimerie impériale, 1858-1869.

Bonaparte, Napoléon, *The Mind of Napoleon. A Selection from his Written and Spoken Words*, ed. and transl. by H.J. Christopher, New York NY, Columbia University Press, 1955.

Bonaparte, Napoleon, Gourgaud, Gaspard, and Montholon, Charles-Tristan, *Memoirs of the History of France During the Reign of Napoleon*, London, H. Colburn and Co., 1823.

Boyer, Abel and Prieur, J.C., *Le Dictionnaire Royal François-Anglois Et Anglois-François* (the Royal Dictionary, French and English, and English and French), 2, London, C. Bathurst, 1773.

Breckenridge, Carol A. *et al.* (eds.), *Cosmopolitanism*, Chapel Hill, Duke University Press, 2002.

Brière, Jean-François, *Haïti et La France, 1804-1848. Le Rêve Brisé*, Paris, Éd. Karthala, 2008.

Briggs, Ronald, *Tropes of Enlightenment in the Age of Bolivar. Simon Rodriguez and the American Essay at Revolution*, Nashville, Vanderbilt University Press, 2010.

Buck-Morss, Susan, *Hegel, Haiti, and Universal History, Illuminations*, Pittsburgh PA, University of Pittsburgh Press, 2009.

Burrow, J.W., *Evolution and Society. A Study of Victorian Social Theory*, Cambridge, Cambridge University Press, 1966.

Bushnell, David, *Simón Bolívar. Hombre De Caracas, Proyecto De América. Una Biografía*, 1ra. ed., Colección Historias Americanas, Buenos Aires, Editorial Biblos, 2002

Böhmer, Justus Henning, *Consultationes et Decisiones iuris*, tomus 2, pars 1, Carl August Böhmer (ed.), Halle, 1734.

Carter, Christine Jane, *Rousseau and the Problem of War*, New York/London, Garland Publishing, 1987.

Carter, J. Kameron, *Race. A Theological Account*, Oxford, Oxford University Press, 2008.

Cavallar, Georg, *The Rights of Strangers. Theories of International Hospitality, the Global Community, and Political Justice since Vitoria*, Burlington, Ashgate, 2002.

Chamberlain, M.E., *The Scramble for Africa*, Harlow, Longman, 1974.

Cheah, Pheng & Robbins, Bruce (eds.), *Cosmopolitics. Thinking and Feeling beyond the Nation*, Minneapolis MN, Minnesota University Press, 1998.

Cheneval, Francis, *La Cité des peuples. Mémoires de cosmopolitismes*, Paris, Cerf, 2005.

Cicero, *De officiis*, with an English translation by Walter Miller, London, Heinemann, 1913.

Cohen, Joshua (ed.), *For Love of Country. Debating the Limits of Patriotism*, Martha C. Nussbaum with Respondents, Boston, Beacon, 1996.

Cohen, Marshall (ed.), *The Philosophy of John Stuart Mill. Ethical, Political and Religious*, New York, Random House Inc., 1961.

Coing, Helmut, *Europäisches Privatrecht*, 2 Vols., Munich, 1985-1989.

Cole, J.P., *The development Gap*, New York, John Wiley & Sons, 1981.

Conrad, Hermann, *Deutsche Rechtsgeschichte, Vol. 2: Neuzeit bis 1806*, Karlsruhe, C.F. Müller Verlag, 1966.

Crampton, Jeremy W. and Elden, Stuart, *Space, Knowledge and Power. Foucault and Geography*, Aldershot, England/Burlington VT, Ashgate, 2007.

Cumberland, Richard, *Traité philosophique des lois naturelles*, Jean Barbeyrac (transl.), Amsterdam, Pierre Mortier, 1744.

Curtin, Philip D. Curtin, *The Atlantic Slave Trade; a Census*, Madison, University of Wisconsin Press, 1969.

D'Anglas, Boissy, *Plan of the New Constitution of the French Republic; To Which Is Prefixed, the Report Presented to the Convention, from the Commission of Eleven*, Edinburgh J. Robertson, No. 4, 1795.

Dante, *Monarchy*, transl. and ed. by Prue Shaw, Cambridge, Cambridge University Press, 1996.

Dario, Ruben, *Cantos de vida y esperanza*, Paris, 1904.

Darjes, Joachim George, *Discours über sein Natur- und Völkerrecht*, 1 Teil, Jena, 1762.

Davidson, Basil, *The Black Man's Burden. Africa and the Curse of the Nation-State*, New York, Three Rivers Press, 1992.

Davison, Roderic H., *Reform in the Ottoman Empire, 1856-1876*, Princeton, Princeton University Press, 1963.

Delagrange Mm. Dalloz, Hennequin, Dupin, *Consultation De Mm. Dalloz, Delagrange, Hennequin, Dupin Jeune Et Autres Jurisconsultes, Pour Les Anciens Colons De St-Domingue* (15 avril 1829), Paris, Impr. de Vve Agasse, 1829.

Delanty, Gerard, *The Cosmopolitan Imagination. The Renewal of Critical Social Theory*, Cambridge, Cambridge University Press, 2009.

Demel, Walter, *Der Bayerische Staatsabsolutismus 1806/08-1817. Staats- und gesellschaftspolitische Motivationen und Hintergründe der Reformära in der ersten Phase des Königreichs Bayern*, Munich, C.H. Beck, 1983

Demel, Walter, *Vom aufgeklärten Reformstaat zum bürokratischen Staatsabsolutismus*, Munich, Oldenbourg, 1993.

Derathé, Robert, *Jean-Jacques Rousseau et la science politique de son temps*, Paris, PUF, 1950.

Deringil, Selim, *The Well-Protected Domains*, London, I.B. Tauris, 1998.

Derrida, Jacques, *On Cosmopolitanism and Forgiveness (Thinking in Action)*, New York, Routledge, 2001.

Diderot, Denis, *Political Writings*, John Hope Manson & Robert Wokler (eds.), Cambridge, Cambridge University Press, 1992.

Dike, Onwuka K., *Trade and Politics in the Niger Delta 1830-1885. An Introduction to the Economic and Political History of Nigeria*, Oxford, Clarendon Press, 1956.

Doeberl, Michael, *Ein Jahrhundert bayerischen Verfassungslebens*, Munich, Lindauer, 1918.

Doeberl, Michael, *Rheinbundverfassung und bayerische Konstitution*, Munich, G. Franz, 1924.

Drescher, Seymour, *Abolition. A History of Slavery and Antislavery*, Cambridge, Cambridge University Press, 2009.

Ehrard, Jean, *Lumières et esclavage. L'esclavage colonial et l'opinion publique en France au XVIIIe siècle*, Brussels, André Versaille, 2008.

Eigen Figal, Sara and Larrimore, Mark J. (eds.), *The German Invention of Race*, Suny Series, Philosophy and Race, Albany, State University of New York Press, 2006.

Elias, T.O., *British Colonial Law A comparative study of the Interaction between English and Local Laws in British Dependencies*, London, Stevens & Sons Limited, 1961.

Elias, T.O., *The Nigerian Legal System*, London, Routledge & Kegan Paul Ltd, 1963.

D'Entrèves, Alessandro Passerin, *Dante as a Political Thinker*, Oxford, Clarendon, 1952.

Erasmus, Desiderius, *Querela pacis undique gentium ejectae profligataeque*, Basel, Joh. Froben, 1517.

Fafunwa, A. Babs, *History of Education in Nigeria*, Ibadan, NPS Educational Publishers, 1995.

Falola, Toyin, *Development Planning and Decolonization in Nigeria*, Gainesville FL, University of Florida Press, 1996.

Falola, Toyin, *Economic Reforms and Modernization in Nigeria, 1945-1965*, Kent OH, The Kent State University Press, 2004.

Fenning, D., *The Royal English Dictionary or a Treasury of the English Language*, 2nd ed., London, Baldwin, Richardson, Crowder, Collins, 1763.

Ferry, Jules François Camille, *Discours et opinions de Jules Ferry*, Tome 5, Paul Robiquet (ed.), Paris, Armand Colin & Cie, 1897.

Fetscher, Iring, *Rousseaus politische Philosophie. Zur Geschichte des demokratischen Freiheitsbegriffs*, 2nd ed., Neuwied am Rhein, Luchterhand, 1968.

Foucault, Michel, *Il faut défendre la société*, Paris, Gallimard, 1997.

Franchescet, Antonio, *Kant and Liberal Internationalism. Sovereignty, Justice and Global Reform*, New York, Palgrave, 2002.

Gallagher, John and Robinson, Ronald, with Denny, Alice, *African and the Victorians. The Official Mind of Imperialism*, London, Macmillan, 1961.

García Bacca, Juan David, *Simón Rodríguez, pensador para América*, Caracas, Editorial de la Presidencia de la República, 1978.

Gavin, R.J. and Betley, J.A., *The Scramble for Africa. Documents on the Berlin West African Conference and Related Subjects 1884/1885*, Ibadan, Ibadan University Press, 1973.

Goldschmidt, Victor, *Anthropologie et politique. Les principes du système de Rousseau* (1974), Paris, Vrin, 1983.

Gott, Richard, *Hugo Chávez and the Bolivarian Revolution*, London, Verso, 2005.

Grases, Pedro, *Simón Rodríguez. Escritos sobre su vida y su obra*, Caracas, Concejo Municipal del Distrito Federal, 1954.

Grotius, Hugo, *Commentary on the Law of Prize and Booty [De jure praedae]*, ed. and with an Introduction by Martine Julia van Ittersum, Indianapolis, Liberty Fund, 2006.

Grotius, Hugo, *De iure belli ac pacis libri tres Aalen*, Scientia Verlag, 1993.

Grotius, Hugo, *Le droit de la guerre et de la paix*, nouvelle traduction par Jean Barbeyrac, Amsterdam, Pierre du Coup, 1724.

Grotius, Hugo, *The Rights of War and Peace*, edited and with an Introduction by Richard Tuck, from the edition by Jean Barbeyrac, Indianapolis, Liberty Fund, 2005.

Habermas, Jürgen, *Der gespaltene Westen. Kleine Politische Schriften X*, Frankfurt a.M., Suhrkamp, 2004.

Hagemeier, Joachim, *Juris publici Europaei ... epistola(e)*, 9 Vols., Frankfurt am Main, 1677-1681, continued by Heinrich Günter Thülemar, 3 Vols., Frankfurt am Main, 1681-1682.

Haggenmacher, Peter, *Grotius et la doctrine de la guerre juste*, Paris, PUF, 1983.

Hanioğlu, M. Şükrü, *A Brief History of the Late Ottoman Empire*, Oxford/Princeton, Princeton University Press, 2008.

Hazareesingh, Sudhir, *The Legend of Napoleon*, London, Granta Books, 2005 [2004].

Hecker, Michael, *Napoleonischer Konstitutionalismus in Deutschland*, Berlin, Duncker & Humblot, 2005.

Hinsley, Francis Harry, *Power and the Pursuit of Peace. Theory and Practice in the History of Relations Between States*, Cambridge, Cambridge University Press, 1963.

Hobbes, Thomas, *De cive* (1642), in Thomas Hobbes, *Opera philosophica quae latine scripsit omnia*, William Molesworth (eds.), (1839-1845), Vol. 2.

Hobbes, Thomas, *Elementa philosophica de Cive*, Amsterdam, Apud Henr. et Viduam Th., 1696.

Hobbes, Thomas, *Le Citoyen ou les fondements de la politique*, French translation by Samuel de Sorbière, Paris, Flammarion, 1982.

Hobbes, Thomas, *Le corps politique*, French translation by Samuel de Sorbière (1652), with an Introduction by Roux, Louis, Saint-Etienne, Publications de l'Université de Saint-Etienne, 1977.

Hobbes, Thomas, *Leviathan*, Richard Tuck (ed.), Cambridge, Cambridge University Press, 2003.

Hobsbawm, E.J., *The Age of Empire, 1875-1914*, New York, Pantheon Books, 1987.

Hoffmann, Stanley and Fidler, David P., *Rousseau on International Relations*, Oxford, Clarendon Press, 1991.

Holland, Thomas Erskine, *The European Concert in the Eastern Question*, 2nd ed., Darmstadt, Scientia Verlag Aalen, 1979.

Hont, Istvan, *Jealousy of Trade. International Competition and the Nation-State in Historical Perspective*, Cambridge Mass./London, The Belknap Press of Harvard University Press, 2005.

Huber, Ernst Rudolf, *Deutsche Verfassungsgeschichte seit 1789. Band 1: Reform und Restauration 1789 bis 1830*, 2nd ed., Stuttgart, W. Kohlhammer, 1967 [1957].

Huber, Ernst Rudolf (ed.), *Dokumente Zur Deutschen Verfassungsgeschichte. 1, Deutsche Verfassungsdokumente 1803-1850*, 3rd ed., Stuttgart [u.a.], W. Kohlhammer, 1978 [1961]).

Hufeland, Gottlieb, *Lehrbuch des in den deutschen Ländern geltenden gemeinen oder subsidiarischen Civilrechts*, I Gießen, 1808.

Hunter, Ian, *Rival Enlightenments. Civil and Metaphysical Philosophy in Early Modern Germany*, Cambridge, Cambridge University Press, 2001.

Ikime, O., *Niger Delta Rivalry and the European Presence 1884-1936*, London, Longmans, 1969.

Jacob, Margaret C., *Strangers Nowhere in the World. The Rise of Cosmopolitanism in Early Modern Europe*, Philadelphia, Univ. of Pennsylvania Press, 2006.

Jardin, André and Chevallier, Jean-Jacques (eds.), *Oeuvres Complètes. Oeuvres, Papiers et Correspondances d'Alexis de Tocqueville*, Vol. 3, Paris, Gallimard, 1962.

Jardin, André and Mayer, J.-P. (eds.), *Oeuvres Complètes. Oeuvres, Papiers et Correspondances d'Alexis de Tocqueville*, Vol. 5, Paris, Gallimard, 1958.

Janvier, Louis Joseph, *Les Constitutions d'Haiti (1801-1885)*, Paris, C. Marpon et E. Flammarion, 1886.

Jersild, Austin, *Orientalism and Empire*, Montreal/Kingston, McGill-Queen's University Press, 2002.

Jouannet, Emmanuelle, *Emer de Vattel et l'émergence doctrinale du droit international classique*, Paris, Pedone, 1998.

Kaipainen, Anu, *Magdaleena ja maailmanlapset*, Porvoo, WSOY, 1969.

Kant, Immanuel, *Grounding for the Metaphysics of Morals*, transl. by James, W. Ellington, Cambridge, MA, Hackett Publishing Company, 1981.

Kant, Immanuel, *Project for a Perpetual Peace. A Philosophical Essay*, London, printed by S. Couchman for Vernor and Hood, 1796.

Kant, Immanuel, *Toward Perpetual Peace and Other Writings on Politics, Peace, and History*, Pauline Kleingeld (ed.), New Haven, Yale University Press, 2006

Katzew, Ilona *et al.* (eds.), *New World Order. Casta Painting and Colonial Latin America*, New York, Americas Society, 1996.

Kennedy, Paul, *The Rise and Fall of the Great Powers. Economic Change and Military Conflict from 1500 to 2000*, New York, Random House, 1987.

Kirsch, Martin, *Monarch und Parlament im 19. Jahrhundert. Der Monarchische Konstitutionalismus als europäischer Verfassungstyp – Frankreich im Vergleich*, Göttingen, Vandenhoeck & Ruprecht, 1999.

Klein, Herbert S., *The Atlantic Slave Trade*, 2nd new ed., New Approaches to the Americas, Cambridge/New York, Cambridge University Press, 2010.

Klippel, Diethelm (ed.), *Naturrecht und Staat. Politische Funktionen des europäischen Naturrechts (17.-19. Jahrhundert)*, Munich, Oldenbourg, 2006.

Knecht, Ingo, *Der Reichsdeputationshauptschluß vom 25. Februar 1803. Rechtmäßigkeit, Rechtswirksamkeit und verfassungsgeschichtliche Bedeutung*, Berlin, Duncker & Humblot, 2007.

Koselleck, Reinhart, *Futures Past. On the Semantics of Historical Time*, transl. and with an introduction by Keith Tribe, New York, Columbia University Press, 2004.

Koskenniemi, Martti, *From Apology to Utopia. The Structure of International Legal Argument*, Reissued with a new epilogue, Cambridge, Cambridge University Press, 2005.

Koskenniemi, Martti, *The Gentle Civilizer of Nations. The Rise and Fall of International Law, 1870-1960*, Cambridge, Cambridge University Press, 2002.

Lagerroth, Fredrik, *1809 års regeringsform: dess ursprung och tolkning*, Stockholm, Norstedt & Söner, 1942.

Lapidus, Ira M., *A History of Islamic Societies*, 2nd ed., Cambridge, Cambridge University Press, 2002.

de Las Cases, Emmanuel-Augustin-Dieudonné-Joseph, *Mémorial de Sainte Hélène. Journal of the Private Life and Conversations of the Emperor Napoleon at Saint Helena*, Vol. 2, 29, 8 [4] Vols., London, H. Colburn and Co, 1823.

Lassudrie-Duchêne, Georges, *Jean-Jacques Rousseau et le Droit des Gens*, Paris, H. Jouve, 1906.

Lastarria, José Victoriano, *Recuerdos literarios*, Santiago de Chile, Ediciones LOM, 2001.

Lenin, V.I., *Imperialism. The Highest Stage of Capitalism*, New York, International Publishers, 1939.

Lewis, Peter, *Growing Apart. Oil, Politics, and Economic Change in Indonesia and Nigeria*, Ann Arbor, MI, University of Michigan Press, 2007.

Ley, Francis, *Alexandre 1er et Sa Sainte-alliance*, Paris, Librairie Fischbacher, 1975.

List, Friedrich, *National System of Political Economy. The Systems and Politics*, 3 Vols., New York, Cosimo Classics, 2005.

Locke, John, *Traité du gouvernement civil*, Simone Goyard-Fabre (ed.), Paris, Garnier Flammarion, 1992.

Locke, John, *Two Treatises of Government*, Peter Laslett (ed.), Cambridge, Cambridge University Press, 2003.

Lord Lugard, *The Dual Mandate in British Tropical Africa*, London, Frank Cass & Co., 1965.

Luxemburg, Rosa, *The Accumulation of Capital* (1913), Agnes Schwarzschild (ed.), London, Routledge and Kegan Paul Ltd, 1951.

De Mably, Gabriel Bonnôt, *Le droit public de l'Europe, fondé sur les traités*, 4th ed., 4 Vols., Genève, 1768.

Mackenzie, Charles, *Notes on Haiti, Made During a Residence in That Republic*, 1st ed., 2 Vols., London, H. Colburn and R. Bentley, 1830.

Maine, Henry Sumner, Sir, *Ancient Law. Its Connection to the History of Early Society*, New York, Cosimo, 2005 [1861].

Malia, Martin, *Alexander Herzen and the Birth of Russian Socialism 1812-1855*, Cambridge, Harvard University Press, 1961.

Manent, Pierre, *Tocqueville and the Nature of Democracy*, transl. by John Waggoner, Lanham, Rowman & Littlefield Publishers Inc., 1996.

Mardin, Şerif, *The Genesis of Young Ottoman Thought. A Study in the Modernization of Turkish Political Ideas*, Syracuse NY, Syracuse University Press, 2000.

Marshall, T.H., *Citizenship and Social Class, and other essays*, Cambridge, Cambridge University Press, 1950.

Martínez, Frédéric, *El nacionalismo cosmopólita. La referencia europea en la construcción nacional en Colombia*, Bogotá, Banco de la República, 1993.

Marx, Karl and Engels, Friedrich, *The Communist Manifesto* (1848), Middlesex, The Echo Library, 2009.

Micheli du Crest, Jacques-Barthélémy, *Discours en forme de Lettres sur le Gouvernement de Genève* (1735), Kenneth Godwin, Guillaume Poisson, Gabriella Silvestrini and Richard Whatmore (eds.), Genève, Slatkine, 2011.

Mill, John Stuart, *On Liberty and Considerations on Representative Government*, R.B. McCallum (ed.), Oxford, Basil Blackwell, 1946.

Mill, John Stuart, *The Spirit of the Age, On Liberty, The Subjection of Women*, New York, W.W. Norton & Company, Inc., 1996.

Mommsen, Wolfgang J., *The Political and Social Theory of Max Weber*, Cambridge UK, Polity Press, 1989.

Montesquieu, Charles de Secondat, *De l'esprit des lois*, X, II, Paris, Garnier Flammarion, 1979.

Montesquieu, Charles de Secondat, *The Spirit of Law*, X, III, Thomas Nugent (transl.), New York, Cosimo Classics, 2011.

Muldoon, James, *Empire and Order. The Concept of Empire 800-1800*, London, Macmillan, 1999.

Muthu, Sankar, *Enlightenment against Empire*, Princeton/Oxford, Princeton University Press, 2003.

Neff, Stephen C., *War and the Law of Nations. A General History*, Cambridge University Press, 2005.

Niven, C. Rex, *A Short History of Nigeria*, London, Longmans, 1965.

Nolte, Paul, *Staatsbildung und Gesellschaftsreform. Politische Reformen in Preußen und den süddeutschen Staaten 1800-1820*, Frankfurt am Main/New York, Campus, 1990.

Nwabueze, B.O., *Constitutional Law of the Nigerian Republic*, London, Butterworths, 1964.

Obilade, A.O., *The Nigerian Legal System*, Ibadan, Spectrum Law Publishing, 2000.

Oeschey, Rudolf, *Die bayerische Verfassungsurkunde vom 26. Mai 1818 und die Charte Ludwigs XVIII. vom 4. Juni 1814. Ein Beitrag zur Lehre vom monarchischen Prinzip. Unter Berücksichtigung der bayerischen Konstitution vom 1. Mai 1808 und deren Vorbildes, der westfälischen Verfassung vom 15. November 1807*, Munich, C.H. Beck, 1914.

Oestmann, Peter, *Rechtsvielfalt vor Gericht. Rechtsanwendung und Partikularrecht im Alten Reich*, Frankfurt am Main, Veröffentlichungen des Max-Planck-Instituts für Europäische Rechtsgeschichte, 2002.

Okonkwo, C.O., *Okonkwo and Naish on Criminal Law in Nigeria*, Ibadan, Spectrum Law Publishing, 1990.

O'Leary, Daniel Florencio, *Bolívar and the War of Independence*, transl. and ed. by Robert F. McNerney, Austin TX, University of Texas Press, 1970.

O'Leary, Daniel Florencio, *Cartas de Sucre al Libertador (1820-1830)*, 2 Vols., Madrid, Editorial-América, 1919.

O'Leary, Daniel Florencio, *Memorias del General O'Leary*, transl. by Simón B. O'Leary, 30 Vols., Caracas, El Monitor, 1883.

Othmer, Sieglinde C., *Berlin und die Verbreitung des Naturrechts in Europa*, Berlin, De Gruyter, 1970.

Pagden, Anthony, *Lords of all the World. Ideologies of Empire in Spain, Britain and France c. 1500-c. 1800*, New Haven/London, Yale University Press, 1995.

Pakenham, Thomas, *The Scramble for Africa. White Man's Conquest of the Dark Continent from 1876 to 1912*, New York, Random House, 1991.

Palmer, Alan, *The Decline and Fall of the Ottoman Empire*, New York, Barnes & Noble Books, 1994.

Pamuk, Şevket, *The Ottoman Empire and European Capitalism, 1820-1913*, Cambridge, Cambridge University Press, 2010 [1987].

Park, A.E.W., *The Sources of Nigerian Law*, Lagos, African Universities Press, 1963.

de Paula Santander, Francisco, *Obra educativa de Santander*, Vol. 1, Luis Horacio López Domínguez (ed.), Bogotá, Fundación Francisco de Paula Santander, 1990.

Perham, Margery, *The Colonial Reckoning. The End of Imperial Rule in Africa In the Light of British Experience*, New York, Alfred A. Knopf, 1962.

Perkins, William A. and Stembridge, Jasper H., *Nigeria. A Descriptive Geography*, Ibadan/London, Oxford University Press, 1963.

Picón Febrés, Gonzalo, *Don Simón Rodríguez. Maestro del libertador*, Caracas, Cooperativa de Artes Gráficas, 1939.

Pierik, Roland, and Werner, Wouter G. (eds.), *Cosmopolitanism in Context. Perspectives from International Law and Political Theory*, Cambridge, Cambridge University Press, 2010.

Pitts, Jennifer, *A Turn to Empire. The Rise of Imperial Liberalism in Britain and France*, Princeton/Oxford, Princeton University Press, 2005.

Prutsch, Markus J., *Die Charte constitutionnelle Ludwigs XVIII. in der Krise von 1830. Verfassungsentwicklung und Verfassungsrevision in Frankreich 1814 bis 1830*, Marburg, Tectum, 2006.

Pufendorf, Samuel, *Gesammelte Werke*, Vol. 4.1-2, Frank Böhling (ed.), Berlin, Akademie Verlag, 1998.

Pufendorf, Samuel, *Le droit de nature et des gens*, trad. par Jean Barbeyrac, Bâle, E. & J.R., Thourneisen, 1732.

Quataert, Donald, *The Ottoman Empire, 1700-1992*, 2nd ed., Cambridge, Cambridge University Press, 2005.

Ramel, Frédérick and Joubert, Jean-Paul, *Rousseau et les relations internationales*, Paris, Harmattan, 2000.

Reibstein, Ernst, *Die Anfänge des neueren Natur- und Völkerrechts. Studien über den 'Controversiae illustres' des Fernandus Vasquius (1559)*, Bern, Haupt, 1949.

Roberts-Wray, Sir Kenneth, *Commonwealth and Colonial Law*, London, Stevens & Sons, 1966.

Robinson, Ronald and Gallagher John, with Denny, Alice, *Africa and the Victorians. The Climax of Imperialism*, New York, Anchor Books, 1968.

Rodney, Walter, *West Africa and the Atlantic Slave Trade*, Nairobi, East African Publishing House, 1967.

Rodríguez, Simón, *Inventamos o erramos*, Caracas, Monte Ávila, 2004.

Rodríguez, Simón, *Obras Completas*, Caracas, 1975.

Rodríguez, Simón, *Simón Rodríguez. Cartas*, Caracas, UNESR, 2001.

Rodríguez, Simón, *Sociedades Americanas en 1828: cómo serán y cómo podrian ser en los siglos venideros*, Arequipa, s.n. 1828.

Rodríguez, Simón, *Sociedades americanas en 1828*, Lima, Imprenta del Comercio por J. Monterola, 1842.

Roggerone, Giuseppe Agostino, *Saint-Pierre et Rousseau. Confederazione, democrazia, utopia*, Milan, Franco Angeli, 1985.

Rosales Sánchez, Juan, *La república de Simón Rodríguez*, Caracas, Fundación Editorial El Perro y La Rana, 2007.

Rotteck, Carl von, *Lehrbuch des Vernunftsrechts und der Staatswissenschaften*, Stuttgart, Hallberg, 1829-1835, Vol. 2 (1830).

Rousseau, Jean-Jacques, *Correspondance Complète de Jean-Jacques Rousseau*, Ralph A. Leigh (ed.), Ginevra/Oxford, The Voltaire Foundation, 1965-1998.

Rousseau, Jean-Jacques, *Emile, or on Education*, Christopher Kelly and Allan Bloom (eds.), Lebanon, Dartmouth College Press, 2010.

Rousseau, Jean-Jacques, *Emilius; or, a Treatise of Education*, 3 Vols., Edinburgh, printed for J. Dickson and C. Elliot, 1773.

Rousseau, Jean-Jacques, *Œuvres complètes de Jean-Jacques Rousseau*, Bernard Gagnebin & Marcel Raymond (eds.), 5 Vols., Paris, Gallimard, 1959-1995.

Rousseau, Jean-Jacques, *Principes du droit de la guerre. Écrits sur la paix perpétuelle*, Bruno Bernardi and Gabriella Silvestrini (eds.), Blaise Bachofenand Céline Spector (dir.), Paris, Vrin, 2008.

Ruiz, Gustavo Adolfo, *Simón Rodríguez. Maestro de escuela de primeras letras*, Caracas, Academia Nacional de Historia, 1990.

Rumazo González, Alfonso, *Simón Rodríguez, maestro de América*, Caracas, Biblioteca Ayacucho, 2005.

Said, Edward W., *Orientalism*, New York, Vintage Books, 2003.

Samper, José María, *Viajes de un colombiano en Europa*, 2 Vols., Paris, Impr. de E. Thunot, 1862.

Sarmiento, Domingo Faustino, *Facundo. Civilization and Barbarism*, trans. by Kathleen Ross, Berkeley, University of California Press, 2003.

Schennach, Martin Paul, *Gesetz und Herrschaft. Zur Entstehung des Gesetzgebungsstaates am Beispiel Tirols*, Köln [u.a.], Böhlau, 2010.

Schmid, Alois (ed.), *Die bayerische Konstitution von 1808. Entstehung – Zielsetzung – Europäisches Umfeld*, Munich, C.H. Beck, 2008.

Schmidt, Georg, *Geschichte des Alten Reiches. Staat und Nation in der Frühen Neuzeit 1495-1806*, Munich, C.H. Beck, 1999.

Schmidt, James and Oksenberg Rorty, Amélie (eds.), *Kant's 'Idea for a Universal History with a Cosmopolitan Aim'. A Critical Guide*, Cambridge, Cambridge University Press, 2009.

Schœlcher, Victor, *Vie De Toussaint-Louverture*, 2nd ed., Paris, P. Ollendorff, 1889.

Schröder, Jan, *Recht als Wissenschaft. Geschichte der juristischen Methodenlehre vom Humanismus bis zur Historischen Schule (1500-1850)*, Munich, C.H. Beck Verlag, 2001.

Schultze, A., *The Sultanate of Bornu*, originally published in German in 1913, translated by P.A. Benton, London, Frank Cass & Co. Ltd, 1968.

Schäfer, Frank L., *Juristische Germanistik. Eine Geschichte der Wissenschaft vom einheimischen Privatrecht*, Frankfurt am Main, Klostermann, 2008.

Sellin, Volker, *Die geraubte Revolution. Der Sturz Napoleons und die Restauration in Europa*, Göttingen, Vandenhoeck & Ruprecht, 2001.

de Sepúlveda, Juan Ginés, *Democrate secondo, ovvero sulle giuste cause di guerra*, Domenico Taranto (ed.), with the original Latin text, Macerata, Quodlibet, 2009.

Seton-Watson, Hugh, *The Russian Empire 1801-1917*, Oxford, Oxford University Press, 1967.

Siedentop, Larry, *Tocqueville*, Oxford, Oxford University Press, 1994.

Skinner, Quentin, *Liberty before Liberalism*, Cambridge, Cambridge University Press, 1998.

Skinner, Quentin, *The Foundations of Modern Political Thought. Vol. I: The Renaissance*, Cambridge, Cambridge University Press, 1978.

Smith, Adam, *An Inquiry into the Nature and Causes of the Wealth of Nations*, Hamburg, Management Laboratory Press, 2008.

Smith, Adam, *An Inquiry into the Nature and Causes of the Wealth of Nations*, New York, Modern Library Edition, 1937.

Spector, Céline, *Montesquieu. Pouvoirs, richesses et sociétés*, Paris, PUF, 2004.

Stein, Peter G., *Römisches Recht in Europa. Die Geschichte einer Rechtskultur*, Frankfurt am Main, Fisher, 1996.

Stein, Peter, *Roman Law in European History*, Cambridge, Cambridge University Press, 1999.

Stephens, Thomas M., *Dictionary of Latin American Racial and Ethnic Terminology*, 2nd ed., Gainesville, University Press of Florida.

Strauss, Leo, *Natural Right and History*, Chicago, Chicago University Press, 1950.

Tamuno, T.N., *The Evolution of the Nigerian State. The Southern Phase, 1898-1914*, London, Longmans, 1972.

Temple, Charles Lindsay, *Native Races and their Rulers. Sketches and Studies of Official Life and Administrative Problems in Nigeria*, London, Frank Cass and Co., 1968.

Temple, C.L., *Notes on the Tribes, Province, Emirates and States of the Northern Provinces of Nigeria*, New York, Barnes & Noble, 1922.

Tocqueville, Alexis de, *Democracy in America*, ed. and transl. by Harvey C. Mansfield & Delba Winthrop, Chicago, The University of Chicago Press, 2000.

Tocqueville, Alexis de, *Selected Letters on Politics and Society*, Roger Boesche (ed.), transl. by James Toupin and Roger Boesche, Berkeley, University of California Press, 1985.

Tocqueville, Alexis de, *The Old Regime and the Revolution*, François Furet and Françoise Mélonio (eds.), transl. by Alan S. Kahan, Chicago, University of Chicago Press, 1988.

Tocqueville, Alexis de, *Writings on Empire and Slavery*, ed. and transl. by Jennifer Pitts, Baltimore/London, The John Hopkins University Press, 2001.

Tómas y Valiente, Francisco, *Manual de historia del derecho español*, 4th ed., Technos, 1997 [1983].

Trouillot, Michel-Rolph, *Silencing the Past, Power and the Production of History*, Boston, Beacon Press, 1995.

Tully, James, *An Approach to Political Philosophy. Locke in contexts*, Cambridge, Cambridge University Press, 1993.

Ullmann, Hans-Peter, *Staatsschulden und Reformpolitik. Die Entstehung moderner öffentlicher Schulden in Bayern und Baden 1780-1820*, 2 Vols., Göttingen, Vandenhoeck & Ruprecht, 1986.

Urquhart, David, *The Spirit of the East*, 2 Vols., London, Henry Colburn Publisher, 1838.

Urquhart, David, *Turkey and Its Resources. Its Municipal Organisation and Free Trade*, London, Sounders and Otley, 1833.

Uslar Pietri, Arturo, *La isla de Róbinsón*, Barcelona, Editorial Seix Barral, 1982.

Vandeleur, Seymour, D.S.O. Lieutenant and Scots Guards, *Campaigning on the Upper Nile and Niger*, London, Methuen & Co., 1898.

de Vargas, Pedro Fermín, *Pensamientos políticos y memorias sobre la población del Nuevo Reino de Granada*, Manuel José Forero (ed.), Bogotá, Banco de la República, 1953.

de Vattel, Emer, *Le droit des gens ou principes de la loi naturelle*, London, 1758.

de Vattel, Emer, *The Law of Nations*, Béla Kapossy and Richard Whatmore (eds.), Indianapolis, Liberty Fund, 2008

Venturi, Franco, *Italy and the Enlightenment. Studies in a Cosmopolitan Century*, transl. by Susan Corsi, London, Longman, 1972.

Vieira Posada, Edgar, *La Integración De América Latina. Del Congreso Anfictiónico De Panamá En 1826 a Una Comunidad Latinoamericana O Sudamericana De Naciones En El Año 2010*, Colección Biblioteca Del Profesional, Bogotá, Editorial Pontificia Universidad Javeriana, 2004.

von Hazzi, Joseph, *Ueber die Standpuncte der baierischen Verfassungs-Urkunde von 1818 in Beziehung anderer Constitutionen*, Munich, J. Lindauer, 1819.

Wallerstein, Immanuel, *European Universalism. The Rhetoric of Power*, New York, New Press, 2006.

Waltz, Kenneth, *Man, the State and War. A Theoretical Analysis*, New York, Columbia University Press, 1959.

Walzer, Michael, *Interpretation and Social Criticism*, Cambridge MA, Harvard University Press, 1987.

Wilson, Holly L., *Kant's Pragmatic Anthropology. It's Origin, Meaning, and Critical Significance*, Albany, State University of New York Press, 2006.

Windenberger, Joseph-Lucien, *Essai sur le système de politique étrangère de J.-J. Rousseau. La République confédérative des petits États*, Paris, Picard et fils, 1899.

Zenkovskii, Vasilii Vasil'evick, *Russian Thinkers and Europe*, Ann Arbor, J.W. Edwards Publisher, 1953.

Ziegler, Karl-Heinz, *Völkerrechtsgeschichte*, 2nd ed., Munich, C.H. Beck Verlag, 2007.

Zimmermann, Fritz, *Bayerische Verfassungsgeschichte vom Ausgang der Landschaft bis zur Verfassungsurkunde von 1818. Ein Beitrag zur Auseinandersetzung Deutschlands mit den Ideen der Französischen Revolution und Restauration.* Erster Teil. Vorgeschichte und Entstehung der Konstitution von 1808, Munich, C.H. Beck, 1940.

Book chapters and articles

Abraham, Garth, "Africa and its Boundaries, a Legal Overview from Colonialism to the African Union," in Jeffrey Herbst and Greg Mills (eds.), *Big African State*, Johannesburg, Wits University Press, 2006, pp. 273-290.

Acemoglu, Daron, Johnson, Simon and Robinson, James A., "The Colonial Origins of Comparative Development. An Empirical Investigation," 91 *The American Economic Review* (2001), pp. 1369-1401.

Akintoye, S.A., "The Ondo Road Eastwards of Lagos, c. 1870-1895," 10 *The Journal of African History* (1969), pp. 581-589.

Allot, A.N., "The Authority of English Decisions in Colonial Courts," 1 *Journal of African Law* (1957), pp. 23-39.

Allot, A.N., "Towards a definition of 'Absolute ownership'," 5 *Journal of African Law* (1961), pp. 99-102.

Andrés-Lasheras, Jesús, "Simón Rodríguez en sus cartas," in Simón Rodríguez, *Simón Rodríguez. Cartas*, Caracas, UNESR, 2001, pp. 17-106.

Archibugi, Daniel, "Immanuel Kant, Cosmopolitan Law and Peace," 1 *European Journal of International Relations* (1995), pp. 429-456.

Armitage, David, "John Locke, Carolina, and the Two Treatises of Government," 32 *Political Theory* (2004), pp. 602-627.

Atanda, J.A., "The Wars and Imperial Conquests of Yorubaland," in Adeagbo Akinjogbin (ed.), *War and Peace in Yorubaland 1793-1893*, Ibadan, Heinemann Educational Books, 1998, pp. 307-320.

Bachofen, Blaise, "La nation, la patrie, le pays. La question de l'appartenance politique chez Rousseau," 50 *Annales de la Société Jean-Jacques Rousseau* (2012), pp. 267-298.

Bachofen, Blaise, "Les raisons de la guerre, la raison dans la guerre," in Blaise Bachofen and Céline Spector (eds.), *Jean-Jacques Rousseau, Principes du droit de la guerre. Écrits sur la paix perpétuelle*, Paris, Vrin, 2008, pp. 131-192.

Badia, Juan Ferrando, "Die Spanische Verfassung von 1812 und Europa," *Der Staat: Zeitschrift für Staatslehre, öffentliches Recht und Verfassungsgeschichte* 2 (1963), pp. 153-180.

Beauvois, Frédérique, "L'indemnité De Saint-Domingue. 'Dette D'indépendance' Ou 'Rançon De L'esclavage'?," 10 *French Colonial History* (2009), pp. 109-124.

Beck, Ulrich, "The Cosmopolitan Manifesto," in Ulrich Beck, *World Risk Society*, Cambridge UK, Polity Press, 1999, pp. 1-18.

Beinart, William, Brown, Karen and Gilfoyle, Daniel, "Experts and Expertise in Colonial Africa Reconsidered. Science and the Interpenetration of Knowledge," *African Affairs*, Advance Access Publication, 28 May 2009, pp. 413-433.

Bell, Duncan, "Republican Imperialism. J.A. Froude and the Virtue of Empire," XXX *History of Political Thought* (2009), pp. 166-191.

Bernardi, Bruno and Silvestrini, Gabriella, "Principes du droit de la guerre," 46 *Annales de la Société Jean-Jacques Rousseau* (2005), pp. 201-280.

Bernasconi, Robert, "Who Invented the Concept of Race. Kant's Role in the Enlightenment Construction of Race," in Robert Bernasconi (ed.), *Race, Blackwell Readings in Continental Philosophy*, Malden Mass., Blackwell, 2001, pp. 11-36.

Bloch, Michael, "Möglichkeit und Unmöglichkeit internationaler Politik. Rousseaus Auffassung des Krieges," 58 *Deutsche Zeitschrift für Philosophie* (2010), pp. 288-306.

Bois, Jean-Pierre, *L'Europe à l'époque moderne. XVIe-XVIIIe siècle*, Paris, Colin, 2004, pp. 186-199.

Bolívar, Simón, "Address to the Angostura Congress, February 15, 1819, the Day of the Installation," in Janet Burke and Ted Humphrey (eds.), *Nineteenth-Century Nation Building and the Latin American Intellectual Tradition.* A Reader, Indianapolis, Hackett Publishing Company, 2007.

Bolívar, Simón, "Decreto Sobre Libertad De Los Esclavos – Carúpano, 2 De Junio De 1816," in Vicente Lecuna (ed.), *Bolívar, Simón. Proclamas Y Discursos Del Libertador, 1811-1830*, Biblioteca De Autores Y Temas Mirandinos, 1983.

Bolívar, Simón, "Latin-American Correspondence author(S). Simon Bolivar and Alexandre Sabès Pétion," 7 *Phylon* (1940-1956) (1946).

Bonaparte, Napoléon, "“Aux Citoyens De Saint-Domingue" Paris, 4 Nivose an VIII (25 Decembre, 1799)," *Correspondence De Napoléon I; Publiée Par Ordre De L'empereur Napoléon III*, Paris, H. Plon, J. Dumaine, 1858.

Brauneder, Wilhelm, "Europäisches Privatrecht – aber was ist es?," 15 *Zeitschrift für Neuere Rechtsgeschichte* (1993), pp. 225-235.

Brunschwig, Henri, "Anglophobia and French African Policy," in Prosser Gifford and William Roger Louis (eds.), *France and Britain in Africa. Imperial Rivalry and Colonial Rule*, New Haven/London, Yale University Press, 1971, pp. 3-34.

Buck-Morss, Susan, "Hegel and Haiti," 26 *Critical Inquiry* (2000), pp. 821-865.

Cavallar, Georg, "'La société générale du genre humain'. Rousseau on Cosmopolitanism, International Relations, and Republican Patriotism," in Kitromilides, Paschalis M. (ed.), *From Republican Polity to National Community. Reconsiderations of Enlightenment Political Thought*, Oxford, Voltaire Foundation, 2003, pp. 89-109.

Chang, Ha-Joon, "The Economic Theory of the Developmental State," in Meredith Woo-Cumings (ed.), *The Developmental State*, New York, Cornell University Press, 1998, pp. 182-199.

Cheah, Pheng, "The Cosmopolitical – Today," Cheah, Pheng & Robbins, Bruce (eds.), *Cosmopolitics. Thinking and Feeling beyond the Nation*, Minneapolis MN, Minnesota University Press, 1998, pp. 30-38.

Cicero, "On The Laws," in Cicero, *On the Commonwealth and On the Laws*, James E.G. Zetzel (ed.), Cambridge, Cambridge University Press, 1999, pp. 105-175.

Condorcet, "Rapport et projet de décret sur l'organisation générale de l'instruction publique (1792)," in Célestin Hippeau (ed.), *L'instruction publique en France pendant la Révolution*, Paris, Klincksieck, 1990.

Corrales, Manuel Ezequiel (ed.), *Homenaje de Colombia al Libertador en su primer centenario, 1783-1883*, Bogotá, Medardo Rivas 1884.

Couture, Jocelyne and Nielsen, Kai, "Cosmopolitanism and the Compatriot Priority Principle," in Gillian Brock and Harry Brighouse (eds.), *The Political Philosophy of Cosmopolitanism*, Cambridge, Cambridge University Press, 2005, pp. 180-197.

Cúneo, Dardo, "Aproximación a Simón Rodríguez," in Simón Rodríguez, *Inventamos o erramos*, Caracas, Monte Ávila, 2004, pp. ix-xli.

Dippel, Horst, "Die Bedeutung der spanischen Verfassung von 1812 für den deutschen Frühliberalismus und Frühkonstitutionalismus," in Martin Kirsch and Pierangelo Schiera (eds.), *Denken und Umsetzung des Konstitutionalismus in Deutschland und anderen europäischen Ländern in der ersten Hälfte des 19. Jahrhunderts*, Berlin, Duncker & Humblot, 1999, pp. 219-237.

Dipper, Christof, "Die politische Funktionalität des italienischen Naturrechts in der zweiten Hälfte des 18. Jahrhunderts," in Vanda Fiorillo and Frank Grunert (eds.), *Das Naturrecht der Geselligkeit. Anthropologie, Recht und Politik im 18. Jahrhundert*, Berlin, Duncker & Humblot, 2009, pp. 135-157.

Dorigny, Marcel, "Aux Origines. L'indépendance D'Haïti Et Son Occultation," in *La Fracture Coloniale. La Société Française Au Prisme De L'héritage Colonial*, Nicolas Bancel Pascal Blanchard and Sandrine Lemaire (eds.), Paris, La Découverte, 2005.

Duvergier, J.B., "12 Nivose an 6 (1er janvier 1798) 'Loi Concernant L'Organisation Constitutionnelle Des Colonies'," in France (ed.), *Collection Complète Des Lois, Décrets, Ordonnances, Réglemens Et Avis Du Conseil D'État, Publiée Sur Les Éditions Officielles Du Louvre, De L'imprimerie Nationale Par Baudouin Et Du Bulletin Des Lois, De 1788 À 1824 Inclusivement*, 10, Paris, A. Guyot et Scribe, 1825.

Dwyer, Philip, "Remembering and Forgetting in Contemporary France. Napoleon, Slavery and the French History Wars," 26 *French Politics, Culture & Society* (2008), pp. 110-122.

Ehrensaft, Philip, "The Political Economy of Informal Empire in Pre-Colonial Nigeria, 1807-1884," 6 *Canadian Journal of African Studies/Revue Canadienne des Études Africaines* (1972), pp. 451-490.

Eigen Figal, Sara and Larrimore, Mark J., "Introduction. The German Invention of Race," in Sara Eigen Figal and Mark J. Larrimore (eds.), *The German Invention of Race, Suny Series, Philosophy and Race*, Albany, State University of New York Press, 2006, pp. 1-22.

Eldem, Edhem, "Istanbul. From Imperial to Peripheralized Capital," in Edhem Eldem *et al.* (eds.), *The Ottoman City between East and West. Aleppo, Izmir, and Istanbul*, Cambridge, Cambridge University Press, 1999, pp. 135-206.

Elias, T.O., "Colonial Courts and the Doctrine of Judicial Precedent," 18 *The Modern Law Review* (1955), pp. 356-370.

Eltis, David and Richardson, David, "The 'Numbers Game' and Routes to Slavery," *Routes to Slavery. Direction, Ethnicity, and Mortality in the Transatlantic Slave Trade*, Studies in Slave and Post-Slave Societies and Cultures, London, Portland OR, Frank Cass, 1997, pp. 1-15.

Farr, James, ""So Vile and Miserable an Estate": The Problem of Slavery in Locke's Political Thought," 14 *Political Theory* (1986), pp. 263-289.

Fehrenbach, Elisabeth, "Verfassungs- und sozialpolitische Reformen und Reformprojekte in Deutschland unter dem Einfluss des Napoleonischen Frankreich," in Helmut Berding and Hans-Peter Ullmann (eds.), *Deutschland zwischen Revolution und Restauration*, Düsseldorf, Königstein/Ts, Athenäum, Droste, 1981.

Filmer, Robert, Sir, "Observations on MR Hobbes' Leviathan: or his Artificial Man a Commonwealth," in Johann P. Sommerville (ed.), *Patriarcha and Other Writings*, Cambridge, Cambridge University Press, 1991.

Fink, Carolyn E., "The Saint Domingue Slave Revolution and the Unfolding of Independence 1791-1804," in David Patrick Geggus and Norman Fiering (eds.), *The World of the Haitian Revolution (Blacks in the Diaspora)*, Bloomington, Indiana University Press, 2009, pp. 179-196.

Fleury, Thibaut, "Le droit des gens dans la pensée de Jean-Jacques Rousseau," *Annales de Philosophie du Droit, Institut Michel Villey* (2006), pp. 295-335.

Florovsky, Anton, "Dostoyevsky and the Slavonic Question," 26 *Slavonic and East European Review* (1930), pp. 411-423.

Foucault, Michel, "The Art of Telling the Truth," in Lawrence D. Kritzman (ed.), *Politics, Philosophy, Culture. Interviews and Other Writings, 1977-1984*, New York, Routledge, 1988.

Gaffield, Julia, "Complexities of Imagining Haiti. A Study of National Constitutions 1801-1807," 41 *Journal of Social History* (Fall 2007), pp. 81-103.

Gallagher, John and Robinson, Ronald, "The Imperialism of Free Trade," William Roger Louis (ed.), *Imperialism. The Robinson and Gallagher Controversy*, New York, New Viewpoints, 1976, pp. 53-72.

Geggus, D., "The Naming of Haiti," 71 *New West Indian Guide/Nieuwe West-Indische Gids* (1997), pp. 43-68.

Gerschenkron, Alexander, "The Rate of Growth in Russia. The Rate of Industrial Growth in Russia, Since 1885," 7 *The Journal of Economic History* (1947), pp. 144-174.

Glauser, Wayne, "Three Approaches to Locke and the Slave Trade," 51 *Journal of the History of Ideas* (1990), pp. 199-216.

Grases, Pedro, "Simón Rodríguez, pionero de la educación republicana," in Buenaventura Delgado Criado (ed.), *Historia de la educación en España y América. La educación en la España contemporánea (1789-1975)*, Madrid, Ediciones Morata, 1994.

Gueye, M., "African Initiatives and Resistance in West Africa, 1880-1914," in A. Adu Boahen (ed.), *General History of Africa. Volume VII Africa under Colonial Domination 1880-1935*, Abridged Edition, Ibadan, Heinemann Educational Books LTD, 1990, pp. 55-71.

Gundre Frank, Andre, "The Development of Underdevelopment", XVIII *Monthly Review* (1966), pp. 17-30.

Hamowy, Roland, "Tocqueville on Socialism," translation of part of Alexis de Tocqueville's speech of September 12, 1848 before the Constituent Assembly, 1 *New Individualist Review* (1961), pp. 18-23.

Hoffmann, Stanley, "Rousseau, la guerre et la paix," 5 *Annales de Philosophie politique* (1965), pp. 195-240.

Inalcik, Halil, "Capital Formation in the Ottoman Empire," 29 *The Journal of Economic History* (1969), pp. 97-140.

Jenson, Deborah, "Dessaline's American Proclamations of the Haitian Independence," 15 *The Journal of Haitian Studies* (2009), pp. 72-102.

Kant, Immanuel, "On the Different Races of Man (1775)," in Emmanuel Chukwudi Eze (ed.), *Race and the Enlightenment. A Reader*, Cambridge Mass., Blackwell, 1997, pp. 38-48.

Kant, Immanuel, "Of the different races of human beings (1775)," *Anthropology, History, and Education*, The Cambridge Edition of the Works of Immanuel Kant, Robert B. Louden and Günter Zöller (eds.), Cambridge UK/New York, Cambridge University Press, 2007, pp. 82-97.

Kant, Immanuel, "On the feeling of the beautiful and sublime (1764)," *Anthropology, History, and Education*, The Cambridge Edition of the Works of

Immanuel Kant, Robert B. Louden and Günter Zöller (eds.), Cambridge UK/New York, Cambridge University Press, 2007, pp. 18-62.

Kant, Immanuel, "Idea for a Universal History with a Cosmopolitan Intent," in *Perpetual Peace and Other Essays on Politics, History, and Moral Practice*, transl. by Ted Humphrey, Indianapolis, Hackett Publishing Company, 1983, pp. 29-40.

Kant, Immanuel, "Idea for a Universal History with a Cosmopolitan Purpose," in Hans S. Reiss (ed.), *Kant. Political Writings*, 2nd enl. ed., Cambridge Texts in the History of Political Thought, Cambridge, Cambridge University Press, 1991, pp. 41-53.

Kant, Immanuel, "On the Common Saying. This may be True in Theory, but is Does not Apply in Practice," Hans S. Reiss (ed.), *Kant. Political Writings*, 2nd enl. ed., Cambridge Texts in the History of Political Thought, Cambridge, Cambridge University Press, 1991, pp. 61-92.

Kant, Immanuel, "On the Relationship of Theory to Practice in Political Right," in Hans S. Reiss (ed.), *Kant. Political Writings*, 2nd enl. ed., Cambridge Texts in the History of Political Thought, Cambridge, Cambridge University Press, 1991, pp. 87-92.

Kant, Immanuel, "Perpetual Peace," in Hans S. Reiss (ed.), *Kant's Political Writings*, Cambridge, Cambridge University Press, 1996.

Kant, Immanuel, "Perpetual Peace. A Philosophical Sketch," in Hans S. Reiss (ed.), *Kant. Political Writings*, 2nd enl. ed., Cambridge Texts in the History of Political Thought, Cambridge, Cambridge University Press, 1991, pp. 93-130.

Kant, Immanuel, "The Contest of the Faculties," in Hans S. Reiss (ed.), *Kant. Political Writings*, 2nd enl. ed., Cambridge Texts in the History of Political Thought, Cambridge, Cambridge University Press, 1991, pp. 176-190.

Kant, Immanuel, "Toward Perpetual Peace (1795)," in *Practical Philosophy*, The Cambridge edition of the works of Immanuel Kant, Mary J. Gregor (transl. & ed.), Cambridge, Cambridge University Press, 1999, pp. 311-351.

Kasaba, Reşat, "Treaties and Friendships. British Imperialism, the Ottoman Empire, and China in the 19th Century," 4 *Journal of World History* (1993), pp. 215-241.

Kavanagh, Thomas, "Rousseau's The Levite of Ephraim: Synthesis within a "Minor" Work," in Patrick Riley (ed.), *The Cambridge Companion to Rousseau*, Cambridge, Cambridge University Press, 2001, pp. 397-417.

Kleingeld, Pauline, "Six Varieties of Cosmopolitanism in Late Eighteenth-Century Germany," 60 *Journal of the History of Ideas* (1999), pp. 505-524.

Koskenniemi, Martti, "International Community from Dante to Vattel," in Vincent Chetail and Peter Haggenmacher, *Vattel's International Law in a 21st Century Perspective*, Leiden, Brill, 2011, pp. 49-74.

Koskenniemi, Martti, "International Law in Europe. Between Tradition and Renewal," 16 *European Journal of International Law* (2005), pp. 113-124.

Laitin, D.D., "Hegemony and Religious Conflict. British Imperial Control and Political Cleavages in Yorubaland," in P.B. Evans, D. Rueschemeyer and T. Skocpol (eds.), *Bringing the State Back In*, Cambridge, Cambridge University Press, 1985, pp. 285-316.

Lalatta Costerbosa, Marina, "Guerra e libertà in Jean-Jacques Rousseau. L'impossibilità di un progetto per la pace internazionale," 15 *Teoria politica* (1999), pp. 125-141.

Larrère, Catherine, "L'état de guerre et la guerre entre les états. Jean-Jacques Rousseau et la critique du Droit naturel," *La Bataille, l'Armée, la Gloire, Actes du Colloque de Clermont-Ferrand*, 1983, Clermont-Ferrand, Association des Publications de Clermont II, 1985.

Leibniz, "Mars Christianissimus," in Patrick Riley (ed.), *Political Writings*, Cambridge, Cambridge University Press, 1981, pp. 121-145.

Lieven, Dominic, "Empire on Europe's Periphery. Russian and Western Comparisons," in Alexei Miller and Alfred J. Reiber (eds.), *Imperial Rule*, Budapest, CEU Press, pp. 133-149.

Louis, William Roger, "The Berlin Congo Conference," in Prosser Gifford and William Roger Louis (eds.), *France and Britain in Africa. Imperial Rivalry and Colonial Rule*, New Haven/London, Yale University Press, 1971, pp. 167-220.

Lugard, Baron, "Native Policy in East Africa," 9 *Foreign Affairs* (1930), pp. 65-78.

Lugard, Frederick D., "Northern Nigeria," 23 *The Geographical Journal* (1904), pp. 1-27.

Lugard, Lord, "Africa and the Powers," 35 *Journal of the Royal African Society* (1936), pp. 4-17.

Lugard, Lord, "British Policy in Nigeria," 10 *Africa Journal of the International African Institute* (1937), pp. 377-400.

Lugard, Lord, "Colonial Administration," 41 *Economica* (1933), pp. 248-263.

Lugard, Lord, "Education and Race Relations," 32 *Journal of the African Society* (1933), pp. 1-11.

Lugard, Lord, "Slavery in All Its Forms," 6 *The Journal of the International African Institute* (1933), pp. 1-14.

Lugard, Lord, "The Basis of the Claim for Colonies," 15 *International Affairs* (1936), pp. 3-25.

Lugard, Lord, "The Claim to Colonies," 35 *Journal of the Royal African Society* (1936), pp. 115-122.

Luig, Klaus, "Universales und partikulares Recht in den 'Meditationes ad Pandectas' von Augustin Leyser," in *Diritto comune e diritti locali nella storia dell' Europa*, Milano, Giuffrè, 1980, pp. 27-48.

Luig, Klaus, "Zur Verbreitung des Naturrechts in Europa," 40 *Tijdschrift voor Rechtsgeschiedenis* (1972), pp. 539-557.

Mahoney, Paul G., "The Common Law and Economic Growth. Hayek Might Be Right," 30 *The Journal of Legal Studies* (2001), pp. 503-525.

Matthewson, Tim, "Jefferson and the Nonrecognition of Haiti," 140 *Proceedings of the American Philosophical Society* (1996) pp. 22-48.

Menin, Marco, "La fin de l'innocence: une lecture du "Lévite d'Éphraïm" de Jean-Jacques Rousseau," 18 *Les Études Rousseau* (2009-2010), pp. 203-225.

Mignolo, Walter, "The Many Faces of Cosmo-polis. Border Thinking and Critical Cosmopolitanism," 12 *Public Culture* (2000), pp. 721-748.

Miliani, Domingo, "Simón Rodríguez. El hombre entre la historia y la ficción," in Beatriz González Stephan (ed.), *Esplendores y miserias del siglo XIX. Cultura y sociedad en América Latina*, Caracas, Monte Avila Editores Latinoamericana, 1995, pp. 25-40.

Miller, Christopher L., "Forget Haiti. Baron Roger and the New Africa," 107 *Yale French Studies, The Haiti Issue: 1804 and Nineteenth-Century French Studies* (2005).

Morison, J. D., "Katkov and Panslavism," 46 *The Slavonic and East European Review* 107 (1968), pp. 422-441.

Möckl, Karl, "Die Bayerische Konstitution von 1808," in Eberhard Weis (ed.), *Reformen im rheinbündischen Deutschland*, Munich, Oldenbourg, 1984, pp. 151-166.

Nabulsi, Karma, "Guerre et inégalité dans la pensée politique de Rousseau," *Les études philosophiques* (October 2007), pp. 413-424.

Nettleford, Rex, "The Haitian Revolution and the Struggle against Slavery. Challenges to Knowledge, Ignorance, and Silence," 58 *International Social Science Journal* (2006), pp. 195-202.

Newbury, C.W., "The Tariff Factor in Anglo-French West Africa Partition," in Prosser Gifford and William Roger Louis (eds.), *France and Britain in Africa. Imperial Rivalry and Colonial Rule*, New Haven/London, Yale University Press, 1971, pp. 221-259.

Nussbaum, Martha C., "Patriotism and Cosmopolitanism," in Martha C. Nussbaum (ed.), *For Love of Country. Debating the Limits of Patriotism*, Boston, Beacon, 1996, pp. 3-17.

Nussbaum, Martha Craven, "Kant and Cosmopolitanism," in James Bohman and Marthias Lutz-Bachmann (eds.), *Perpetual Peace. Essays on Kant's Cosmopolitan Ideal*, Cambridge, MIT Press, 1997, pp. 25-58.

Nyers, Peter, "Abject Cosmopolitanism. The Politics of Protection and the Anti-Deportation Movement," *Third World Quarterly* 24 (2003), pp. 1069-1093.

Nys, Ernest, "Le droit des gens et les écrits de Jean-Jacques Rousseau," *Revue de droit international et de législation comparée* IX (1907), pp. 77-89.

Obregón, Liliana, "Construyendo la región americana. Andrés Bello y el derecho internacional," in Beatriz González Stephan and Juan Poblete (eds.), *Andrés Bello y los estudios latinoamericanos*, Pittsburgh PA, Universidad de Pittsburgh, 2009, pp. 189-218.

Owen, Thomas C., "The Russian Industrial Society and the Tsarist Economic Policy, 1867-1905," 45 *The Journal of Economic History* (1985), pp. 587-606.

Pagden, Anthony, "Stoicism, Cosmopolitanism, and the Legacy of European Imperialism," 7 *Constellations* (2002).

Pagni, Andrea, "Versiones y subversiones del canon Europeo en el siglo XIX. Simón Rodríguez, Andrés Bello y Juan Antonio Pérez Bonalde," in Carlos Pacheco, Luis Barrera Linares and Beatriz González Stephan (eds.), Nación y literatura. Itinerarios de la palabra escrita en la cultura venezolana, Caracas, Equinoccio, 2006, pp. 153-175.

Pearce, Robert, "The Colonial Economy. Nigeria and the Second World War," in Barbara Ingham and Colin Simmons (eds.), *Development Studies and Colonial Policy*, London, Frank Cass, 1987, pp. 263-292.

Pempel, T.J., "The Developmental Regime in a Changing World," in Meredith Woo-Cumings (ed.), *The Developmental State, New York, Cornell University Press*, 1998, pp. 137-181.

Perham, Margery, "Lord Lugard. A Preliminary Evaluation," 20 *Africa Journal of the International African Institute* (1950), pp. 228-339.

Pitts, Jennifer, "Empire and Democracy. Tocqueville and the Algeria Question," 8 *The Journal of political Philosophy* (2000), pp. 295-318.

Pufendorf, Samuel, *De jure naturae et gentium libri octo* (1672), in Samuel Pufendorf, *Gesammelte Werke*, Vol. 4, Frank Böhling (ed.), Berlin, Akademie Verlag, 1998.

Raeff, Marc, *Michael Speransky. Statesman of Imperial Russia 1772-1839*, The Hague, Martinus Nijhoff, 1957, pp. 78-160.

Reinhardt, Thomas, "200 Years of Forgetting. Hushing up the Haitian Revolution," 35 *Journal of Black Studies* (2005), pp. 246-261.

Richter, Melvin, "Tocqueville on Algeria," 25 *The Review of Politics* (1963), pp. 362-398.

Robinson, Ronald and Gallagher, John, "The Partition of Africa," in William Roger Louis (ed.), *Imperialism. The Robinson and Gallagher Controversy*, New York, New Viewpoints, 1976, pp. 73-128.

Rodríguez, Simón, "Estracto sucinto de mi obra sobre la educación republicana," in Number 39 *Neo-Granadino*, Bogota, 28 April 1849, p. 132.

Rousseau, Jean-Jacques, "Abstract of Monsieur Abbé de Saint-Pierre's Plan for Perpetual Peace," in Jean-Jacques Rousseau, *The Plan for Perpetual Peace, on the Government of Poland, And Other Writings on History and Politics*, Christopher Kelly (ed.), Lebanon, Dartmouth College Press, 2005.

Rousseau, Jean-Jacques, "Discourse on the Origin and the Foundations of Inequality among Men," in Jean-Jacques Rousseau, *The Discourses and Other Early Political Writings*, Victor Gourevitch (ed.), Cambridge, Cambridge University Press, 1997, pp. 111-231.

Rousseau, Jean-Jacques, "Discourse on Political Economy," in Jean-Jacques Rousseau, *The Social Contract and other later Political Writings*, Victor

Gourevitch (ed.), Cambridge/New York, Cambridge University Press, 1997, pp. 3-38.

Rousseau, Jean-Jacques, "Principles of the Right of War," in Jean-Jacques Rousseau, *Of the Social Contract and Other Political Writings*, Christopher Bertram (ed.), Quintin Hoare (transl.), London, Penguin Books, 2012.

Rousseau, Jean-Jacques, "Prinzipien des Krieges," German translation by Michael Bloch, 58 *Deutsche Zeitschrift für Philosophie* (2010), pp. 307-317.

Rumazo González, Alfonso, "El pensamiento educador de Simón Rodríguez," in Simón Rodríguez, *Obras Completas*, Caracas, 1975.

Rumschöttel, Hermann, "Die Entstehung der bayerischen Konstitution," in Alois Schmid (ed.), *Die bayerische Konstitution von 1808. Entstehung – Zielsetzung – Europäisches Umfeld*, Munich, C.H. Beck, 2008, pp. 211-228.

Rus Rufino, Salvador, "Die Entwicklung des Naturrechts in der spanischen Aufklärung," in Diethelm Klippel (ed.), *Naturrecht und Staat. Politische Funktionen des europäischen Naturrechts (17.-19. Jahrhundert)*, Munich, Oldenbourg, 2006, pp. 59-88.

Sakwa, Richard, "Russia as Eurasia. An Innate Cosmopolitanism," in Gerard Delanty (ed.), *Europe and Asia beyond East and West*, London, Routledge, 2006, pp. 215-227.

Salomon, Noel, "Cosmopolitismo e internacionalismo (1880-1940)," in Leopoldo Zea (ed.), *América Latina en sus ideas*, México, Siglo XXI, 1986.

Schiller, Friedrich, "What is Universal History, and to What End Does One Study It? An Academic Inaugural Address", 1789, in Rolf Saltzer (ed.), *German Essays on History*, New York, Continuum, 1991.

Schröder, Jan, "'Gesetz' und 'Naturgesetz' in der frühen Neuzeit," *Abhandlungen der Geistes- und sozialwissenschaftlichen Klasse, Akademie der Wissenschaften und der Literatur Mainz* 1 (2004), pp. 1-35.

Schröder, Jan, "'Naturrecht bricht positives Recht' in der Rechtstheorie des 18. Jahrhunderts?," in Dieter Schwab *et al.* (eds.), *Staat, Kirche, Wissenschaft in einer pluralistischen Gesellschaft. Festschrift zum 65. Geburtstag von Paul Mikat*, Berlin, Duncker & Humblot, 1989, pp. 419-433.

Schuller, Karen, "From Liberalism to Racism. German Historians, Journalists, and the Haitian Revolution from the Late Eighteenth to the Early Twentieth Century," in David P. Geggus (ed.), *The Impact of the Haitian Revolution in the Atlantic World*, Columbia, University of South Carolina, 2001, pp. 23-43.

Schumpeter, Joseph A., "A Sociological Theory of Imperialism. An Atavism," in Robin W. Winks (ed.), *British Imperialism. Gold, God and Glory*, New York, Holt, Rinehart and Winston, 1963, pp. 82-91.

Silvestrini, Gabriella, "Diritti naturali e diritto di uccidere. Teorie moderne della guerra fra modelli teorici e tradizioni di pensiero," 21 *Filosofia politica* (2007), pp. 425-452.

Silvestrini, Gabriella, "Vattel, Rousseau et la question de la justice de la guerre," in Vincent Chetail & Peter Haggenmacher (eds.), *Vattel's Interna-*

tional Law from a XXIst Century Perspective, Boston, Brill, 2011, pp. 99-127.

Silvestrini, Gabriella, "Guerre juste et droit de résistance dans la tradition protestante du droit naturel," *Genève et la Suisse dans la pensée politique. Actes du Colloque de Genève* (Septembre 2006), Aix-en-Provence, Presses Universitaires d'Aix-Marseille, 2007, pp. 103-116.

Silvestrini, Gabriella, "Justice, War and Inequality. The Unjust Aggressor and the Enemy of the Human Race in Vattel's Theory of the Law of Nations," in Béla Kapossy (ed.), Rival Histories of Emer de Vattel's Law of Nations, 31 *Grotiana* (2010), pp. 44-68.

Talleyrand, "Rapport fait au Roi pendant son voyage de Gand à Paris (June 1815)," in Georges Pallain (ed.), *Correspondance inédite du Prince De Talleyrand et du Roi Louis XVIII pendant le Congrès de Vienne. Publiée sur les manuscrits conservés au dépôt des Affaires étrangères, avec préface, éclaircissements et notes*, 3rd ed., Paris, Londres, Leipzig, E. Plon et cie, 1881, pp. 436-484.

Taylor, Norman W., "Adam Smith's First Russian Disciple," 45 *The Slavonic and East European Review* (1967), pp. 425-438.

Tiainen, Jorma, "Die Bayerische Konstitution von 1808 und die öffentliche Diskussion darüber," *Acta Societatis Historicae Ouluensis* 1, 1967, pp. 166-184.

Turin, S.P., "Nicholas Chernyshevsky and John Stuart Mill," 9 *The Slavonic and East European Review* (1930), pp. 29-33.

Ullmann, Hans-Peter, "Die öffentlichen Schulden in Bayern und Baden 1780-1820," 242 *Historische Zeitschrift* (1986), pp. 31-67.

Uzoigwe, G.N., "European Partition and Conquest of Africa. An Overview," in A. Adu Boahen (ed.), *General History of Africa. Volume VII Africa under Colonial Domination 1880-1935*, Abridged Edition, Ibadan, Heinemann Educational Books LTD, 1990, pp. 10-24.

Vinogradoff, Paul, Sir, "Historical Types of International Law," 1 *Bibliotheca Visseriana*, Leiden, Brill, 1923.

Vitoria, Francisco de, "On Civil Power," *Political Writings*, Anthony Pagden and Jeremy Lawrence (eds.), Cambridge, Cambridge University Press, 1991.

Wegelin, Peter, "Die Bayerische Konstitution von 1808," *Schweizer Beiträge zur Allgemeinen Geschichte* 16, 1958, pp. 142-206.

Welch, Cheryl B., "Colonial Violence and the Rhetoric of Evasion. Tocqueville on Algeria," 31 *Political Theory* (2003), pp. 235-264.

Williams, F.R.A., "Fundamental Rights and the Prospects for Democracy in Nigeria," 115 *University of Pennsylvania Law Review* (1967), pp. 1073-1090.

Williams, M.C., "Rousseau, Realism and Realpolitik," 18 *Millennium: Journal of International Studies* (1989), pp. 188-195.

Dissertations

Doğan, Necmettin, "The Origins of Liberalism and Islamism in the Ottoman Empire, 1908-1914," Dissertation zur Erlangung des Doktorgrades der Philosophie am Institut für Soziologie, Fachbereich Politik – und Sozialwissenschaften der Freien Universität, Berlin, 2006.

Schneider, Michael, *Das Verhältnis des Reichsrechts zum Landesrecht im alten Reich seit dem Beginn der Neuzeit*, Diss. Jur., Tübingen, 2002.

Papers

Bloch, Michael, "Is Rousseau really a Realist? On the Political Theory of Peace and War," Paper presented at the Annual Congress of the Swiss Political Science Association, 7-8 January, 2010, Geneva (December 2009).

Webpages

Bulbul, Yasar, "Transfer of Political Economy by a Traditional Society. Ilm-I tebdir-I menzil in the Ottoman Empire," <www.econ.uba.ar/www/institutos/epistemologia/marco_archivos/ponencias/Actas%20XIII/Trabajos%20Episte/BULBUL_paper.pdf> (visited 8 November 2012).

Commonwealth Secretariat ‹www.thecommonwealth.org/YearbookHomeInternal/138917/› (visited 29 November 2012).

Other Works Cited

The American Whig Review, new series Vol. VIII, New York, Published at 120 Nassau Street, 1851, pp. 156-157.

Congressional Debates, Vol. II, William Jay, View of the action of the Federal Government in Behalf of Slavery, published by the American-Anti-slavery society, 1839.

The debates in the several State conventions, on the adoption of the Federal Constitution as recommended by the General convention at Philadelphia, in 1787 together with the Journal of the Federal Convention, Luther Martin's Letter, Yate's Minute, Congressional Opinions, and others, Vol. IV, Washington, 1836.

"Décret Qui Abolit L'Esclavage Des Nègres Dans Les Colonies. Du 4 Février, 1794," in L. Rondonneau (ed.), *Collection Générale Des Lois, Décrets, Arrêtés, Sénatus-Consultes (1789-1814)*, IV, Paris, Imprimerie Royale, 1818.

Fundamental principles of the science of the European state's-constitution of today and of the peoples that are subjected to European powers and of general state law, 1. Theil, Tübingen, 1732.

"Guerre," *Encyclopédie, ou Dictionnaire raisonné des sciences, des arts et des métiers*, Paris, Briasson, 1751-1780, 35 Vols.

Königliches Dekret vom 7. Dezember 1807, in *Bulletin des lois du Royaume de Westphalie/Gesetz-Bulletin des Königreichs Westphalen* 1808 (1), pp. 1-31.

Konstitution für das Königreich Baiern (25 May 1808), in *Königlich-Baierisches Regierungsblatt* 1806, Columns 985-1000.

Proceedings of the conference on "Integration of Customary and Modern Legal Systems in Africa" directed by Dr Antony Allot at the Institute of African studies at University of Ife from 24 August to 29 August 1964 reported in the 8 *Journal of African Law* (1964), pp. 55-56.

Register of the Debates in Congress of the second Session of the twentieth Congress, volume V, Appendix to Gales & Seaton's Register, Documents relative to the Panama Mission, Washington, 1830.

United States Congress (1826), Executive Proceedings on the Panama Mission: March 14, 1826. *Register of Debates in Congress: Comprising the Leading Debates and Incidents of The First Session of The Nineteenth Congress*, Washington, Vol. II, Gales & Seaton.

Index

'Multiple Europes'

The series 'Multiple Europes' is multiple in two ways: it understands Europe in an interdisciplinary manner with a strong historical perspective, and it understands Europe as being inserted in transnational and global contexts. On both levels, the perspectives on Europe and the very role and understanding of Europe is multiple. The special emphasis of the series thus lies in understanding the pasts of Europe as well as its complex present.

The history of Europe and the history of European integration have influenced each other in the past and will continue to do so in the future. There is an inbuilt tension in the relation between European history and the history of European integration. Europe signifies a space and semantics much broader and more complex than the EU. The relations between ideas of Europe, European history, global history and European integration need to be faced more openly. In order to do this, an open dialogue between academic disciplines is just as necessary as critical self-reflection within each discipline. Furthermore, European history was preoccupied with looking at itself and needs to be connected to global relations.

Series Editor: **Hagen Schulz-Forberg**,
Associate Professor for Global and European History

Series Titles

Cosmopolitanisms in Enlightenment Europe and Beyond, Mónica GARCÍA-SALMONES & Pamela SLOTTE (eds.), No.49, 2013

The European Public Sphere. From Critical Thinking to Responsible Action, Luciano MORGANTI & Léonce BEKEMANS (eds.), No.48, 2012

Intercultural Dialogue and Multi-level Governance in Europe. A Human Rights Based Approach, Léonce BEKEMANS (ed.), No.47, 2012

Imagining Europe as a Global Player. The Ideological Construction of a New European Identity within the EU, Christoffer KØLVRAA, No.46, 2012

Capital City Cultures. Reconstructing Contemporary Europe in Vienna and Berlin, Monika DE FRANTZ, No.45, 2011

Building a European Public Sphere. From the 1950s to the Present / Un espace public européen en construction. Des années 1950 à nos jours, Robert FRANK, Hartmut KAELBLE, Marie-Françoise LÉVY & Luisa PASSERINI (eds./dir.), No.44, 2010

'We belong to them'. Narratives of Belonging, Homeland and Nationhood in Territorial and Non-territorial Minority Settings, Tünde PUSKÁS, No.43, 2008

Imagining Europe. Europe and European Civilisation as Seen from its Margins and by the Rest of the World, in the Nineteenth and Twentieth Centuries, Michael WINTLE (ed.), No.42, 2008

Figures of Authority. Contributions towards a Cultural History of Governance from the Seventeenth to the Twentieth Century, Peter BECKER & Rüdiger VON KROSIGK (eds.), No.41, 2008

Europe and the Historical Legacies in the Balkans, Raymond DETREZ & Barbara SEGAERT (eds.), No.40, 2008

Histoire économique et sociale de la construction européenne, René LEBOUTTE, n° 39, 2008

Collective Traumas. Memories of War and Conflict in 20th-Century Europe, Conny MITHANDER, John SUNDHOLM & Maria HOLMGREN TROY (eds.), No.38, 2007

Reflections on Europe. Defining a Political Order in Time and Space, Hans-Åke PERSSON & Bo STRÅTH (eds.), No.37, 2007

London – Berlin. Authenticity, Modernity, and the Metropolis in Urban Travel Writing from 1851 to 1939, Hagen SCHULZ-FORBERG, No.36, 2006

(Un)Doing Europe. Discourses and Practices of Negotiating the EU Constitution, Michał KRZYŻANOWSKI & Florian OBERHUBER, No.35, 2007

Developing Cultural Identity in the Balkans. Convergence vs. Divergence, Raymond DETREZ & Pieter PLAS (eds.), No.34, 2005

Statehood Before and Beyond Ethnicity. Minor States in Northern and Eastern Europe, 1600-2000, Linas ERIKSONAS & Leos MÜLLER (eds.), No.33, 2005

Berlin en musée. Changements sociopolitiques et usages du patrimoine, Véronique CHARLÉTY, n° 32, 2005

Democratisation in Turkey. The Role of Political Parties, Huri TÜRSAN, No.31, 2004

Unravelling Civilisation. European Travel and Travel Writing, Hagen SCHULZ-FORBERG, No.30, 2005

Nation States and Minority Rights. A Constitutional Law Analysis (provisional title), Christina JOHNSSON, No.29, forthcoming

Living Boundaries. Frontiers and Identity in the Basque Country, Zoe BRAY, No.28, 2004

MIX
Papier | Fördert gute Waldnutzung
FSC® C083411

Kolibri 360 GmbH
Ferdinand-Jühlke-Straße 7
99095 Erfurt, Deutschland
produktsicherheit@kolibri360.de